Dimensions Math
Textbook 4B

Authors and Reviewers
Bill Jackson
Jenny Kempe
Cassandra Turner
Allison Coates
Tricia Salerno

Consultant
Dr. Richard Askey

Singapore Math Inc.

Published by Singapore Math Inc.

19535 SW 129th Avenue
Tualatin, OR 97062
www.singaporemath.com

Dimensions Math® Textbook 4B
ISBN 978-1-947226-11-1

First published 2019
Reprinted 2020

Copyright © 2017 by Singapore Math Inc.
All rights reserved. This book or any portion thereof may not be reproduced or used in any manner whatsoever without the express written permission of the publisher.

Printed in China

Acknowledgments

Editing by the Singapore Math Inc. team.
Design and illustration by Cameron Wray with Carli Fronius.

Preface

The Dimensions Math® Pre-Kindergarten to Grade 5 series is based on the pedagogy and methodology of math education in Singapore. The curriculum develops concepts in increasing levels of abstraction, emphasizing the three pedagogical stages: Concrete, Pictorial, and Abstract. Each topic is introduced, then thoughtfully developed through the use of problem solving, student discourse, and opportunities for mastery of skills.

Features and Lesson Components

Students work through the lessons with the help of five friends: Emma, Alex, Sofia, Dion, and Mei. The characters appear throughout the series and help students develop metacognitive reasoning through questions, hints, and ideas.

The colored boxes and blank lines in the textbook lessons are used to facilitate student discussion. Rather than writing in the textbooks, students can use whiteboards or notebooks to record their ideas, methods, and solutions.

Chapter Opener

Each chapter begins with an engaging scenario that stimulates student curiosity in new concepts. This scenario also provides teachers an opportunity to review skills.

Think

Students, with guidance from teachers, solve a problem using a variety of methods.

Learn

One or more solutions to the problem in **Think** are presented, along with definitions and other information to consolidate the concepts introduced in **Think**.

Do

A variety of practice problems allow teachers to lead discussion or encourage independent mastery. These activities solidify and deepen student understanding of the concepts.

Exercise

A pencil icon ✏️ at the end of the lesson links to additional practice problems in the workbook.

Practice

Periodic practice provides teachers with opportunities for consolidation, remediation, and assessment.

Review

Cumulative reviews provide ongoing practice of concepts and skills.

Emma   Alex   Sofia   Dion   Mei

Contents

Chapter		Lesson	Page
Chapter 10 **Measurement**		Chapter Opener	1
	1	Metric Units of Measurement	2
	2	Customary Units of Length	7
	3	Customary Units of Weight	12
	4	Customary Units of Capacity	16
	5	Units of Time	20
	6	Practice A	23
	7	Fractions and Measurement — Part 1	25
	8	Fractions and Measurement — Part 2	28
	9	Practice B	31
Chapter 11 **Area and Perimeter**		Chapter Opener	33
	1	Area of Rectangles — Part 1	34
	2	Area of Rectangles — Part 2	38
	3	Area of Composite Figures	41
	4	Perimeter — Part 1	46
	5	Perimeter — Part 2	51
	6	Practice	56

Chapter	Lesson	Page
Chapter 12 **Decimals**	Chapter Opener	59
	1 Tenths — Part 1	60
	2 Tenths — Part 2	66
	3 Hundredths — Part 1	72
	4 Hundredths — Part 2	77
	5 Expressing Decimals as Fractions in Simplest Form	83
	6 Expressing Fractions as Decimals	86
	7 Practice A	89
	8 Comparing and Ordering Decimals	91
	9 Rounding Decimals	96
	10 Practice B	102
Chapter 13 **Addition and Subtraction of Decimals**	Chapter Opener	105
	1 Adding and Subtracting Tenths	106
	2 Adding Tenths with Regrouping	109
	3 Subtracting Tenths with Regrouping	113
	4 Practice A	117
	5 Adding Hundredths	119
	6 Subtracting from 1 and 0.1	123
	7 Subtracting Hundredths	126
	8 Money, Decimals, and Fractions	130
	9 Practice B	134
	Review 3	136

Chapter		Lesson	Page
Chapter 14 **Multiplication and Division of Decimals**		Chapter Opener	139
	1	Multiplying Tenths and Hundredths	140
	2	Multiplying Decimals by a Whole Number — Part 1	143
	3	Multiplying Decimals by a Whole Number — Part 2	147
	4	Practice A	151
	5	Dividing Tenths and Hundredths	153
	6	Dividing Decimals by a Whole Number — Part 1	156
	7	Dividing Decimals by a Whole Number — Part 2	160
	8	Dividing Decimals by a Whole Number — Part 3	164
	9	Practice B	168
Chapter 15 **Angles**		Chapter Opener	171
	1	The Size of Angles	172
	2	Measuring Angles	177
	3	Drawing Angles	182
	4	Adding and Subtracting Angles	186
	5	Reflex Angles	190
	6	Practice	195

Chapter		Lesson	Page
Chapter 16 **Lines and Shapes**		Chapter Opener	197
	1	Perpendicular Lines	198
	2	Parallel Lines	202
	3	Drawing Perpendicular and Parallel Lines	206
	4	Quadrilaterals	210
	5	Lines of Symmetry	215
	6	Symmetrical Figures and Patterns	219
	7	Practice	222
Chapter 17 **Properties of Cuboids**		Chapter Opener	225
	1	Cuboids	226
	2	Nets of Cuboids	230
	3	Faces and Edges of Cuboids	234
	4	Practice	238
		Review 4	241
		Review 5	245

Chapter 10

Measurement

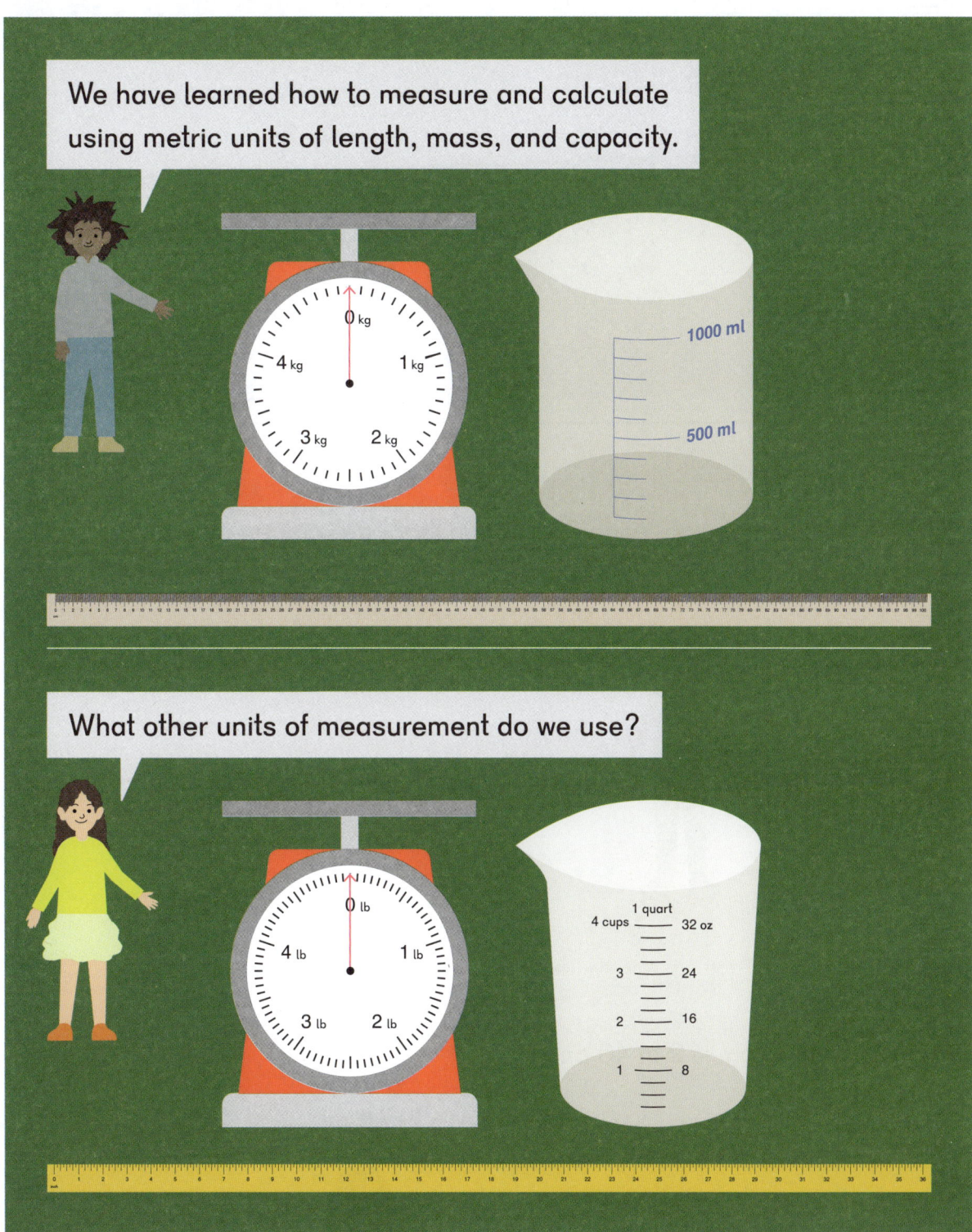

Lesson 1
Metric Units of Measurement

Think

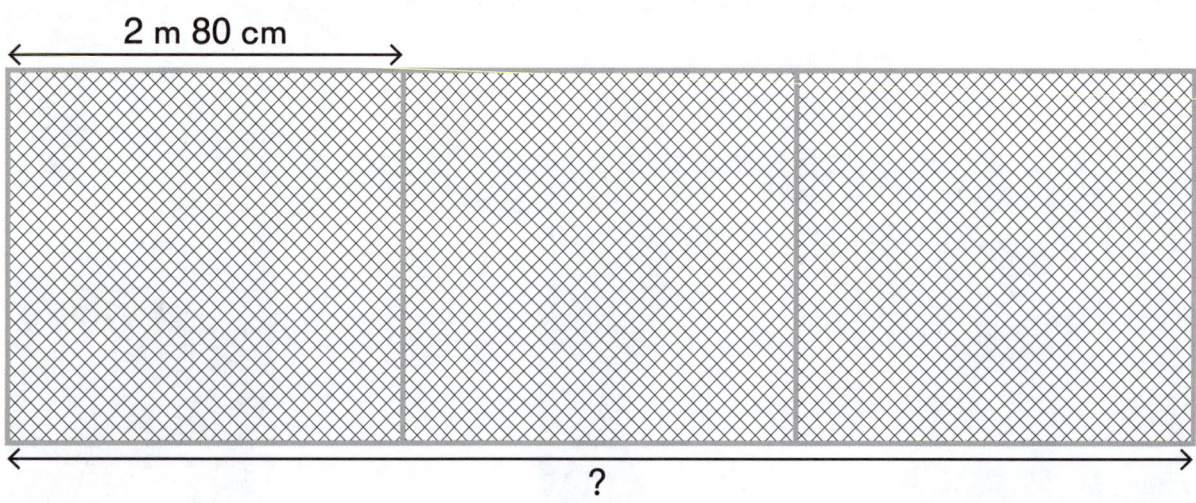

Three sections of fencing, each 2 m 80 cm long, are placed side by side. What is the total length of the fencing?

1 m = 100 cm

Learn

Method 1

3 × 2 m = 6 m

3 × 80 cm = 240 cm = 2 m 40 cm

3 × 2 m 80 cm = 6 m + 2 m 40 cm

                       = 8 m 40 cm

```
   2 m 80 cm
   /      \
  2 m    80 cm
```

2 10-1 Metric Units of Measurement

Method 2

2 m 80 cm = 280 cm

```
  280
×   3
  840
```

840 cm = 8 m 40 cm

The total length of the fencing is _____ m _____ cm.

When we express a measurement in two units, such as 8 m 40 cm, we are expressing the measurement in compound units.

Kilometers (km), meters (m), centimeters (cm), and millimeters (mm) are **metric units** of length.

1 cm = 10 mm
1 m = 100 cm
1 km = 1,000 m

1 m = 1,000 mm

Kilograms and grams are metric units of mass.

1 kg = 1,000 g

Liters and milliliters are metric units of capacity.

1 L = 1,000 mL

Do

1 A rope is 4 m 16 cm long. Express the length of the rope in centimeters.

4 m 16 cm = ☐ cm + 16 cm

= ☐ cm

4 m = 4 × 100 cm

2 An orange pumpkin weighs 7 kg 4 g. A green pumpkin weighs 6,856 g.

(a) Which pumpkin weighs more and by how much?

7 kg = 7 × 1,000 g
7 kg 4 g = ? g

(b) Write 6,856 g in kilograms and grams.

6,856 g = 6,000 g + 856 g

3 A nail is 5 cm 7 mm long. How long is it in millimeters?

5 cm = 5 × 10 mm

4 Amelia and Daren are walking from school to the Botanical Garden.

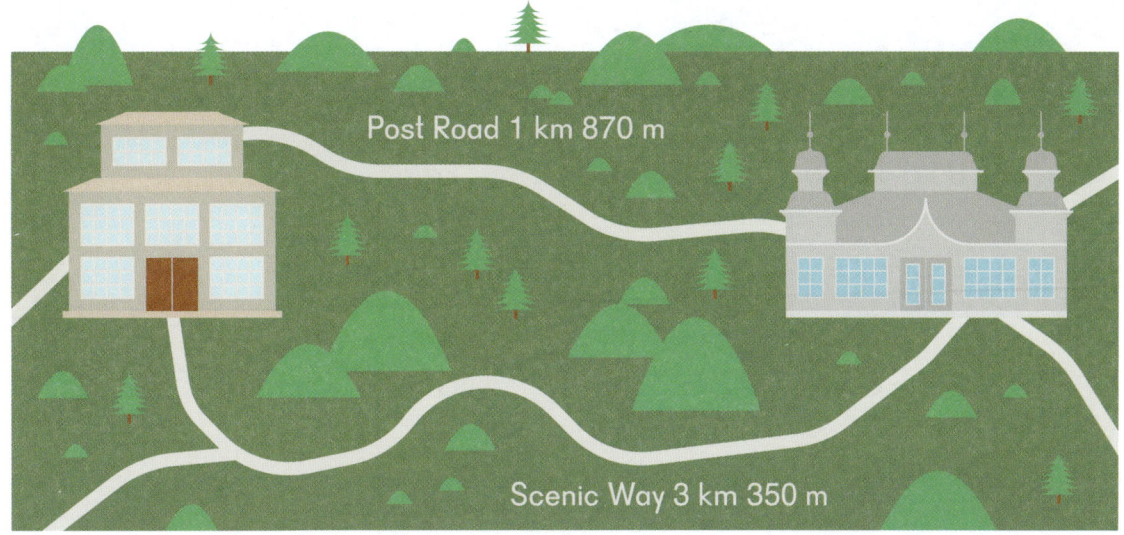

(a) If they walk to the Botanical Garden on Scenic Way and then walk back to school on Post Road, how far will they walk in kilometers and meters?

1 km + 3 km = ?
870 m + 350 m = ?

1,870 + 3,350 = ?

(b) How much longer is Scenic Way than Post Road in kilometers and meters?

3 km 350 m − 1 km = 2 km 350 m
2 km 350 m − 870 m = 1 km 1,350 m − 870 m

3,350 − 1,870 = ?

5. Add or subtract in compound units.

(a) 2 m 45 cm + 4 m 85 cm = ☐ m ☐ cm

(b) 9 kg 150 g − 5 kg 650 g = ☐ kg ☐ g

(c) 8 m 7 cm − 4 m 75 cm = ☐ m ☐ cm

(d) 4 cm 6 mm + 4 cm 6 mm = ☐ cm ☐ mm

(e) 3 L 856 mL + 6 L 199 mL = ☐ L ☐ mL

(f) 8 cm 3 mm − 3 cm 8 mm = ☐ cm ☐ mm

6. Alex filled a barrel with 5 buckets of water. The capacity of the bucket is 2 L 500 mL. Express the total amount of water in the barrel in milliliters and also in liters and milliliters.

7. A yellow ribbon is 2 m 75 cm long. A red ribbon is twice as long as the yellow ribbon. A blue ribbon is twice as long as the red ribbon. How much longer is the blue ribbon than the yellow ribbon in meters and centimeters?

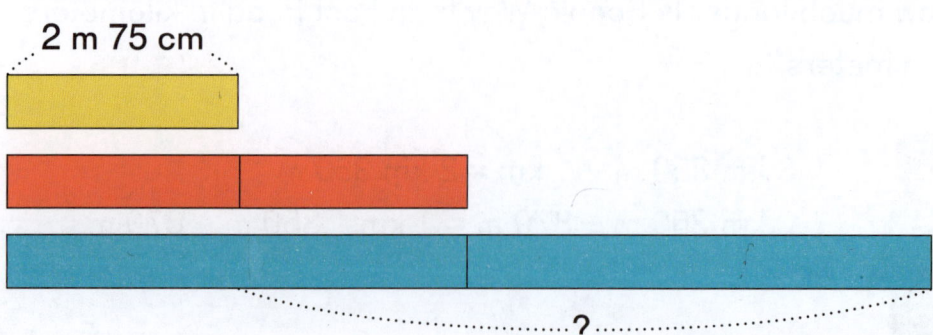

Exercise 1 • page 1

6 10-1 Metric Units of Measurement

Lesson 2
Customary Units of Length

②

Think

Examine a yardstick. Find the markings for feet and inches.

How many feet are in 1 yard?

How many inches are in 1 foot?

Sofia measured her height in feet and inches. Dion measured his height in inches only.

I am 4 feet and 6 inches tall.

I am 51 inches tall.

I wonder who is taller.

(a) How tall is Sofia in inches?

(b) How tall is Dion in feet and inches?

10-2 Customary Units of Length

7

Learn

Yards (yd), feet (ft), and inches (in) are **customary units** of length.

1 ft = 12 in

1 yd is a little less than 1 m.
1 ft is a little more than 30 cm.

1 yd = 3 ft

(a) Sofia is 4 ft 6 in tall.

1 ft = 12 in
4 ft = 4 × 12 in

4 ft = 48 in

4 ft 6 in = 48 in + 6 in = 54 in

Sofia is 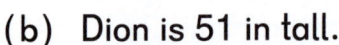 in tall.

(b) Dion is 51 in tall.

51 in = 48 in + 3 in

= 4 ft 3 in

Dion is _____ ft _____ in tall.

A mile (mi) is also a customary unit of length.
1 mi = 5,280 ft
1 mi is a little more than $1\frac{1}{2}$ km.

8   10-2 Customary Units of Length

Do

1 Use a measuring tape.

(a) Measure something that is between 2 and 3 feet long and express the length in feet and inches, and in inches only.

(b) Measure something that is between 5 and 6 feet long and express the length in feet and inches, and in inches only.

(c) Measure something that is between 1 and 3 yards long and express the length in yards, feet, and inches.

2 Copy and complete the table.

ft	1	2		4	5
in	12		36		

3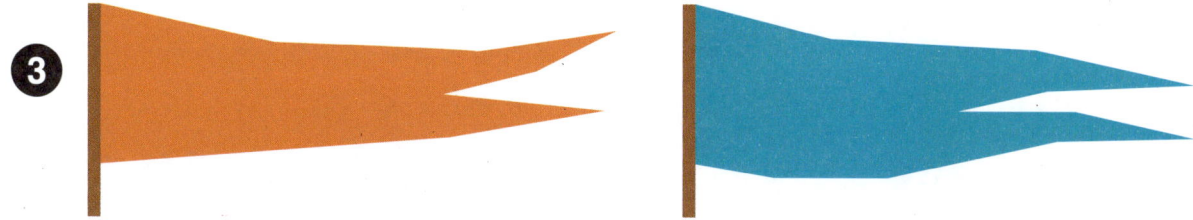

Two flagpoles are placed 3 feet 6 inches apart. Express this length in inches.

3 ft 6 in = ☐ in + 6 in = ☐ in

4 Sofia's cousin is 70 inches tall. How tall is he in feet and inches?

70 in = 60 in + ☐ in = ☐ ft ☐ in

5 A green ribbon is 4 ft 7 in long. A red ribbon is 2 ft 9 in long.

(a) What is their total length?

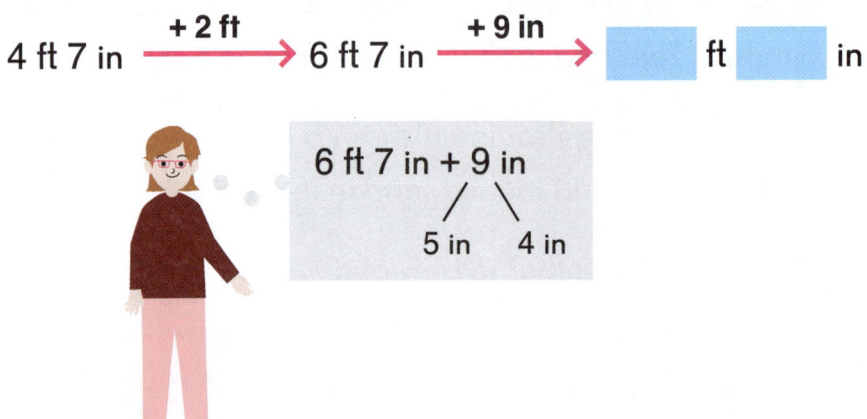

(b) What is the difference in lengths?

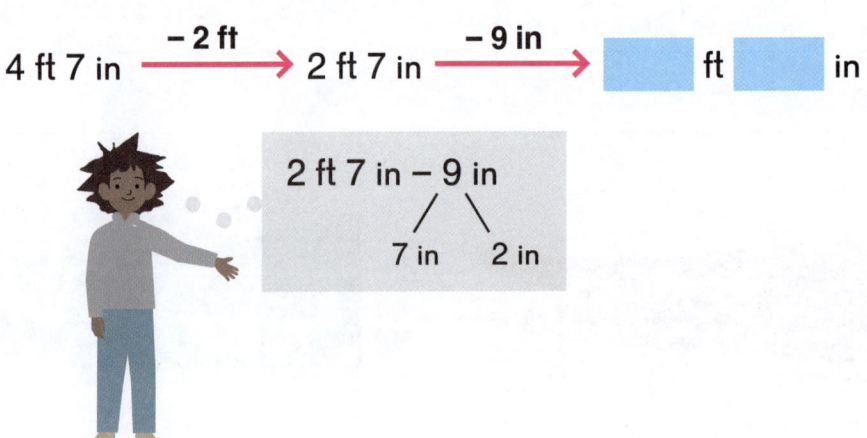

6 The height of the ceiling in a cafeteria is 4 yards 2 feet. Express this height in feet.

4 yd 2 ft = ☐ ft + 2 ft   4 yd = 4 × 3 ft

= ☐ ft

7 A football player ran 20 feet. How far did he run in yards and feet?

20 ft = ▢ yd ▢ ft

20 ÷ 3 is 6 R 2

8 (a) 10 in + 10 in = ▢ ft ▢ in

(b) 6 ft 3 in − 8 in = ▢ ft ▢ in

(c) 2 ft + 2 ft = ▢ yd ▢ ft

(d) 3 yd 1 ft − 2 ft = ▢ yd ▢ ft

(e) 8 ft 8 in + 9 ft 9 in = ▢ ft ▢ in

(f) 11 ft 2 in − 3 ft 9 in = ▢ ft ▢ in

(g) 3 yd 2 ft + 1 yd 2 ft = ▢ yd ▢ ft

9 Linda bought three pieces of cloth. Two of the pieces are each 16 ft long and the third is 2 yd 2 ft long. What is the total length of cloth in yards and feet?

Exercise 2 • page 4

10-2 Customary Units of Length

Lesson 3
Customary Units of Weight

Think

Examine the platform scale. Find the markings for pounds and ounces.

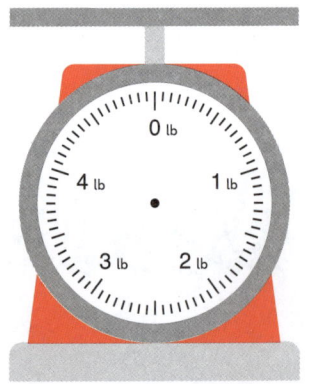

We abbreviate pounds as **lb** and ounces as **oz**. 1 lb = 16 oz

Dion is weighing melons on the platform scale.

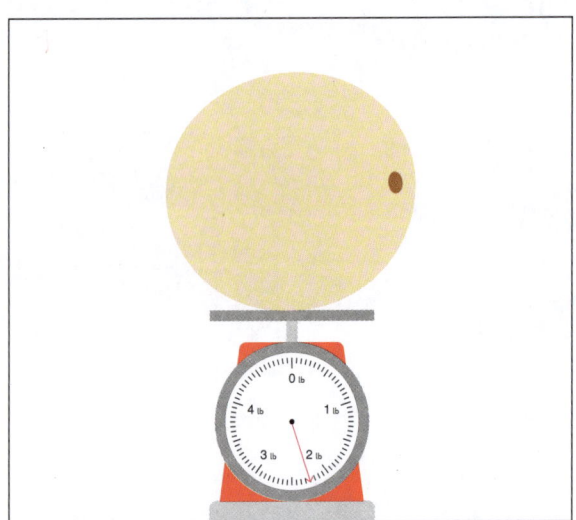

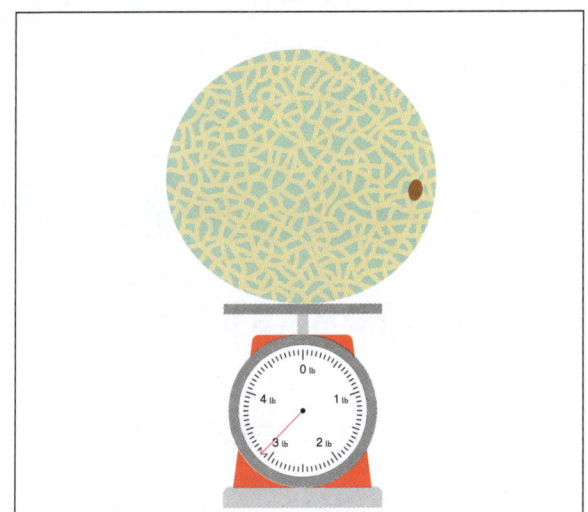

The cantaloupe weights 2 lb 4 oz.

The honeydew melon weighs 3 lb 2 oz.

(a) Express the weight of each melon in ounces.

(b) How many more ounces does the honeydew melon weigh than the cantaloupe?

Learn

(a) 2 lb = 32 oz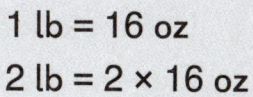

2 lb 4 oz = 32 oz + 4 oz = 36 oz

The cantaloupe weighs _____ oz.

3 lb = 48 oz

3 lb 2 oz = 48 oz + 2 oz = 50 oz

The honeydew melon weighs _____ oz.

(b) 50 oz − 36 oz = 14 oz

The honeydew melon weighs _____ oz more than the cantaloupe.

Pounds (lb) and ounces (oz) are customary units of weight.

1 lb = 16 oz

1 pound is about $\frac{1}{2}$ kilogram.
1 ounce is about 28 grams.

10-3 Customary Units of Weight

Do

1 Use a platform scale. Find something that weighs between 1 and 2 lb. Express the weight in pounds and ounces, and in ounces only.

2 Copy and complete the table.

lb	1	2		4	5
oz	16		48		

3 A kitten weighs 3 lb 10 oz. Express the weight of the kitten in ounces.

3 lb 10 oz = ☐ oz + 10 oz = ☐ oz

4 A squash weighs 34 oz. Express the weight of the squash in pounds and ounces.

34 oz = 32 oz + ☐ oz = ☐ lb ☐ oz

5 One package weighs 3 lb 9 oz and another package weighs 1 lb 11 oz.

(a) What is the total weight of both packages?

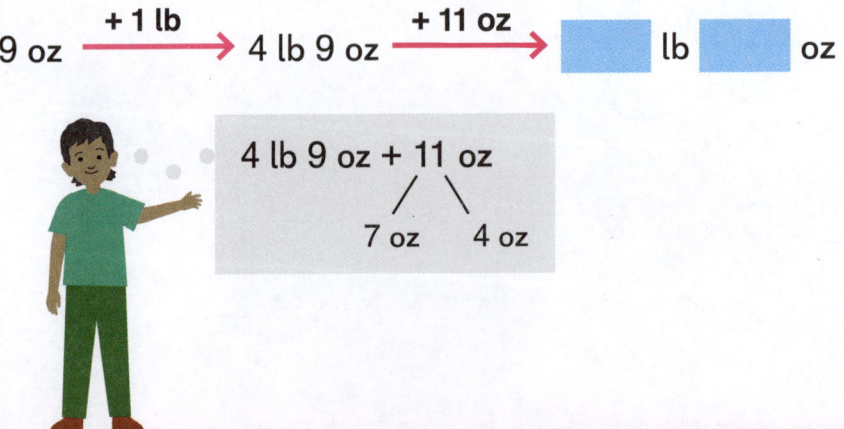

14   10-3 Customary Units of Weight

(b) What is the difference in weight between the two packages?

3 lb 9 oz —−1 lb→ 2 lb 9 oz —−11 oz→ ☐ lb ☐ oz

2 lb 9 oz − 11 oz
   /   \
  9 oz   2 oz

6 Add or subtract in compound units.

(a) 12 oz + 6 oz

(b) 1 lb 10 oz + 14 oz

(c) 4 lb 5 oz + 1 lb 15 oz

(d) 1 lb − 7 oz

(e) 3 lb 4 oz − 10 oz

(f) 6 lb 1 oz − 3 lb 8 oz

7 A bag of apples weighs 2 lb 8 oz. A bag of plums weighs 1 lb 14 oz.

(a) What is the total weight of the bags of fruit in pounds and ounces?

(b) What is the difference in weight between the bags of fruit in ounces?

8 A math textbook weighs 1 lb 6 oz. A math workbook weighs 1 lb 3 oz. What is the combined weight of 5 textbooks and 5 workbooks in pounds and ounces?

Exercise 3 • page 8

Lesson 4
Customary Units of Capacity

Think

Examine a 1-cup and a 1-quart measuring cup. Find the markings for cups and fluid ounces.

We abbreviate quarts as qt, cups as c, and fluid ounces as fl oz.
1 c = 8 fl oz
1 qt = 4 c

A small bottle has a capacity of 2 c 6 fl oz.

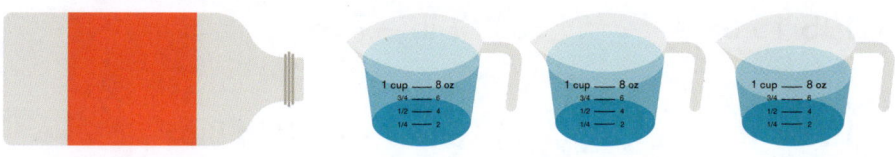

A large bottle has a capacity of 2 qt 1 c.

(a) Express the capacity of the small bottle in fluid ounces.

(b) Express the capacity of the large bottle in cups.

(c) Express the capacity of the large bottle in fluid ounces.

Learn

(a) 2 c = 16 fl oz

   2 c 6 fl oz = 16 fl oz + 6 fl oz

   = 22 fl oz

   1 c = 8 fl oz
   2 c = 2 × 8 fl oz

   The small bottle has a capacity of _____ fl oz.

(b) 2 qt = 8 c

   1 qt = 4 c
   2 qt = 2 × 4 c

   2 qt 1 c = 8 c + 1 c = 9 c

   The large bottle has a capacity of _____ c.

(c) 9 c = 72 fl oz

   The large bottle has a capacity of _____ fl oz.

Fluid ounces (fl oz), cups (c), pints (pt), quarts (qt), and gallons (gal) are customary units of capacity.

1 c = 8 fl oz
1 pt = 2 c
1 qt = 4 c
1 qt = 2 pt
1 gal = 4 qt

1 cup is a little more than 200 mL.
1 quart is a little less than 1 L.
1 gallon is almost 4 L.

Some items, such as milk, can be bought in half-gallons. 1 half-gallon = 2 quarts

Do

1 8 cups of water are poured into a 1-gallon jug.

(a) Express the amount of water in fluid ounces.

(b) Express the amount of water in pints.

(c) Express the amount of water in quarts.

(d) How many more cups of water are needed to fill the jug to 1 gal?

2 A bottle has a capacity of 4 qt 2 c. Express the capacity of the bottle in cups.

4 qt 2 c = ☐ c + 2 c = ☐ c

3 Emma used 38 quarts of water to fill a fish tank. How much water is in the tank in gallons and quarts?

38 qt = ☐ gal ☐ qt

38 ÷ 4 is 9 R ?

4 Teaspoons (tsp) and tablespoons (tbsp) are customary units of measurement used in cooking. How many teaspoons equal 1 cup?

1 c = 16 tbsp
1 tbsp = 3 tsp

5. A pitcher has 2 qt 3 c of mango juice and a bottle has 4 qt 2 c of pineapple juice.

   (a) How much juice is there altogether?

   (b) How much more pineapple than mango juice is there?

   (c) Both juices are poured into a 2 gal punch bowl and mixed together. How much ginger ale must be added to fill the bowl?

6. There are 24 bottles of water in a pack. Each bottle has 20 fl oz of water. A large bottle for a water dispenser has 5 gal of water. How much more water is in the large bottle than in all the bottles in the 24-pack?

7.

Anna is selling jars of salad dressing at the farmers market. Each jar needs 1 cup of oil, 1 cup of vinegar, 3 tbsp of mustard, and other spices. The olive oil comes in gallon bottles and the vinegar in quart bottles. Each bottle of mustard has 1 cup of mustard. How many bottles of oil, vinegar, and mustard does she need to buy to make 20 jars of salad dressing?

Exercise 4 • page 11

10-4 Customary Units of Capacity

Lesson 5
Units of Time

Think

A runner ran the Boston Marathon in 2 h 19 min.

1 hour = 60 minutes
1 minute = 60 seconds

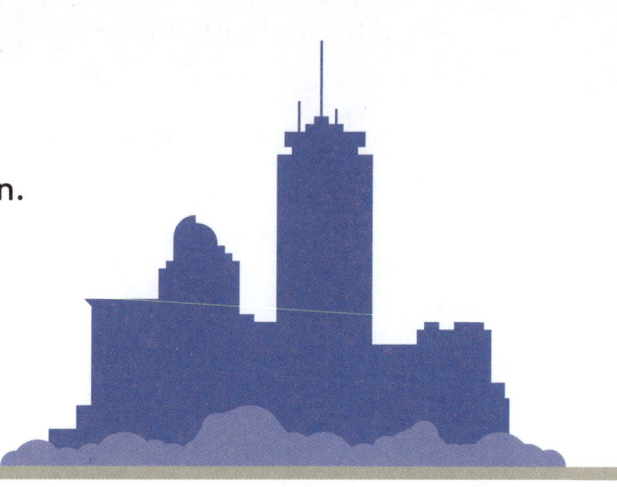

(a) How many minutes did he take to run the marathon?

(b) How many seconds did he take to run the marathon?

Learn

(a) 2 h 19 min = 120 min + 19 min = 139 min

2 h = 2 × 60 min

It took him _____ minutes to run the marathon.

(b) 139
   × 60
   8,340

It took him _____ seconds to run the marathon.

Hours (h), minutes (min), and seconds (s) are units of time.

Days, weeks, months, and years are also units of time.

Do

1 Copy and complete the table.

min	1	2		4	
s	60		180		300

2 A train ride took 8 h 32 min. How long was the ride in minutes?

8 h 32 min = ⬚ min + 32 min

= ⬚ min

8 h = 8 × 60 min

3 June spent 145 minutes at the pool. How long did she spend at the pool in hours and minutes?

145 min = 120 min + ⬚ min = ⬚ h ⬚ min

4 Chad ran the 300-meter sprint in 76 seconds on Saturday. On Sunday, he ran the 300-meter sprint in 1 min 23 s. On which day did he run faster, and how many seconds faster?

76 s = ? min ? s

1 min 23 s = ? s

10-5 Units of Time

5. Sofia's watch shows the seconds as well as the minutes. When she looked at her watch, it was 10:12:40. The next time she looked at her watch, it was 10:15:32. How many seconds passed?

10:12:40 means 10 h 12 min 40 s

6. It is 4:47 p.m.

   (a) What time will it be in 130 minutes?

   (b) What time was it 130 minutes ago?

7. (a) How many minutes are there in a day?

   (b) How many minutes are there in a week?

8. Alex spends 1 h 15 min practicing piano each day.

   (a) How many hours and minutes does he spend practicing the piano in one week?

   (b) How many minutes does he spend practicing the piano in one week?

9. How many days are there in a month that begins and ends on a Monday?

Each month has 28, 29, 30, or 31 days.

Exercise 5 • page 14

Lesson 6
Practice A

P 6

1 Find the values.

(a) 9 m 10 cm = ☐ cm

(b) 4 km 857 m = ☐ m

(c) 2 L 7 mL = ☐ mL

(d) 8 kg 52 g = ☐ g

2 Add or subtract in compound units.

(a) 4 ft 9 in + 2 ft 10 in

(b) 7 ft 2 in – 4 ft 6 in

(c) 10 yd – 5 yd 2 ft

(d) 10 yd 1 ft – 1 yd 2 ft

(e) 4 gal 3 qt + 1 gal 3 qt

(f) 3 c 2 fl oz – 7 fl oz

(g) 4 h – 12 min

(h) 3 h 16 min + 4 h 55 min

3 How many inches are in one yard?

4 1 mile is equal to 5,280 feet. How many yards are in one mile?

5 A snake is 3 ft 9 in long. How long is the snake in inches?

6 A football player ran 12 yards 2 feet. How many feet did he run?

7 A basketball hoop is 10 ft high. How high is it in yards and feet?

8 A basketball court is 84 feet long and 50 feet wide. What is the perimeter of the basketball court in yards and feet?

9 An athlete threw a discus 215 ft. How far did he throw the discus in yards and feet?

10 Two packages weigh 5 lb 4 oz each and two other packages weigh 3 lb 12 oz each. How much do the four packages weigh altogether?

11 A local television station charges $200 for every 30-second commercial. How much will a commercial that lasts 1 minute 30 seconds cost?

12 The length of a basketball court is 31 yd 1 ft. The length of a hockey rink is 66 yd 2 ft.

(a) What is the difference between the length of the basketball court and the length of the hockey rink in yards and feet?

(b) What is the difference between the lengths in feet?

Exercise 6 • page 17

Lesson 7
Fractions and Measurement — Part 1

Think

Mei is measuring and cutting ribbons to wrap presents.

$\frac{2}{3}$ ft

$\frac{3}{4}$ ft

10 in

(a) Express the length of the red and blue ribbons in inches.

(b) Express the length of the green ribbon as a fraction of 1 foot.

Learn

(a) $\frac{2}{3}$ ft = $\frac{2}{3}$ × 12 in = 8 in

The red ribbon is _____ in long.

$\frac{3}{4}$ ft = $\frac{3}{4}$ × 12 in = 9 in

The blue ribbon is _____ in long.

(b) $\frac{10}{12} = \frac{5}{6}$

10 in = $\frac{5}{6}$ ft

The green ribbon is _____ ft long.

$\frac{2}{3}$ × 12

1 ft = 12 in
10 in is what fraction of 12 in?

Do

① (a) A string is $\frac{2}{3}$ yd long. Express the length of the string in feet.

$\frac{2}{3}$ yd = $\frac{2}{3}$ × 3 ft

= ☐ ft

1 yd = ? ft

(b) A desk is $\frac{4}{5}$ m wide. Express the width of the desk in centimeters.

$\frac{4}{5}$ m = $\frac{4}{5}$ × ☐ cm = ☐ cm

(c) A melon weighs $\frac{3}{8}$ lb. Express the weight of the melon in ounces.

$\frac{3}{8}$ lb = $\frac{3}{8}$ × ☐ oz = ☐ oz

(d) A cat sleeps about $\frac{2}{3}$ of a day. About how many hours a day does a cat sleep?

$\frac{2}{3}$ day = $\frac{2}{3}$ × ☐ h = ☐ h

② Express 75 cm as a fraction of 1 m. Express the fraction in simplest form.

$\frac{75}{100}$ = $\frac{☐}{☐}$

1 m = 100 cm
75 out of 100 is ?

75 cm = $\frac{☐}{☐}$ m

3. Express 20 min as a fraction of 2 hours.

$\frac{20}{120} = \frac{\square}{\square}$

20 minutes is $\frac{\square}{\square}$ of 2 hours.

2 h = 120 min
20 min out of 120 min is ?

4. (a) $\frac{5}{6}$ ft = ☐ in   (b) $\frac{1}{2}$ qt = ☐ c

   (c) $\frac{1}{3}$ yd = ☐ ft   (d) $\frac{3}{10}$ m = ☐ cm

   (e) $\frac{3}{4}$ gal = ☐ qt   (f) $\frac{4}{5}$ L = ☐ mL

5. (a) 25 cm = $\frac{\square}{\square}$ m   (b) 12 oz = $\frac{\square}{\square}$ lb

   (c) 25 min = $\frac{\square}{\square}$ h   (d) 250 m = $\frac{\square}{\square}$ km

6. Jessie swam $\frac{3}{4}$ km on Saturday and the same distance on Sunday. Express how far he swam altogether in kilometers and meters.

7. A pole is 3 m long. It is stuck into the ground so that 2 m 10 cm is above ground. What fraction of the length of the pole is below ground?

Exercise 7 • page 20

10-7 Fractions and Measurement — Part 1   27

Lesson 8
Fractions and Measurement — Part 2

Think

Crotalus, the zoo's rattlesnake, is $3\frac{2}{3}$ ft long.

(a) How long is Crotalus in feet and inches?

(b) How long is Crotalus in inches?

Learn

(a) $3\frac{2}{3}$ ft = 3 ft + $\frac{2}{3}$ ft

$\frac{2}{3}$ ft = $\frac{2}{3}$ × 12 in

= 3 ft + 8 in

= 3 ft 8 in

Crotalus is _____ ft _____ in long.

(b) 3 ft = 3 × 12 in = 36 in

$\frac{2}{3}$ ft = 8 in

$3\frac{2}{3}$ ft = 36 in + 8 in

= 44 in

Crotalus is _____ in long.

Do

1 Crotalus weighs $2\frac{1}{2}$ lb.

(a) How much does he weigh in pounds and ounces?

(b) How much does he weigh in ounces?

2 lb = 2 × 16 oz
$\frac{1}{2}$ lb = $\frac{1}{2}$ × 16 oz

2 Crotalus's rattle is 4 inches long. What fraction of his length is his rattle?

$3\frac{2}{3}$ ft = 44 in

$\frac{4}{44}$ = ☐/☐

To express a part as a fraction of the whole, both the part and the whole have to be in the same units.

3

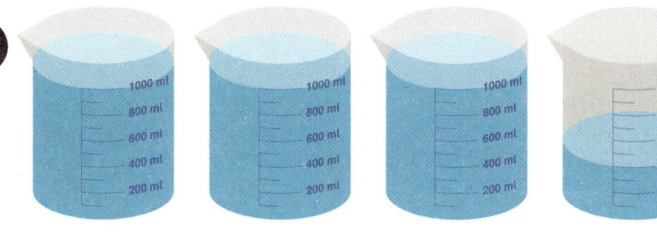

The total amount of water is $3\frac{2}{5}$ L. How many milliliters of water are there?

3 L = 3 × ☐ mL = ☐ mL

$\frac{2}{5}$ L = $\frac{2}{5}$ × ☐ mL = ☐ mL

$3\frac{2}{5}$ L = ☐ mL

10-8 Fractions and Measurement — Part 2

4 (a) $3\frac{1}{4}$ km = ☐ km ☐ m

   (b) $3\frac{3}{4}$ qt = ☐ qt ☐ c

5 (a) $2\frac{3}{5}$ m = ☐ cm   (b) $1\frac{3}{4}$ days = ☐ h

   (c) $2\frac{1}{2}$ c = ☐ fl oz   (d) $1\frac{3}{8}$ lb = ☐ oz

   (e) $4\frac{7}{10}$ L = ☐ mL   (f) $2\frac{5}{12}$ h = ☐ min

   (g) $3\frac{3}{5}$ min = ☐ s   (h) $2\frac{1}{2}$ qt = ☐ pt

6 A tree is $5\frac{3}{5}$ meters tall. How tall is the tree in meters and centimeters?

7 Rowan ran $2\frac{1}{2}$ km on Saturday and $3\frac{3}{4}$ km on Sunday. How many meters did she run altogether?

8 Emiliano had $3\frac{1}{4}$ c of milk. He used $1\frac{1}{2}$ c of milk to make a milk shake. How many fluid ounces of milk does he have left?

9 Ximena exercised for $1\frac{3}{4}$ hours. She spent the last 15 minutes of that time stretching. What fraction of her time exercising was spent stretching?

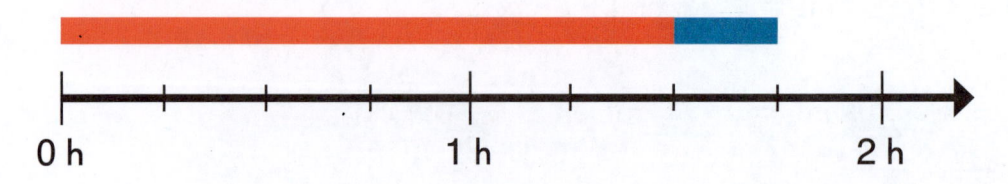

Exercise 8 • page 23

30   10-8 Fractions and Measurement — Part 2

Lesson 9
Practice B

1 (a) $\frac{3}{4}$ ft = ___ in (b) $\frac{2}{3}$ yd = ___ ft

(c) $\frac{4}{5}$ km = ___ m (d) $\frac{9}{10}$ m = ___ cm

(e) $\frac{3}{4}$ kg = ___ g (f) $\frac{3}{10}$ L = ___ mL

(g) $\frac{5}{12}$ h = ___ min (h) $\frac{4}{5}$ min = ___ s

2 (a) $3\frac{1}{4}$ h = ___ h ___ min

(b) $3\frac{3}{4}$ c = ___ c ___ fl oz

3 (a) $2\frac{3}{4}$ lb = ___ oz (b) $4\frac{1}{2}$ gal = ___ qt

(c) $2\frac{1}{2}$ h = ___ min (d) $4\frac{2}{5}$ min = ___ s

(e) $7\frac{1}{3}$ yd = ___ ft (f) $2\frac{3}{5}$ kg = ___ g

4 (a) 10 oz = $\frac{\square}{\square}$ lb

(b) 4 cm = $\frac{\square}{\square}$ m

5 (a) Express $\frac{3}{4}$ km in centimeters.

(b) Express $\frac{3}{4}$ day in minutes.

6   Samantha's arm span measures $5\frac{2}{3}$ ft. How long is her arm span in inches?

7   There is $\frac{3}{4}$ gal of milk left in a gallon jug. How many quarts of milk have been used already?

8   Aaron was asleep for 10 hours. What fraction of the day was he awake?

9   A bag of red grapes weighs $\frac{5}{8}$ lb. A bag of green grapes weighs $\frac{3}{4}$ lb. How much do the grapes weigh altogether in ounces?

10 Hailey spent $\frac{3}{4}$ hour practicing programming and $1\frac{1}{2}$ hours practicing drums. How many more minutes did she spend practicing drums than practicing coding?

11 Last week, Jasmine did her homework for $\frac{3}{4}$ hour a day for 5 days. How much time did she spend doing her homework last week in hours and minutes?

12 There are 4 bottles that each contains $\frac{2}{5}$ L of juice. How much juice is in all of the bottles in liters and milliliters?

Exercise 9 • page 26

Chapter 11

Area and Perimeter

We are finding the area and perimeter of things in the classroom.

25 ft

30 ft 6 in

6 ft

4 ft

The perimeter is the distance around a figure. How can we find the perimeter of the whiteboard?

The sides of a square window are all the same length. How can we find the area and perimeter?

$4\frac{1}{2}$ ft

$4\frac{1}{2}$ ft

What kinds of units do we use to express area and perimeter?

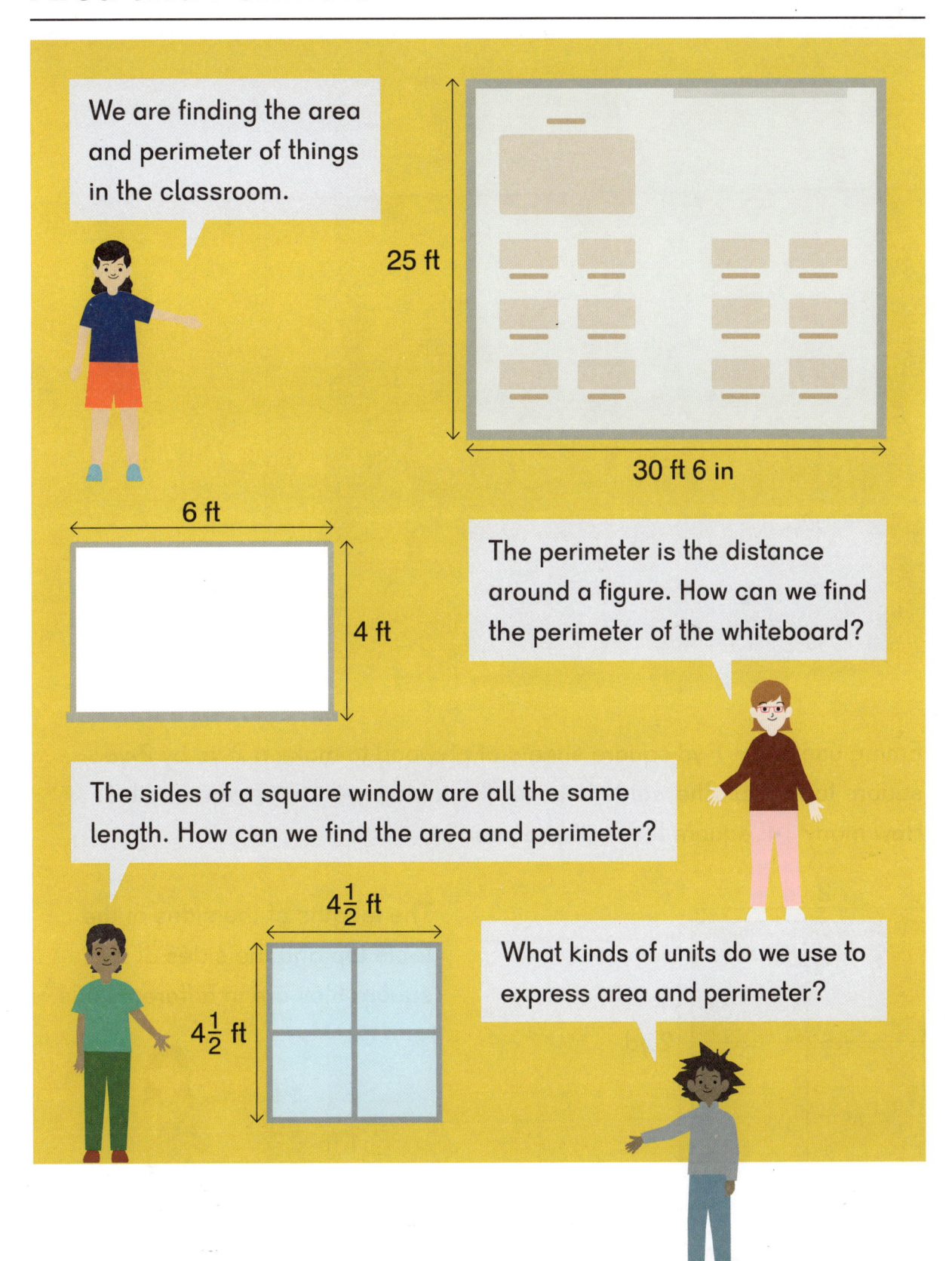

Lesson 1
Area of Rectangles — Part 1

Think

Emma used four 1-yd square sheets of plywood to make a 2-yd by 2-yd square table top. She wants to cover the table top with 1-ft square tiles. How many 1-ft square tiles will she need?

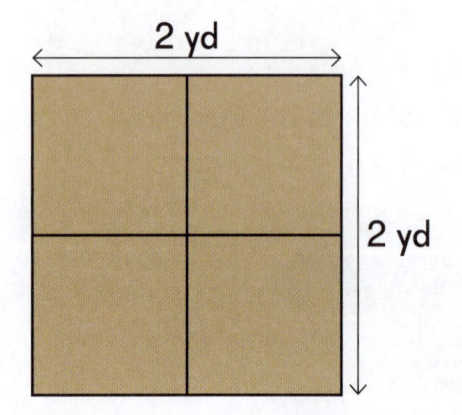

The lengths of the sides of the table top and the sides of the square tiles are in different units.

Learn

Method 1

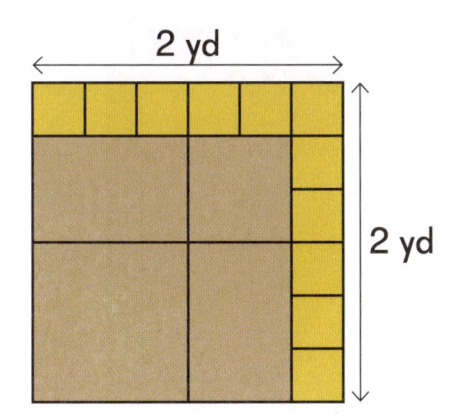

2 yd
2 yd

2 yd = 6 ft

6 × 6 = 36

There are 36 square feet in 4 square yards.

Method 2

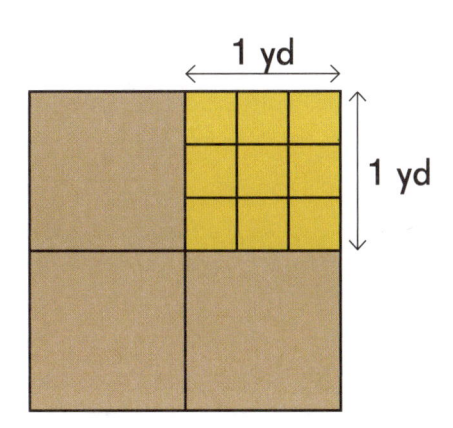

1 yd
1 yd

1 yd = 3 ft
1 yd² = 3 ft × 3 ft
1 yd² = 9 ft²

Number of square feet in 1 square yard: 3 × 3 = 9

Number of square feet in 4 square yards: 4 × 9 = 36

She will need _____ 1-ft square tiles to cover the table top.

Do

1 How many 1-in squares are needed to cover an area of 1 ft² ?

1 ft = 12 in

12 × 12 = ☐

1 ft² = ☐ in²

_____ 1-in squares will cover an area of 1 ft².

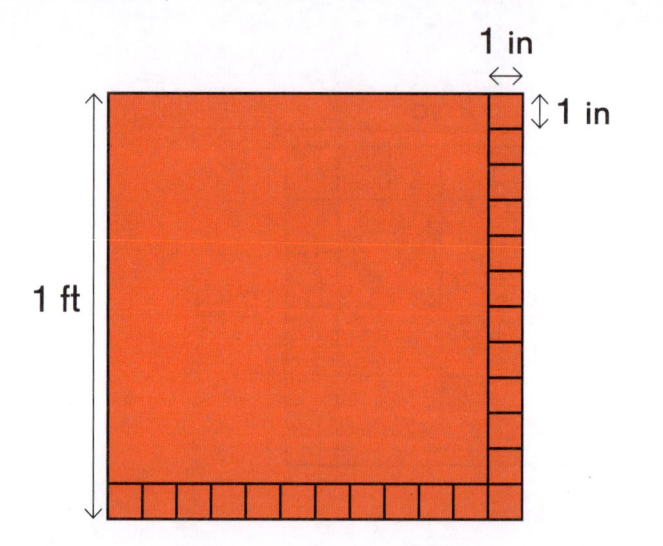

2 Express the area of 1 square meter in square centimeters.

100 × 100 = ☐

1 m² = ☐ cm²

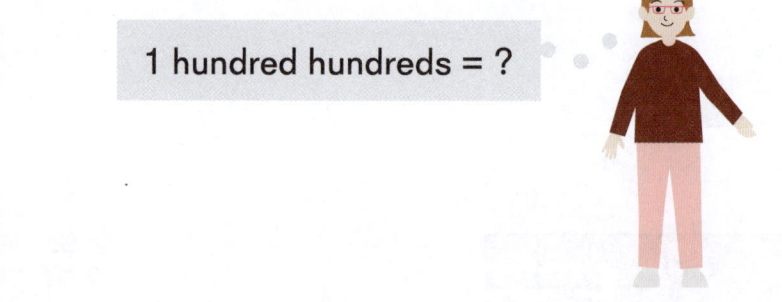

1 hundred hundreds = ?

3 A contractor is tiling a rectangular floor with 1-ft square tiles. How many tiles will she need to cover the floor?

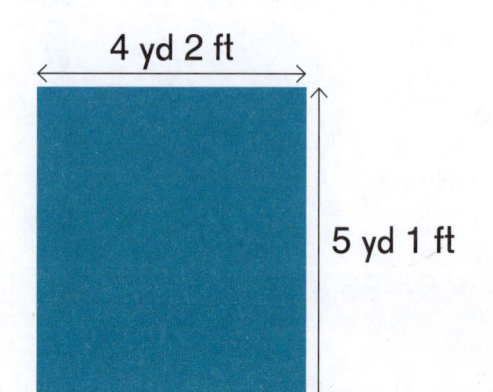

4 yd 2 ft

5 yd 1 ft

4 yd 2 ft = ? ft
5 yd 1 ft = ? ft

36 11-1 Area of Rectangles — Part 1

4. Express the area of the rectangle in square centimeters.

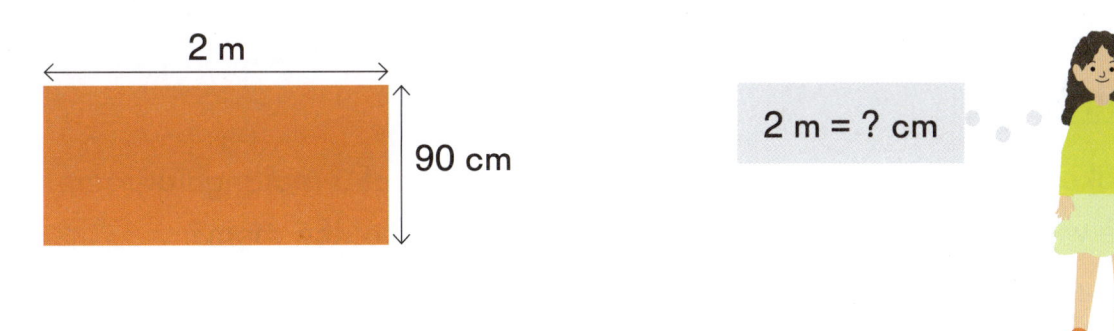

2 m

90 cm

2 m = ? cm

5. Express the area of the rectangle in square yards.

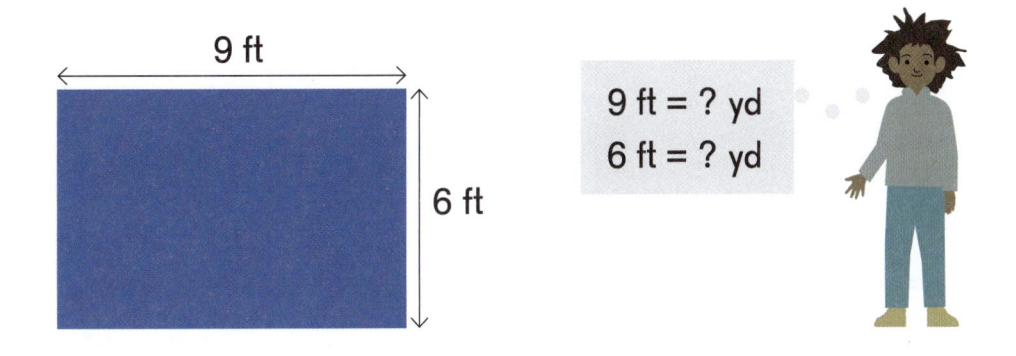

9 ft

6 ft

9 ft = ? yd
6 ft = ? yd

6. A rectangular canvas for a painting is $\frac{3}{4}$ m long and $\frac{1}{2}$ m wide. Express its area in square centimeters.

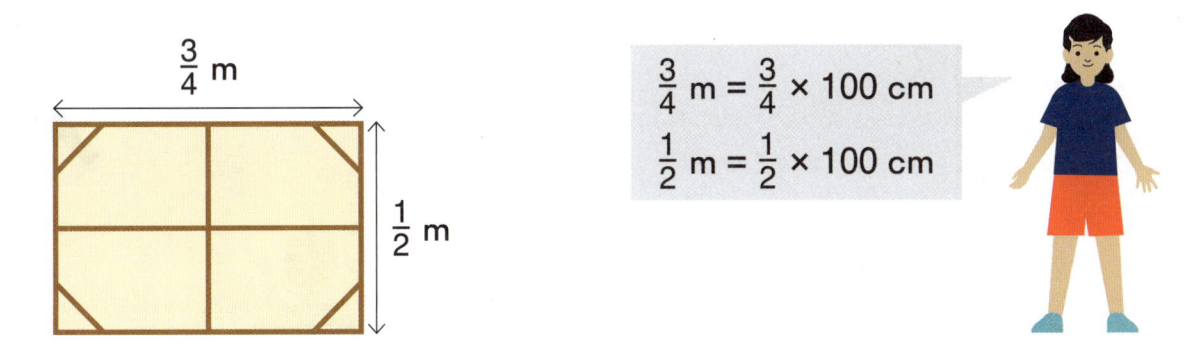

$\frac{3}{4}$ m

$\frac{1}{2}$ m

$\frac{3}{4}$ m = $\frac{3}{4}$ × 100 cm
$\frac{1}{2}$ m = $\frac{1}{2}$ × 100 cm

7. A square rug has sides measuring 4 ft. Express the area of the rug in square inches.

Exercise 1 • page 29

11-1 Area of Rectangles — Part 1

Lesson 2
Area of Rectangles — Part 2

Think

It takes 96 one-foot square tiles to cover the floor of a rectangular room. The width of the room is 8 feet. What is the length of the room?

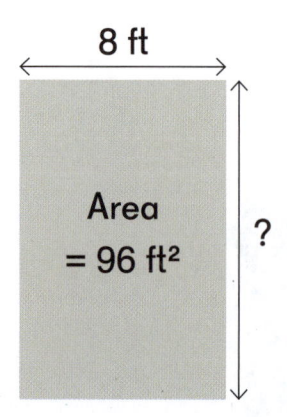

Learn

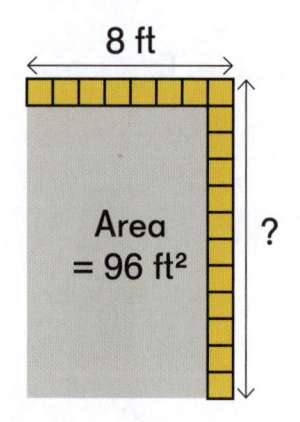

Area of Rectangle = Length × Width
Area of Rectangle ÷ Width = Length

8 × ? = 96

96 ÷ 8 = 12

Length = 12 ft

The length of the room is _____ ft.

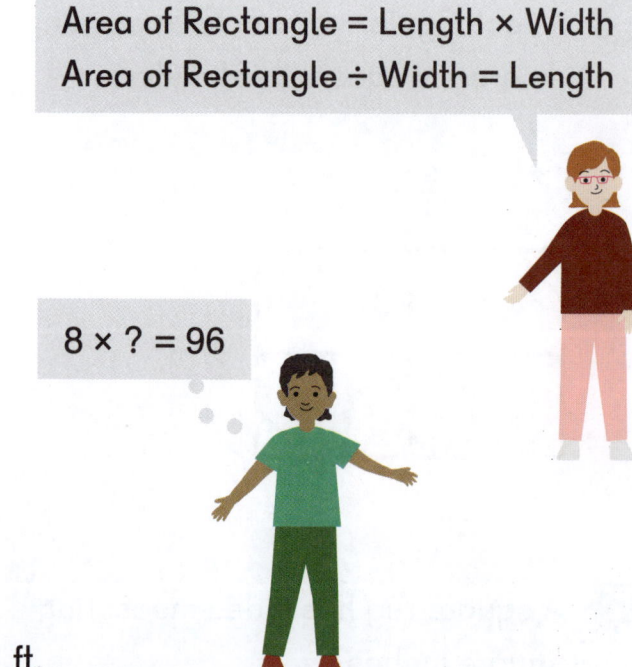

Do

1 Find the length of the rectangle.

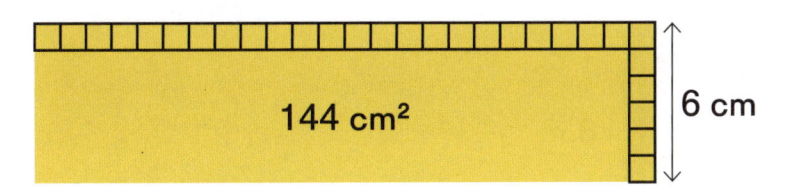

144 cm², 6 cm

144 ÷ 6 = ☐

Length = ☐ cm

2 Find the unknown length.

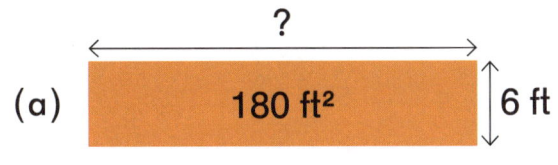

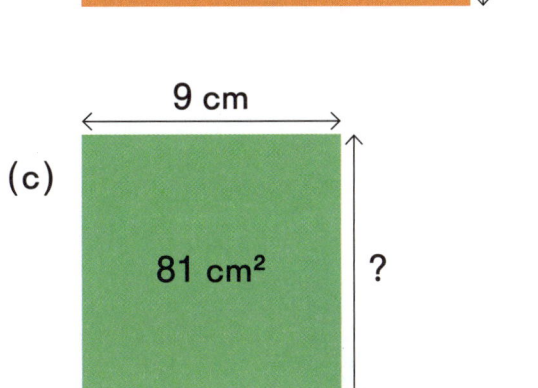

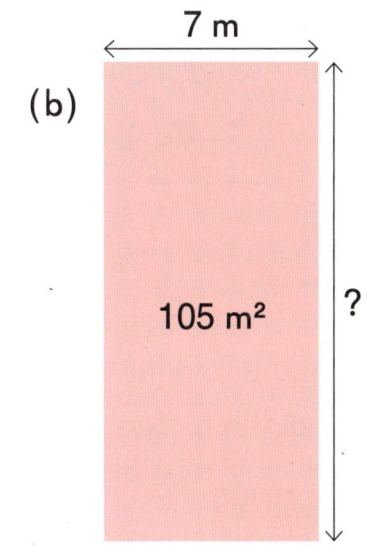

(a) ?, 180 ft², 6 ft

(b) 7 m, 105 m², ?

(c) 9 cm, 81 cm², ?

3 Find the unknown length in feet.

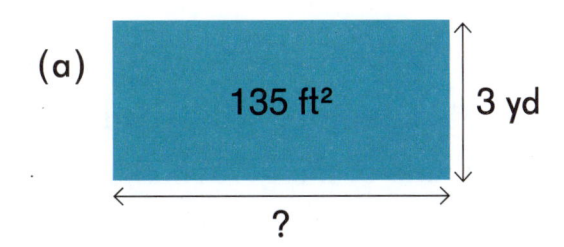

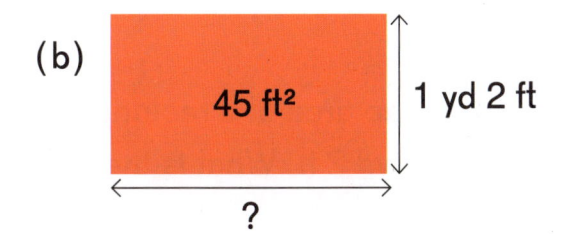

(a) 135 ft², 3 yd, ?

(b) 45 ft², 1 yd 2 ft, ?

11-2 Area of Rectangles — Part 2

4. The area of a volleyball court is 128 m². The width of the court is 8 m. What is the length of the court?

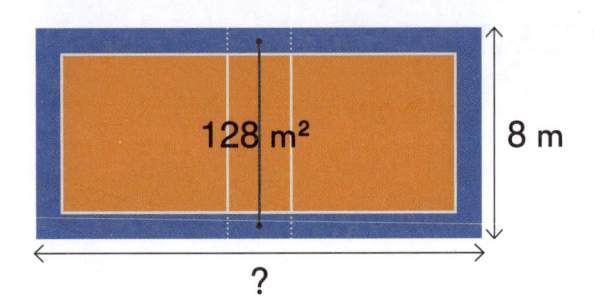

5. Emma's backyard is in the shape of a rectangle. It has an area of 153 ft² and a width of 9 ft. What is the length of her backyard?

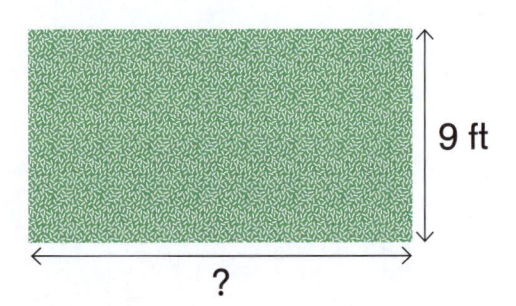

6. The square and the rectangle have the same area. Express the unknown length of the rectangle in inches.

$\frac{2}{3}$ ft = ? in

7. The area of a rectangular garden is 72 ft². One side of the garden is 2 yd 2 ft. What is the length of the other side of the garden in feet?

Exercise 2 • page 32

Lesson 3
Area of Composite Figures

Think

A builder is building a cement patio around a rectangular pool. The dimensions of the pool and the patio are shown below. What is the area of the cement patio in square yards?

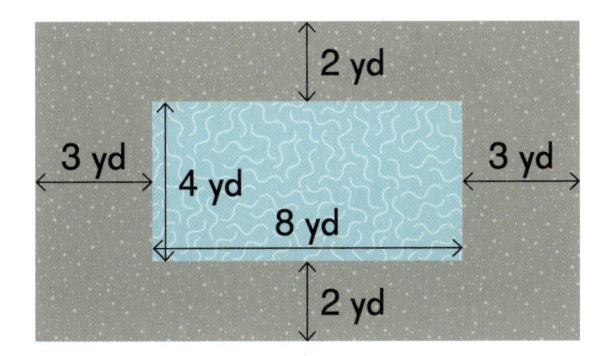

Learn

Method 1

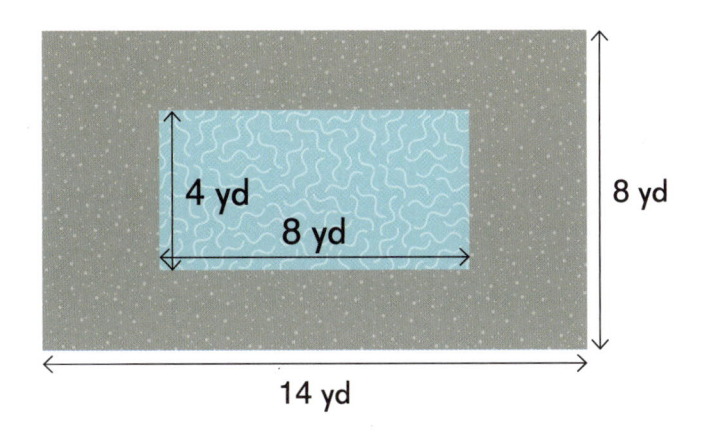

I subtracted the area of the pool from the total area.

Area of large rectangle = 14 × 8 = 112 yd²

Area of pool = 8 × 4 = 32 yd²

Area of patio = 112 − 32 = 80 yd²

11-3 Area of Composite Figures

Method 2

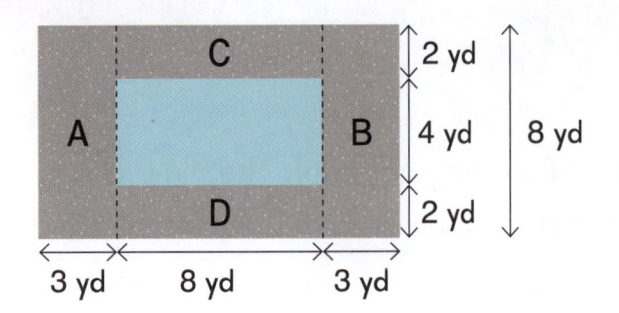

I split the area of the patio into smaller rectangles.

Which rectangles have the same area?

Areas of Rectangles A and B:

8 × 3 = 24 yd²

Total area of Rectangles A and B:

2 × 24 = 48 yd²

Areas of Rectangles C and D:

8 × 2 = 16 yd²

Total area of Rectangles C and D:

2 × 16 = 32 yd²

Area of Patio:

48 + 32 = 80 yd²

What is the area in square feet?

The area of the cement patio is _____ yd².

Do

① Some workers are replacing the grass around the school basketball court. How many square meters of sod will they need?

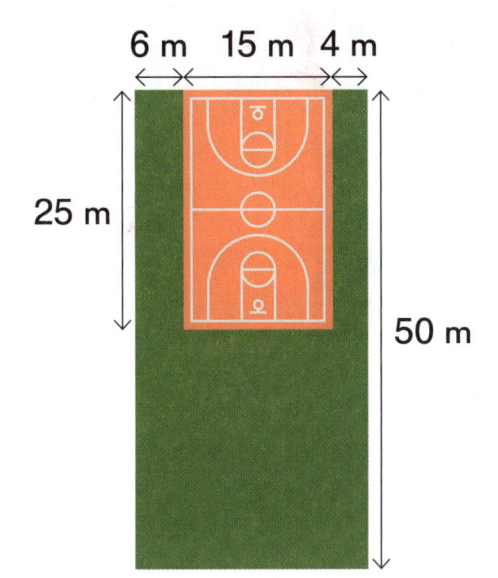

6 m   15 m   4 m

25 m

50 m

We could divide the area of the grass into rectangles, or we could subtract the area of the court from the total area.

② Mei and her mom are putting in new countertops in their kitchen. They are also tiling the floor with 1-ft square tiles.

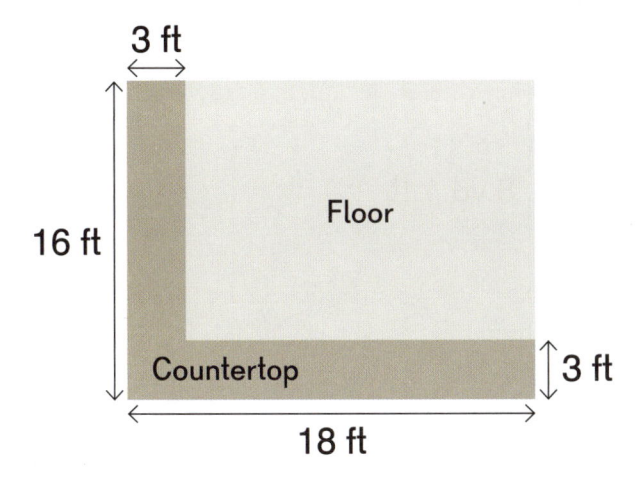

3 ft

16 ft

Floor

Countertop   3 ft

18 ft

(a) How many square feet of countertop do they need?

(b) How many 1-ft square tiles do they need for the floor?

11-3 Area of Composite Figures

3. The shape below is made of rectangles. Find the area of the shape in square inches.

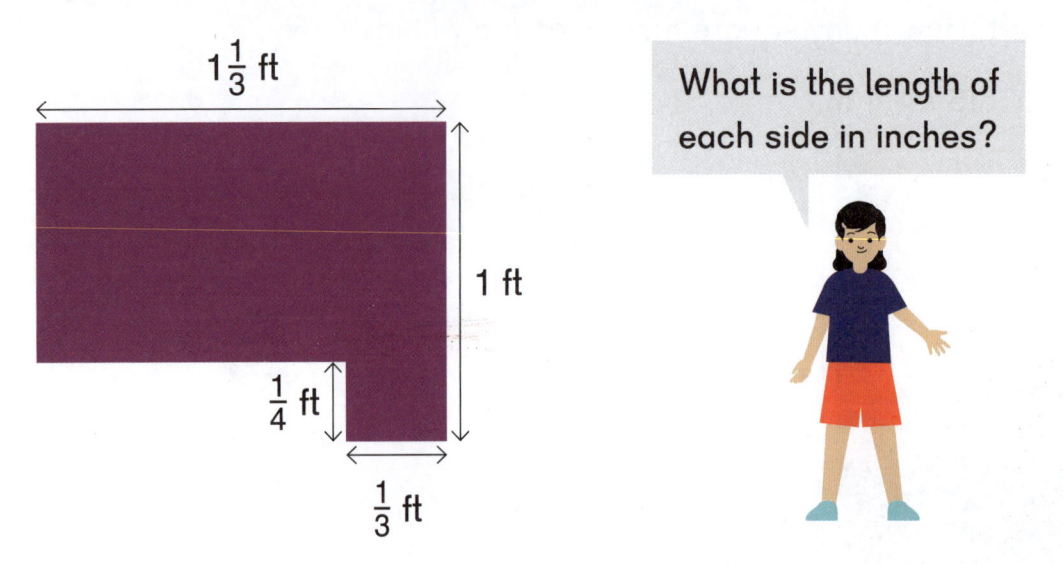

$1\frac{1}{3}$ ft

1 ft

$\frac{1}{4}$ ft

$\frac{1}{3}$ ft

What is the length of each side in inches?

4. Dion's backyard has a rectangular patio with a lawn around it.

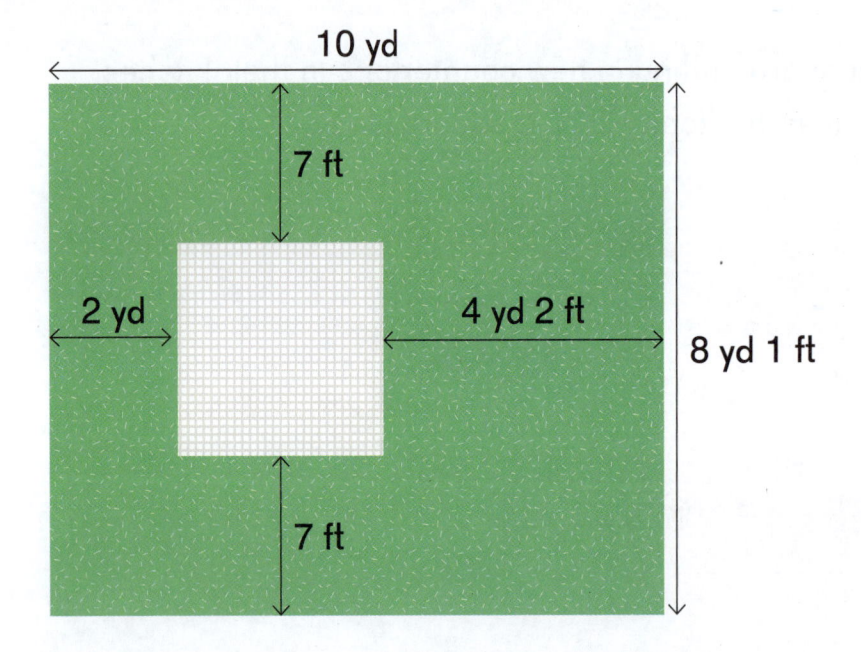

10 yd

7 ft

2 yd

4 yd 2 ft

8 yd 1 ft

7 ft

(a) What is the area of the patio in square feet?

(b) What is the area of the lawn in square feet?

5 A wall in a room has a square window and a door. Alex wants to paint the wall blue. How many square feet of the wall will he paint?

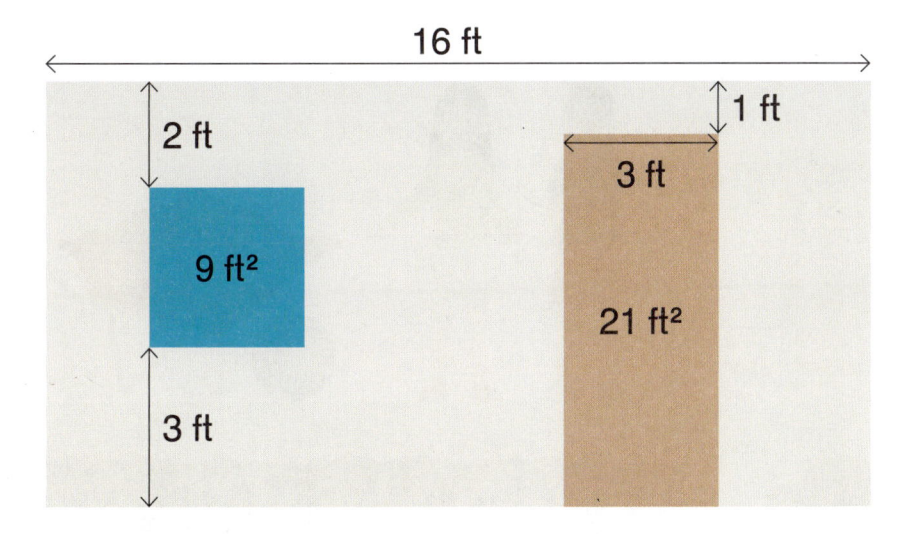

16 ft

2 ft

1 ft

3 ft

9 ft²

21 ft²

3 ft

6 Mei glued 3 square pieces of red paper, each with an area of 64 cm², on a large sheet of paper and colored the rest of the paper green. What is the area of the paper that is colored green?

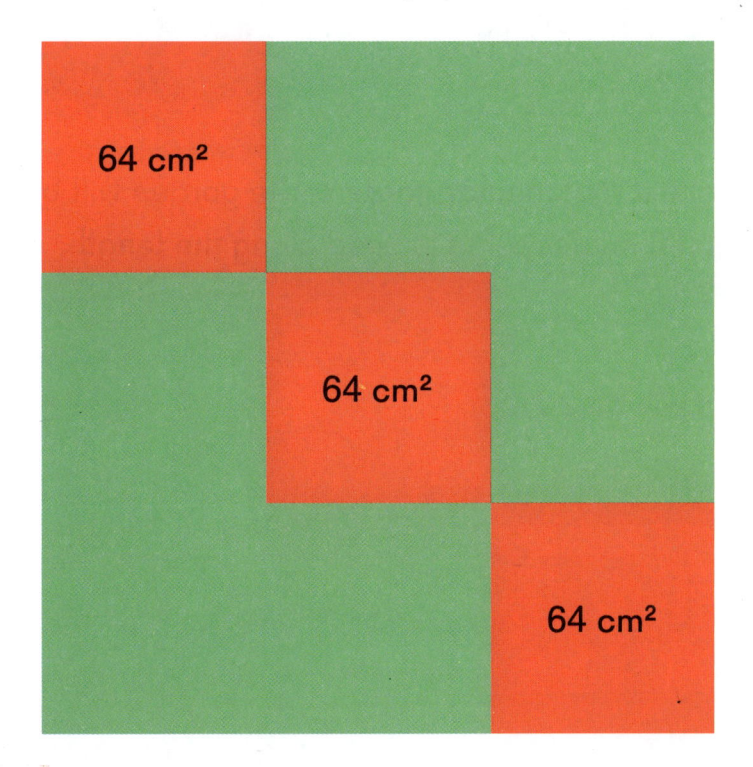

64 cm²

64 cm²

64 cm²

Exercise 3 • page 35

11-3 Area of Composite Figures

Lesson 4
Perimeter — Part 1

Think

Mei and Sofia are helping make a rectangular garden. The garden will be enclosed by 20 m of fencing. If 6 m of fencing is used along the length, how wide can the garden be?

> The perimeter of the garden will be 20 m.

Learn

Method 1

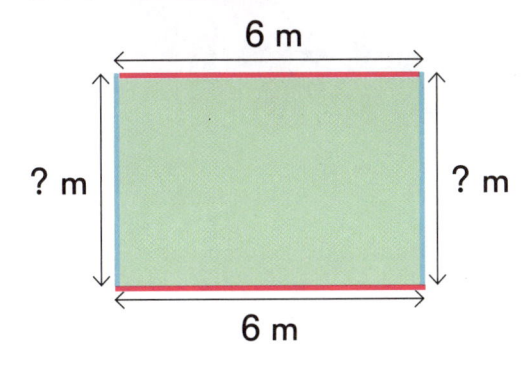

6 m
? m   ? m
6 m

The perimeter of a rectangle is equal to twice the length plus twice the width.

2 × Length = 2 × 6 = 12 m

2 × Width = 20 − 12 = 8 m

Width = 8 ÷ 2 = 4 m

Method 2

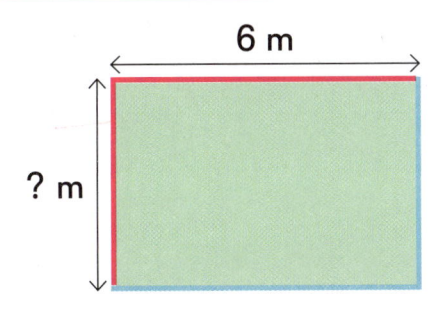

6 m
? m

The perimeter of a rectangle is equal to twice the sum of the length and width.

Perimeter = 20 m

Length + Width = 20 ÷ 2 = 10 m

Width = 10 − 6 = 4 m

They can make the garden _____ m wide.

Do

1 Find the perimeter of the rectangle.

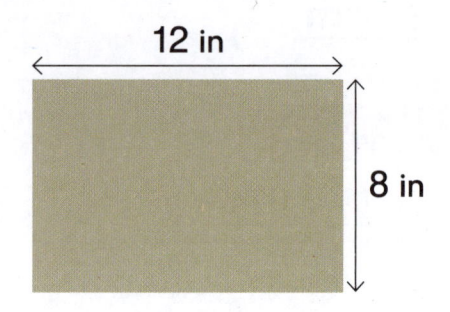

(a) 2 × Length = 2 × 12 = ☐ in

  2 × Width = 2 × 8 = ☐ in

  Perimeter = ☐ + ☐ = ☐ in

(b) Length + Width = 12 + 8 = ☐ in

  Perimeter = 2 × ☐ = ☐ in

2 A rectangle has a perimeter of 26 cm and a width of 5 cm. Find the length of the rectangle.

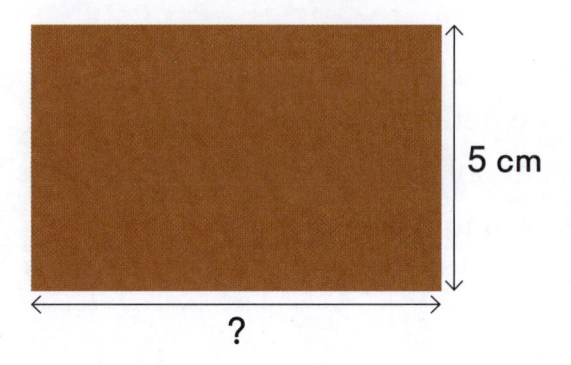

(a) Length + Width = 26 ÷ 2 = ☐ cm

  Length = ☐ − ☐ = ☐ cm

(b) 2 × Length = 26 − ☐ = ☐ cm

  Length = ☐ ÷ 2 = ☐ cm

3 A square has a perimeter of 36 in. What is the area of the square?

4 × Length of side = 36 in

Length of side = 36 ÷ 4 = ☐ in

Area = ☐ × ☐ = ☐ in²

4 Find the unknown lengths.

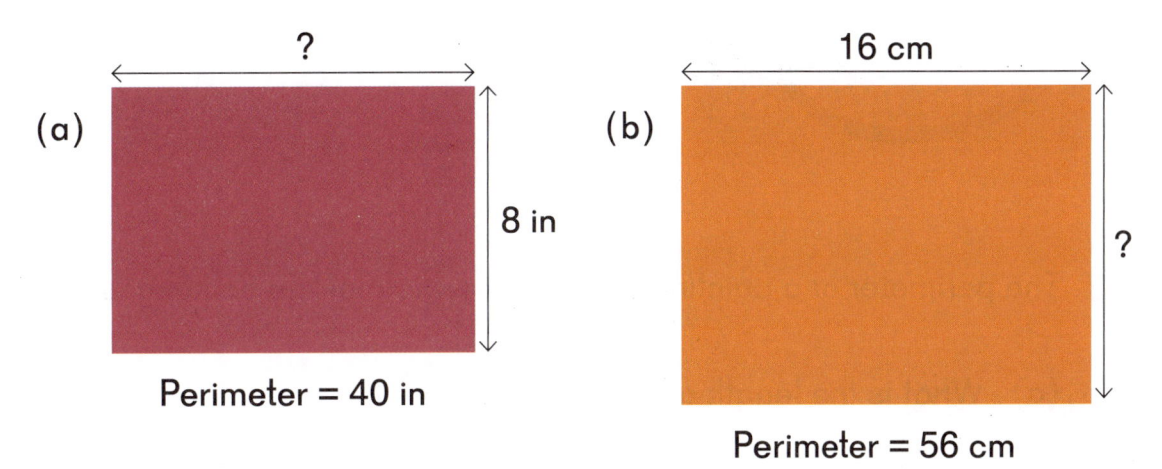

(a) ? / 8 in / Perimeter = 40 in

(b) 16 cm / ? / Perimeter = 56 cm

5 In the figures below, the square and the rectangle have the same area. The perimeter of the square is 40 cm. What is the length of the rectangle?

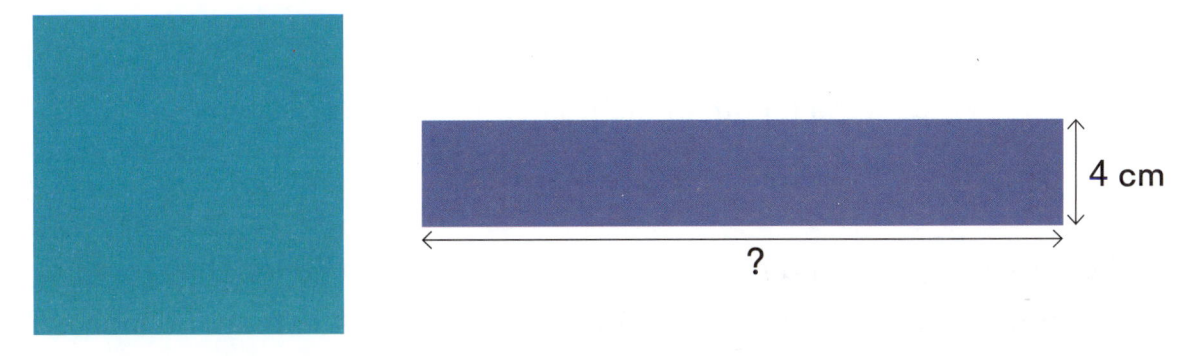

Perimeter = 40 cm

4 cm / ?

11-4 Perimeter — Part 1

6 The perimeter of a tennis court is 228 feet. The width of the court is 12 yards.

(a) What is the length of the court in feet?

(b) What is the length of the court in yards?

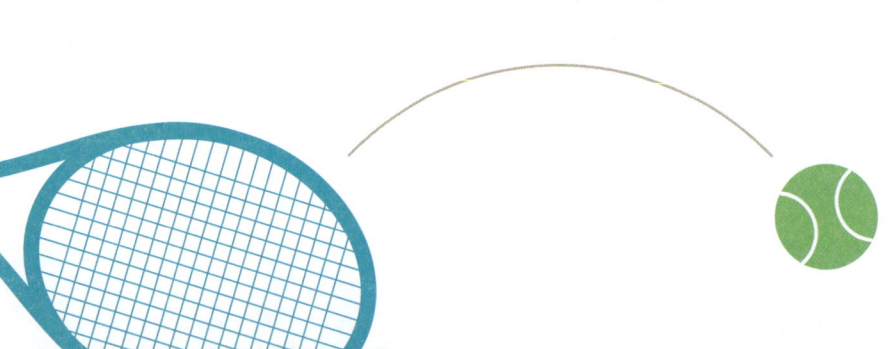

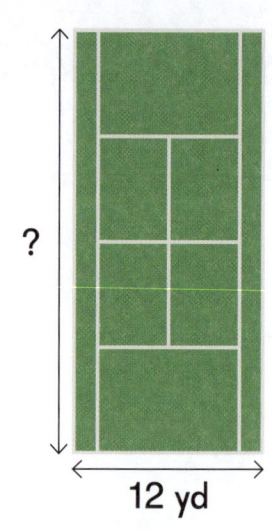

7 The perimeter of a painting is 18 ft. The width of the painting is $4\frac{1}{2}$ ft.

(a) What is the length of the painting in feet?

$2 \times \text{Length} = 18 - 4\frac{1}{2} - 4\frac{1}{2}$

(b) What is the length of the painting in inches?

8 The perimeter of a rectangular picture frame is 70 in. The length of the frame is 1 ft 8 in. What is the width of the frame in feet and inches?

Exercise 4 • page 39

Lesson 5
Perimeter — Part 2

Think

The dimensions of a puppy pen at the pet shelter is shown here. What is the perimeter of the puppy pen?

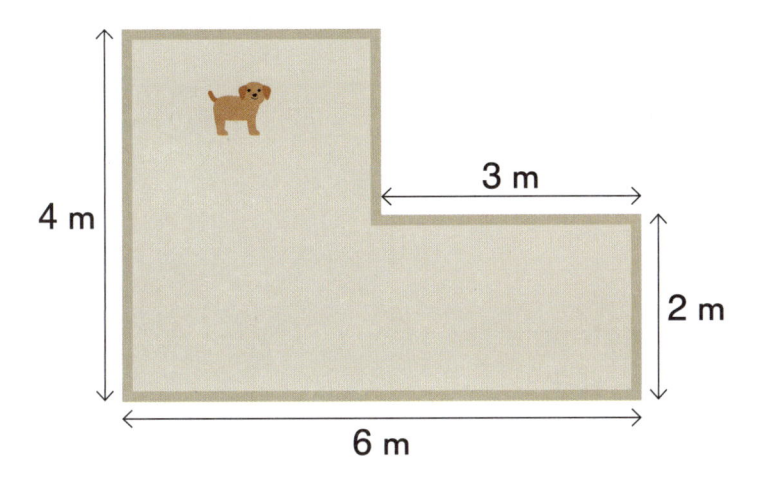

Learn

Method 1

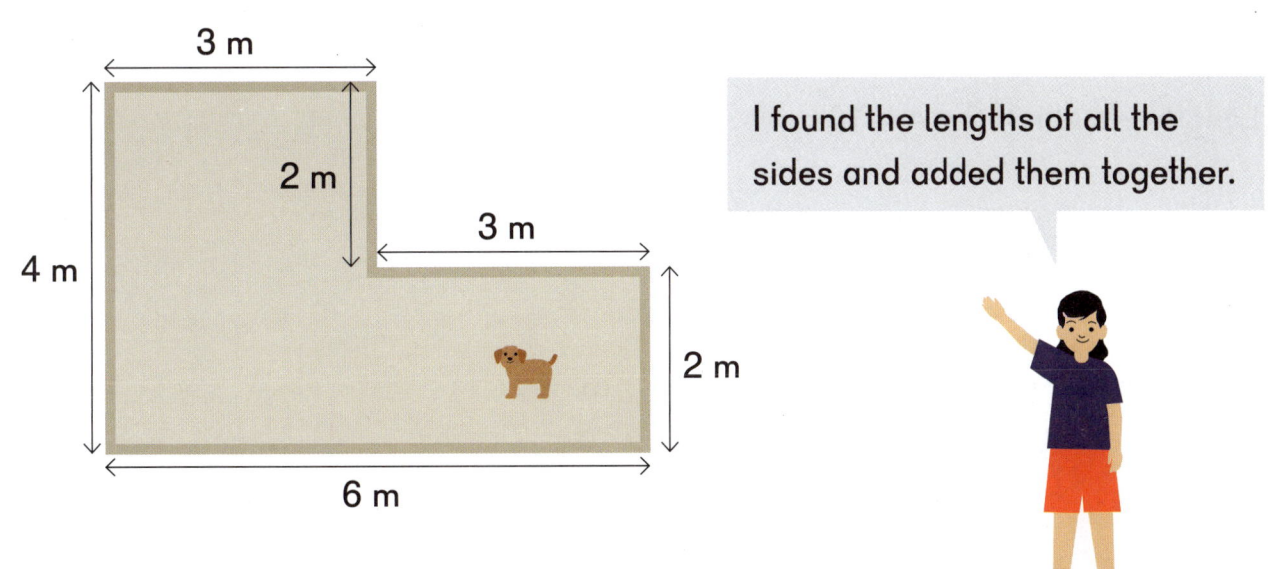

I found the lengths of all the sides and added them together.

Perimeter = 4 + 3 + 2 + 3 + 2 + 6 = 20 m

Method 2

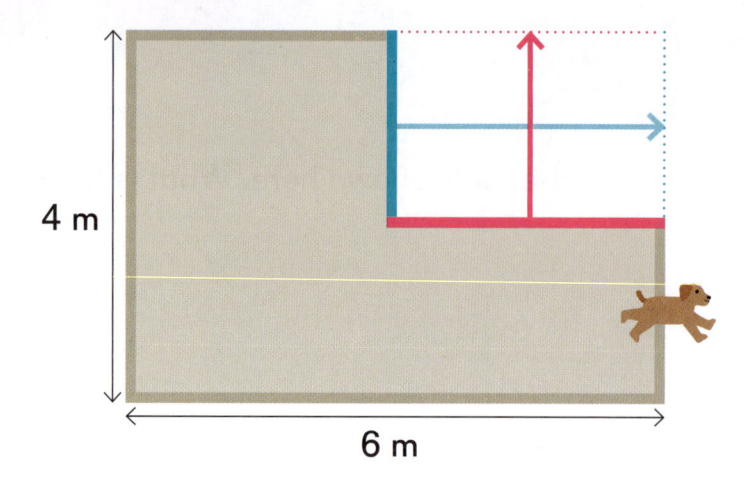

4 m

6 m

I moved some sides out to form a large rectangle. The area changes, but the perimeter does not.

Length + Width = 6 + 4 = 10 m

Perimeter = 2 × 10 = 20 m

The perimeter of the puppy pen is _____ m.

Do

1 Find the perimeter of the figure in meters and centimeters.

28 cm
12 cm
25 cm
16 cm

Which method has easier calculations in this case?

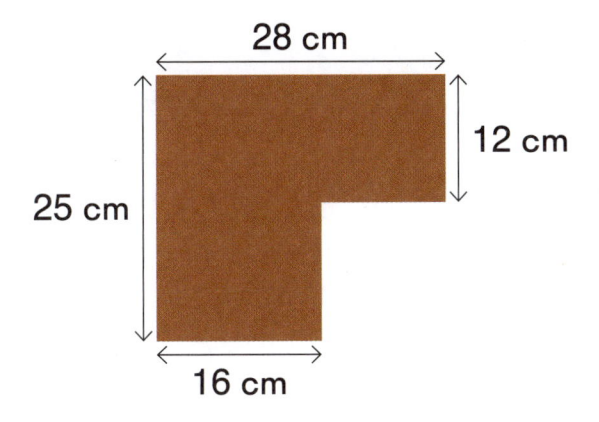

2 Find the perimeter of the figure.

9 ft
5 ft
$2\frac{1}{4}$ ft
$2\frac{1}{2}$ ft

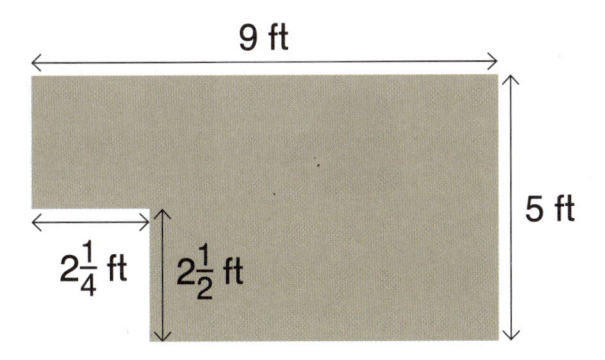

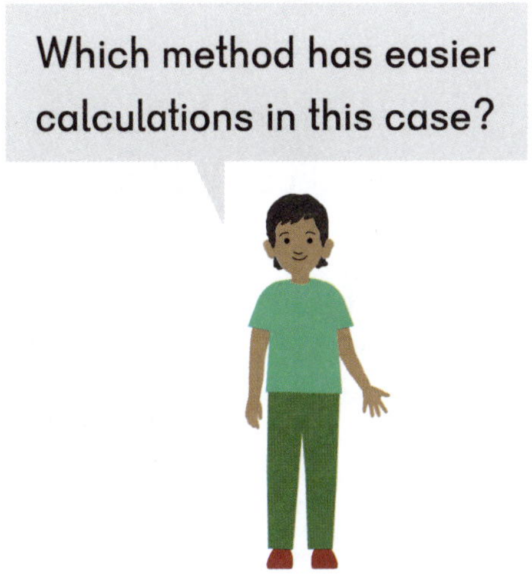

3 Find the perimeter of the figure in meters and centimeters.

25 cm
30 cm
65 cm
1 m 10 cm

11-5 Perimeter — Part 2

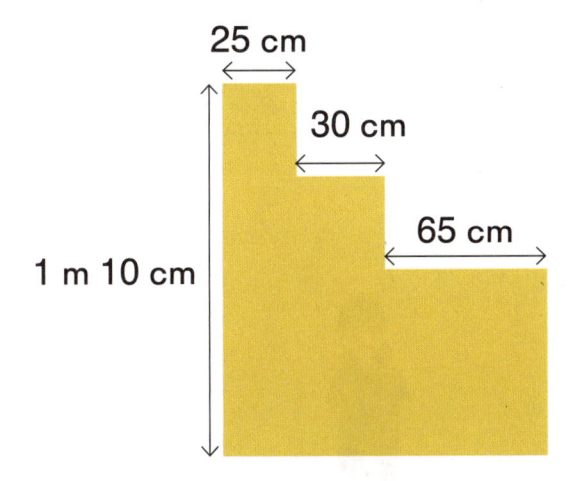

④ Mr. Bhatia is putting a fence around his garden. What is the total feet of fencing that he will need?

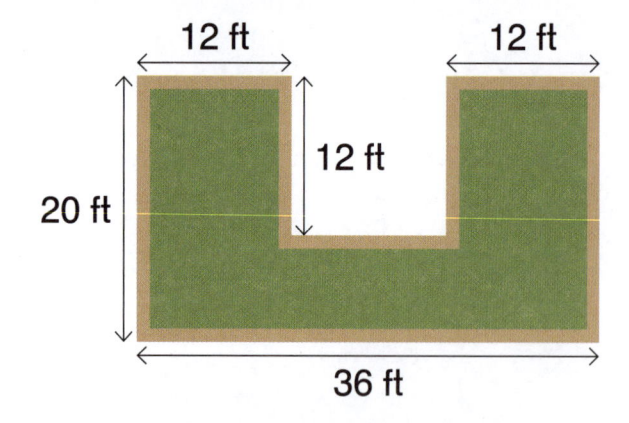

12 ft   12 ft
12 ft
20 ft
36 ft

I just need to find one length, then I can add all the sides.

I can find the perimeter of the large rectangle, then add in the two 12-ft sides.

⑤ The following figure is made from rectangles. Find the perimeter of the figure in centimeters.

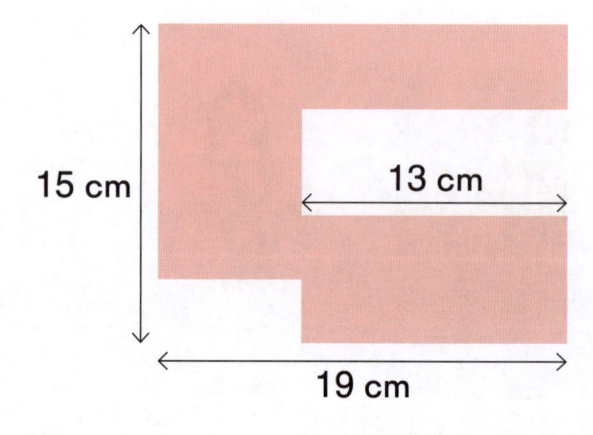

15 cm
13 cm
19 cm

54   11-5 Perimeter — Part 2

6. Dion made this letter E by overlapping four strips of paper each 4 inches wide and 15 inches long. What is the perimeter?

7. (a) Find the perimeter of the figure below in feet.

   (b) Express the perimeter of the figure below in inches.

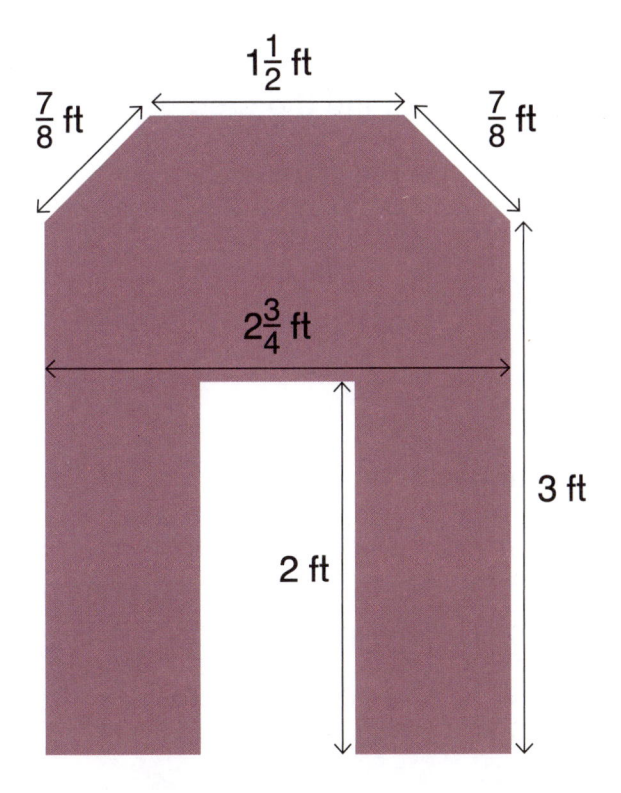

Exercise 5 • page 42

Lesson 6
Practice

P 6

1 How many square feet are in a 2-yard square?

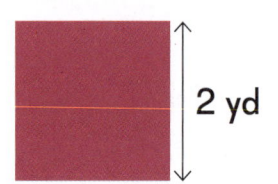

2 yd

2 Express the area of the rectangle in square feet.

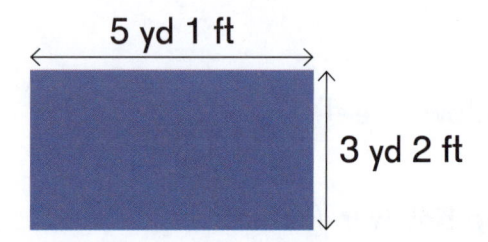

5 yd 1 ft

3 yd 2 ft

3 The rectangle has a perimeter of 40 in. Find the area of the rectangle.

6 in

4 Find the perimeter of each rectangle.

(a) 9 cm

Area = 63 cm²

(b) 2 yd 1 ft

Area = 42 ft²

5 Find the area and perimeter of each shape.

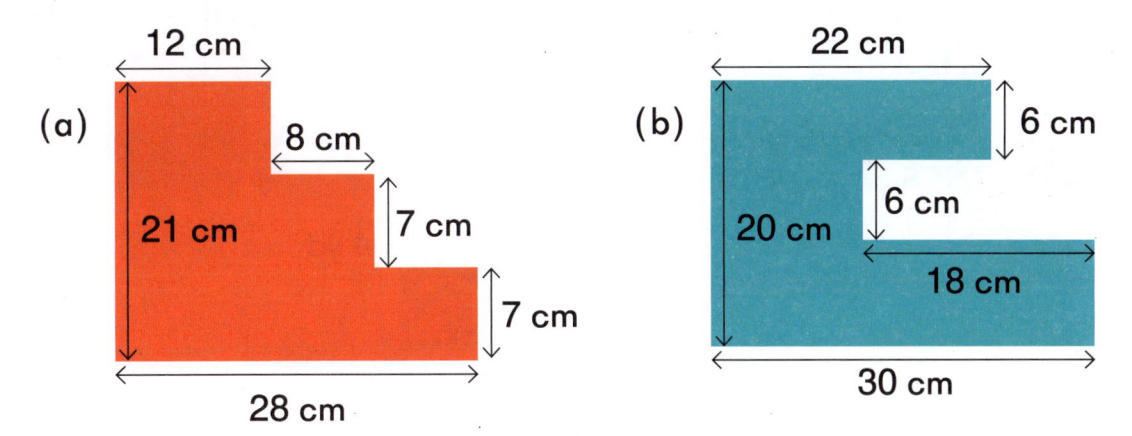

(a) 12 cm, 8 cm, 21 cm, 7 cm, 7 cm, 28 cm

(b) 22 cm, 6 cm, 20 cm, 6 cm, 18 cm, 30 cm

6 Find the perimeter of the figure in meters.

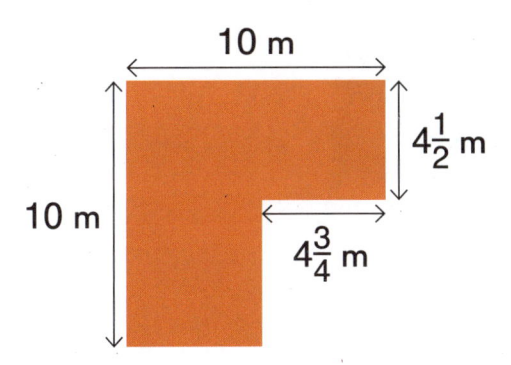

10 m, $4\frac{1}{2}$ m, 10 m, $4\frac{3}{4}$ m

7 A rectangular swimming pool measures 16 m by 10 m. It has a path 2 m wide around it. Find the area of the path in square meters.

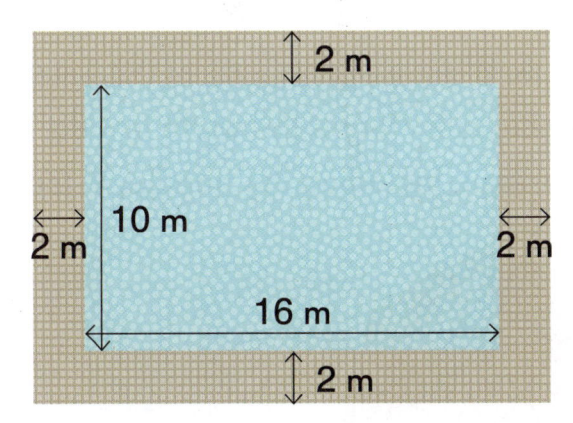

2 m, 10 m, 2 m, 2 m, 16 m, 2 m

11-6 Practice

8) This garden shown below has a rock garden in the center and a flower garden around the rock garden. What is the area of the flower garden in square feet?

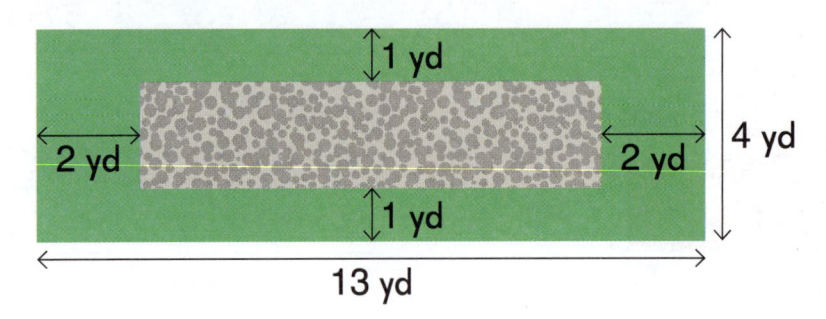

9) Find the perimeter of the figure in centimeters.

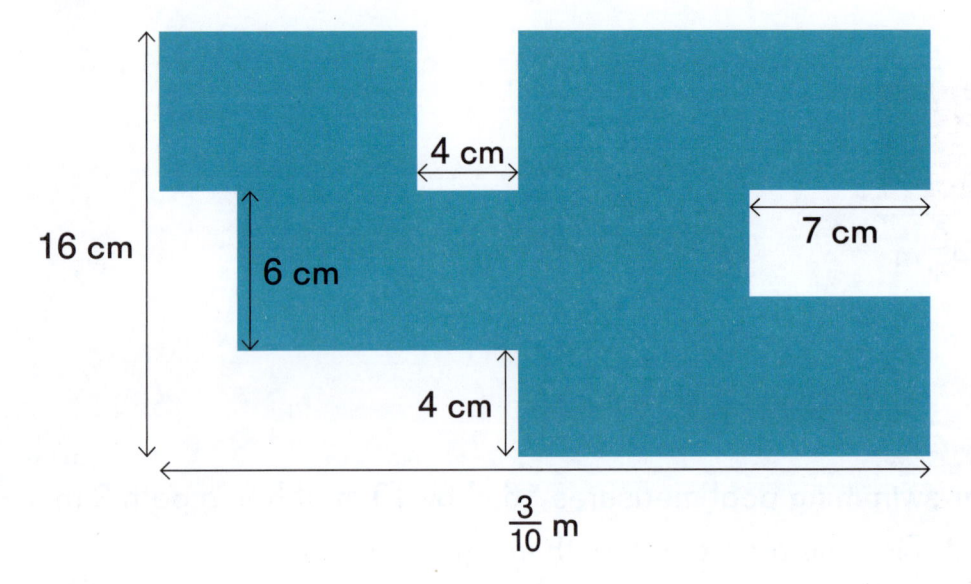

10) Alex made a cardboard stop sign for a game. Each side of the octagon is $1\frac{1}{2}$ ft long. The length of the handle is $2\frac{1}{2}$ ft and the width is $\frac{1}{2}$ ft. What is the perimeter of the whole sign, including the handle, in inches?

Exercise 6 • page 45

Chapter 12

Decimals

Where have you seen decimals?

0.47 kg

Sparkling WATER
750 ML | 25.4 Fl oz

00:13.02
LAP 1 00:12.67
LAP 2 00:13.02

$1,299.98

Lesson 1
Tenths — Part 1

Think

Dion divided a 1-m paper tape into 10 equal length parts.

0 m   1 m

(a) 1 part is what fraction of 1 meter?

(b) 3 parts is what fraction of 1 meter?

(c) 7 parts is what fraction of 1 meter?

(d) How many meters is 7 parts and 3 parts together?

Learn

(a) When 1 m is divided into 10 equal parts, each part is $\frac{1}{10}$ m.

We can express fractions in tenths as **decimals**.

$\frac{1}{10}$ m = 0.1 m

0.1 is read as **zero point one** or **one tenth**.

1 tenth = 0.1 m
↑
decimal point

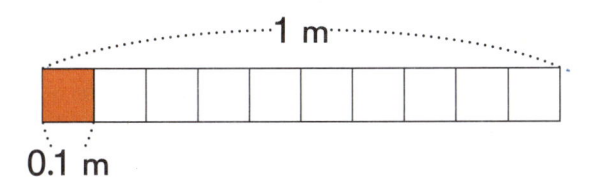

1 m

0.1 m

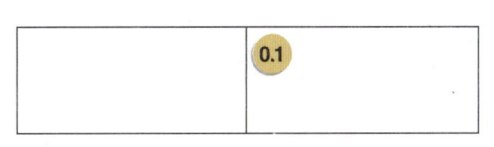

The unit of measurement that is 0.1 m is called a **decimeter (dm)**. 1 m = 10 dm, so 1 dm = 0.1 m.

Ones	Tenths
0	1

There are 0 ones and 1 tenth in 0.1.

(b) Three parts is $\frac{3}{10}$ m. $\frac{3}{10}$ expressed as a decimal is 0.3.

$\frac{3}{10}$ m = 0.3 m

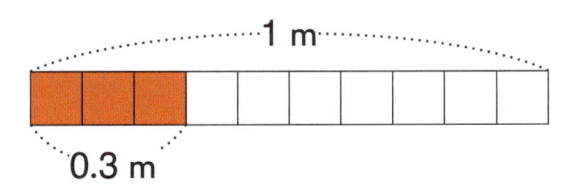

1 m

0.3 m

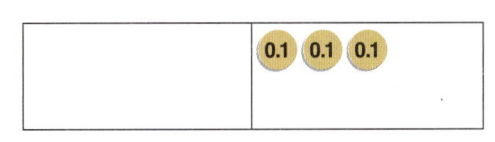

0.3 is read as **zero point three** or **three tenths**.

Ones	Tenths
0	3

There are 0 ones and 3 tenths in 0.3.

12-1 Tenths — Part 1

(c) Seven parts is $\frac{7}{10}$ m. $\frac{7}{10}$ expressed as a decimal is 0.7.

$\frac{7}{10}$ m = 0.7 m

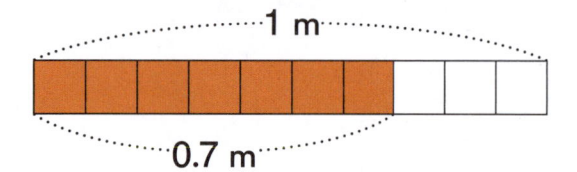

Ones	Tenths
0	7

There are 0 ones and 7 tenths in 0.7.

(d) Seven parts and three parts is 1 m.

0.7 + 0.3 = 1

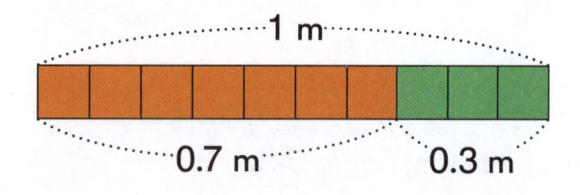

10 tenths = 1.0 = 1

Ones	Tenths
1	0

Numbers such as 3, 250, and 9,455 are whole numbers. Numbers such as 0.7, 5.8, and 42.5 are **decimal** numbers. We can use decimals to write fractions with denominators of 10, 100, 1,000, etc.

Do

1 (a) Express the amount of water in liters as a fraction and a decimal.

$\frac{8}{10}$ L = **0** . **8** L

(b) Express the weight of the lemons in kilograms as a fraction and as a decimal.

$\frac{7}{10}$ kg = **0** . **7** kg

2 Write each fraction as a decimal.

(a) $\frac{9}{10}$ = **0** . **9**

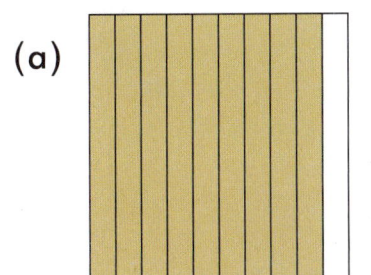

9 tenths

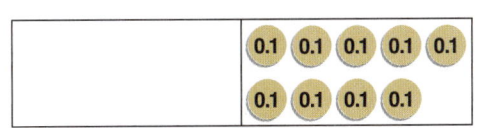

Ones	Tenths
0 .	9

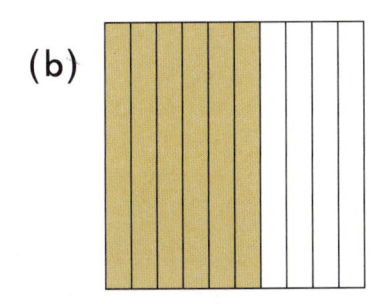

(b) $\frac{6}{10}$ = **0** . **6**

6 tenths

Ones	Tenths
0 .	6

12-1 Tenths — Part 1

3. Express each number as a fraction with a denominator of 10 and as a decimal.

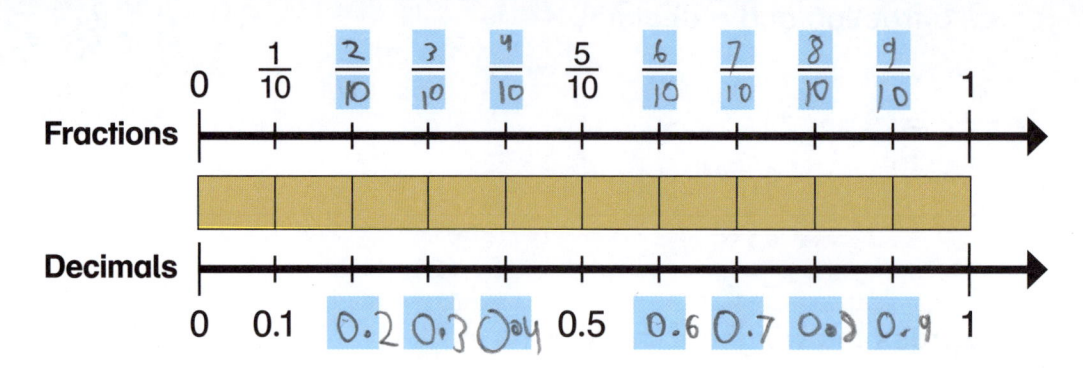

Fractions: 0, 1/10, 2/10, 3/10, 4/10, 5/10, 6/10, 7/10, 8/10, 9/10, 1

Decimals: 0, 0.1, 0.2, 0.3, 0.4, 0.5, 0.6, 0.7, 0.8, 0.9, 1

4. Find the missing values.

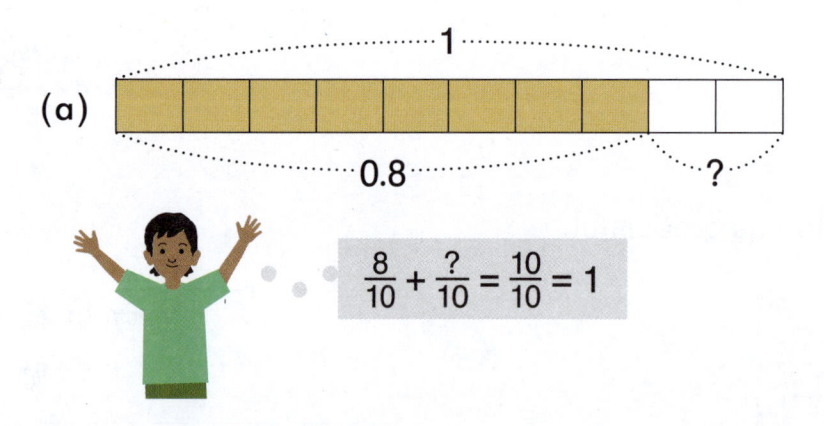

(a) 0.8 and ?

$$\frac{8}{10} + \frac{?}{10} = \frac{10}{10} = 1$$

0.8 and 0.2 make 1.

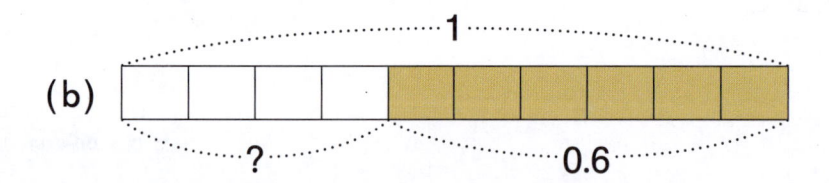

(b) ? and 0.6

0.4 and 0.6 make 1.

(c) 0.7 + 0.3 = 1

(d) 1 − 0.5 = 0.4

5. Express each fraction as a decimal and each decimal as a fraction in tenths.

(a) $\frac{1}{10}$ = 0.1 (b) $\frac{2}{10}$ 0.2 (c) $\frac{4}{10}$ 0.4 (d) $\frac{8}{10}$ 0.8

(e) 0.5 $\frac{5}{10}$ (f) 0.6 $\frac{6}{10}$ (g) 0.8 $\frac{8}{10}$ (h) 0.2 $\frac{2}{10}$

6. Order the numbers from least to greatest.

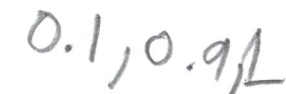

(a) 0.7, 0.2, 0.4   (b) 0.1, 1, 0.9

0.2, 0.4, 0.7   0.1, 0.9, 1

7. Express the length of the fly in centimeters as a decimal.

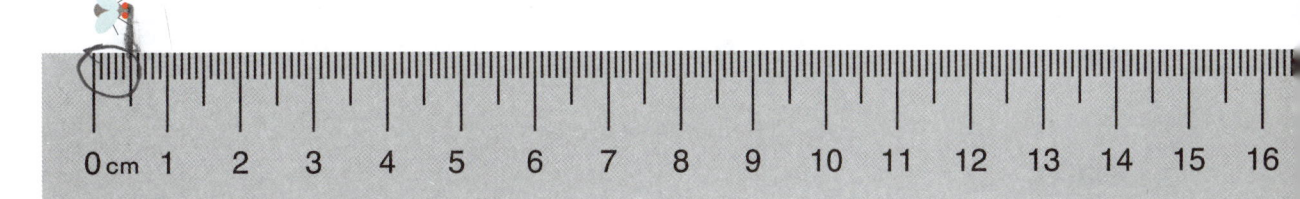

The fly is 5 mm long.
1 cm = 10 mm
1 mm = 0.1 cm
5 mm = ? cm

8. Express the distance between Alex's house and the school in kilometers as a decimal.

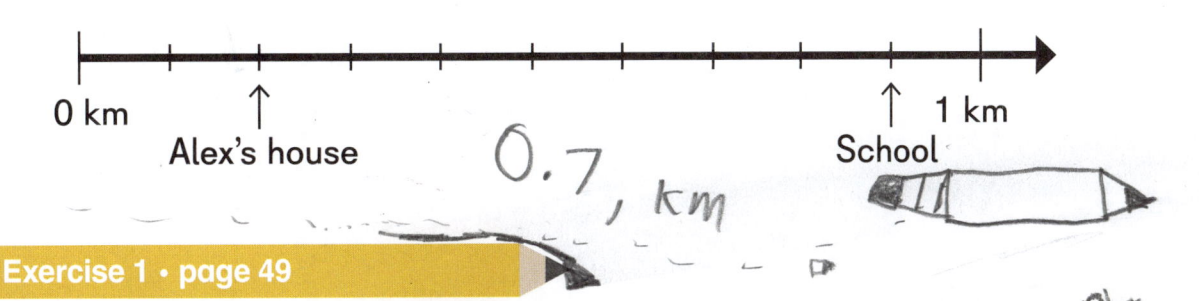

0.7 km

Exercise 1 • page 49

12-1 Tenths — Part 1

Lesson 2
Tenths — Part 2

Think

Express the height of each animal in meters using decimals.

Learn

There are 10 increments between 0 m and 1 m so each increment is 0.1 m.

$\frac{3}{10}$ m = 0.3 m

1 m

$1 + \frac{3}{10} = 1\frac{3}{10} = 1.3$

1 one 3 tenths = 1.3

1.3 = 1 + 0.3

The zebra is 1.3 m tall.

Ones	Tenths
1	3

We read 1.3 as **one point three** or **one and three tenths**.

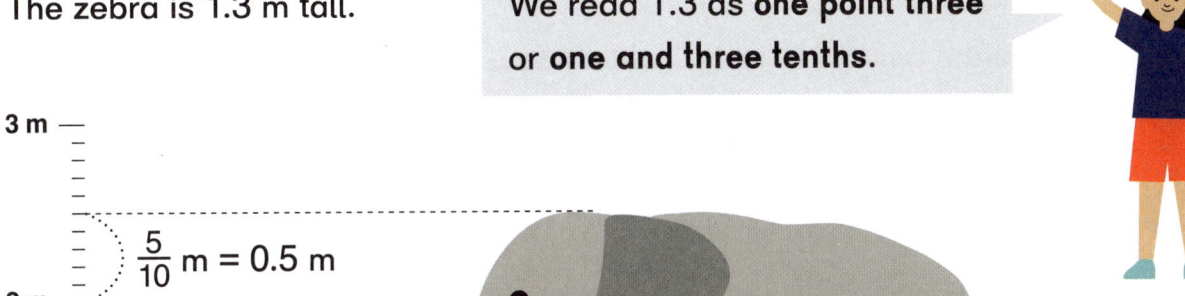

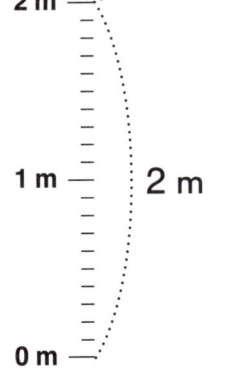

$\frac{5}{10}$ m = 0.5 m

2 m

$2 + \frac{5}{10} = 2\frac{5}{10} = 2.5$

2 ones 5 tenths = 2.5

2.5 = 2 + 0.5

The elephant is _____ m tall.

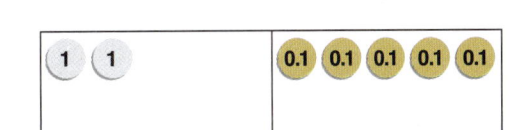

Ones	Tenths
2	5

We read 2.5 as **two point five** or **two and five tenths**.

12-2 Tenths — Part 2

Do

1

Express the amount of water in liters as a decimal.

4.7 L

2 Express each improper fraction as a mixed number and as a decimal.

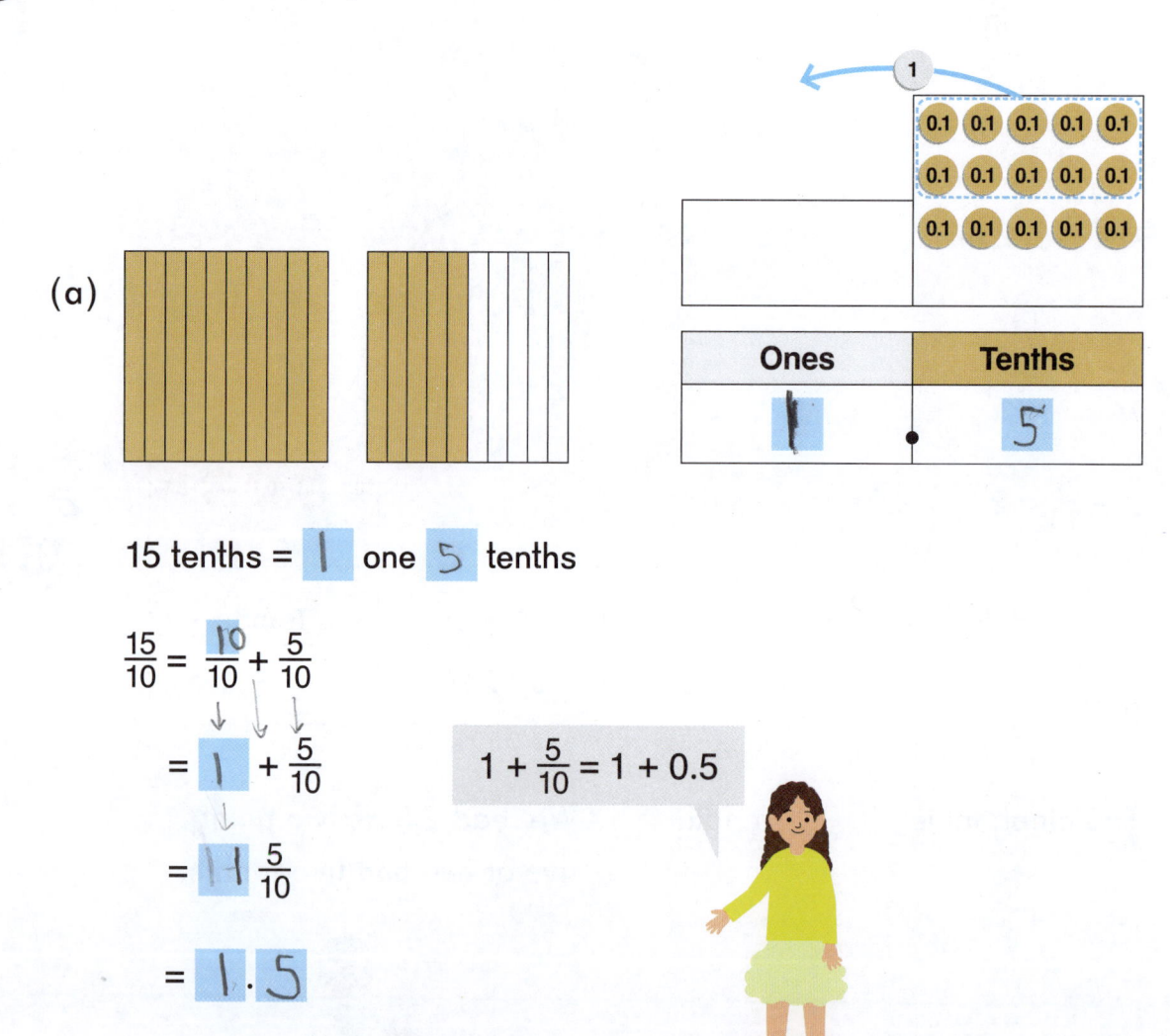

(a)

15 tenths = 1 one 5 tenths

Ones	Tenths
1	5

$$\frac{15}{10} = \frac{10}{10} + \frac{5}{10}$$

$$= 1 + \frac{5}{10}$$

$$= 1\frac{5}{10}$$

$$= 1.5$$

$1 + \frac{5}{10} = 1 + 0.5$

(b)

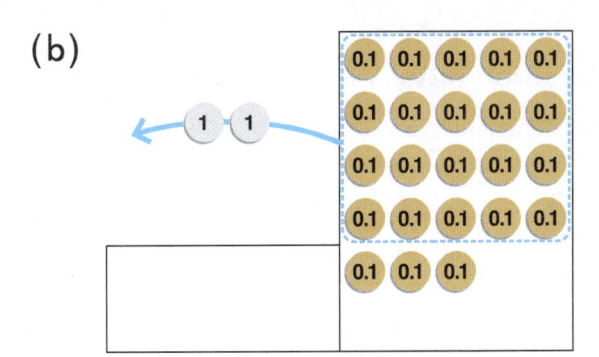

Ones	Tenths
2	3

23 tenths = 2 ones 3 tenths

$\frac{23}{10} = \frac{20}{10} + \frac{3}{10} = 2\frac{3}{10} = 2.3$

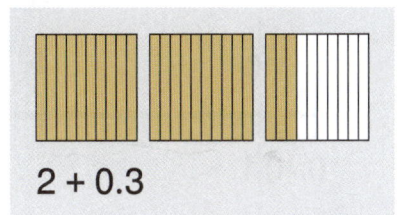

2 + 0.3

(c)

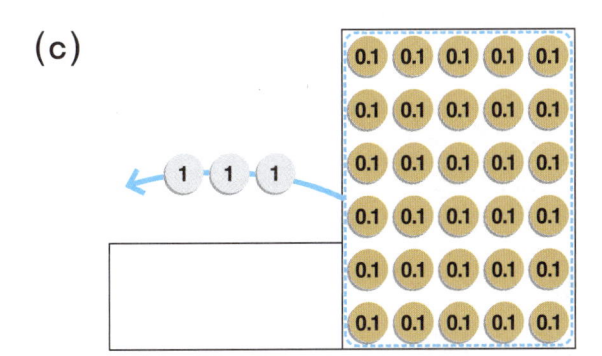

Ones	Tenths
3	0

30 tenths = 3 ones 0 tenths

$\frac{30}{10} = 3$

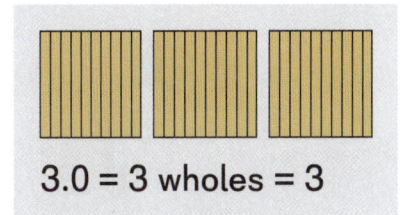

3.0 = 3 wholes = 3

3 Write the number represented by each letter as a decimal and as a fraction or mixed number with a denominator of 10.

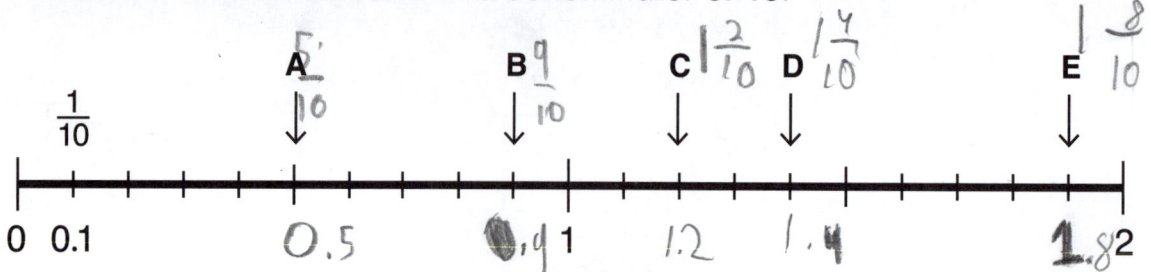

A $\frac{5}{10}$ B $\frac{9}{10}$ C $1\frac{2}{10}$ D $1\frac{4}{10}$ E $1\frac{8}{10}$

$\frac{1}{10}$

0   0.1   0.5   0.9   1   1.2   1.4   1.8   2

4 Write the numbers as decimals and as mixed numbers.

(a) → 5.6

$5.6 = 5\frac{6}{10}$

(b) → 15.8

$15.8 = 15\frac{8}{10}$

(c) → 30.5

$30.5 = 30\frac{5}{10}$

70   12-2 Tenths — Part 2

5 (a) 9 + 0.5 = ☐ (b) 10 + 6 + 0.5 = ☐

(c) 50 + 0.8 = ☐ (d) 500 + 70 + 0.4 = ☐

(e) 0.1 + 2 = ☐ (f) 0.6 + 40 + 8 = ☐

6 (a) 4.8 = ☐ + 0.8 (b) 9.2 = ☐ + 0.2

(c) 35.7 = 30 + 5 + ☐ (d) 60.5 = 60 + ☐

(e) 29.2 = ☐ + 29 (f) 0.7 + ☐ = 200.7

7 Write the numbers as decimals.

(a) 4 tenths   4/10 = 0.4

(b) 50 tenths   5.0

(c) 52 tenths   10   5.2

(d) 10 ones 32 tenths   10.32

8 Billy ran 2 km in the morning and 0.6 km in the afternoon. He wants to run a total of 3 km that day. How much farther does he need to run?

(a) How many kilometers has he run so far?

(b) How many more kilometers does he still need to run?

Exercise 2 • page 52

Lesson 3
Hundredths — Part 1

Think

Dion divided a 1 m strip into 10 equal parts. Then he divided one of those parts into 10 smaller equal parts.

0 m   0.1 m   1 m

(a) When 0.1 m is divided into 10 equal parts, what fraction of 1 m is 1 part? How can we express this length as a decimal?

> When we expressed $\frac{1}{10}$ of 1 as a decimal we wrote a 0 in the ones place and a 1 to the right of the decimal point. So to express $\frac{1}{10}$ of 1 tenth as a decimal...

(b) What fraction of 1 m is 7 of these smaller parts? How can we express this length as a decimal?

> I wonder how many cm these lengths are.

Learn

(a) When 0.1 m is divided into 10 equal parts, each part is $\frac{1}{100}$ m.

Since there are 100 cm in 1 m, 1 cm is $\frac{1}{100}$ m.

$$\div 10 \begin{cases} 100 \text{ cm} = 1 \text{ m} \\ 10 \text{ cm} = \frac{1}{10} \text{ m} \\ 1 \text{ cm} = \frac{1}{100} \text{ m} \end{cases} \div 10$$

We can write fractions expressed in hundredths as decimals.

$\frac{1}{100}$ m = 0.01 m

We read 0.01 as **zero point zero one** or **one hundredth**.

1 cm = 0.01 m

(b) 7 parts is $\frac{7}{100}$ of 1 m.

$\frac{7}{100}$ m = 0.07 m

Ones	Tenths	Hundredths
0	0	7

There are 0 ones, 0 tenths, and 7 hundredths in 0.07.

The hundredths place is also called the **second decimal place**. The tenths place is called the **first decimal place**.

0.07

12-3 Hundredths — Part 1   73

Do

1 (a) How many 0.01 m are in 0.1 m?

0.01 m

0 m   0.1 m

? hundredths = 1 tenth

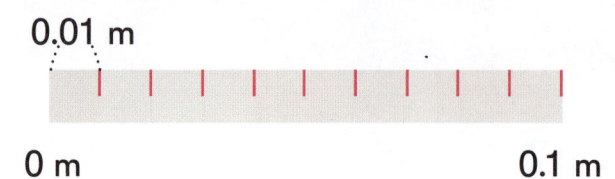

(b) What is the sum of 0.07 m and 0.03 m?

0.07 m + 0.03 m = ☐.☐ m

(c) How many 0.01 m are in 1 m?

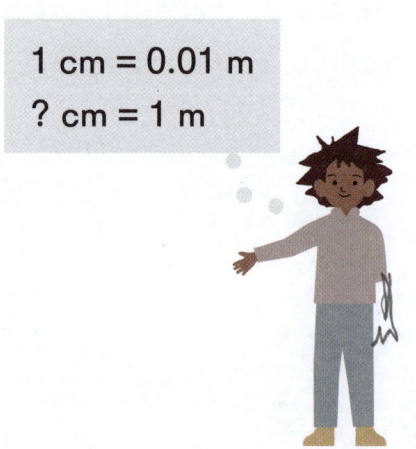

1 cm = 0.01 m
? cm = 1 m

2 Express each fraction as a decimal.

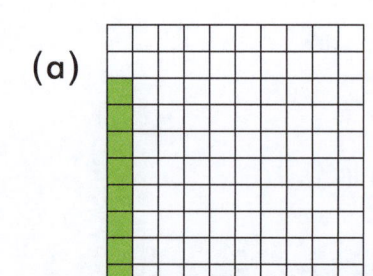

(a)

Ones	Tenths	Hundredths
0 .	0	8

$\frac{8}{100}$ is 0.08 hundredths.

12-3 Hundredths — Part 1

(b)

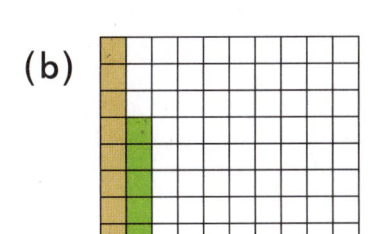

$\frac{17}{100}$ is 1 tenth ▢ hundredths.

$\frac{17}{100} = \frac{10}{100} + \frac{7}{100} = \frac{1}{10} + \frac{7}{100} = 0.17$

We read 0.17 as **zero point one seven** or **seventeen hundredths**.

(c)

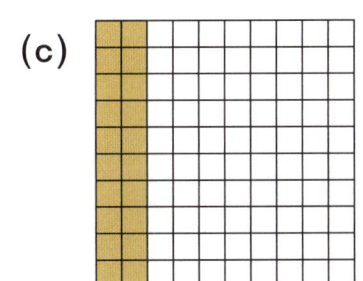

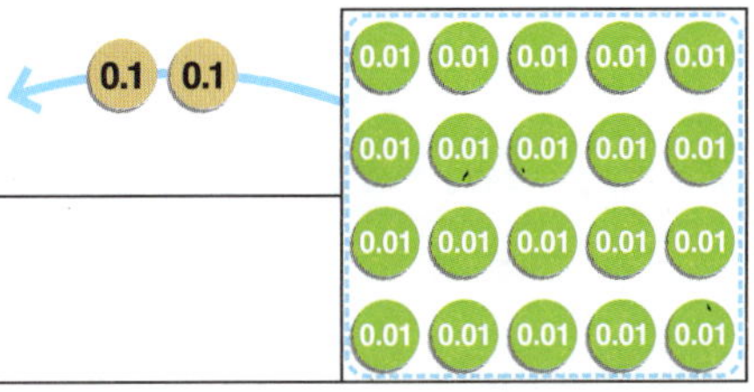

Ones: 0 Tenths: 2 Hundredths: 0

$\frac{20}{100}$ is 0.2 tenths.

0.20 = 0.2

12-3 Hundredths — Part 1

3. Write the number represented by each letter as a decimal and as a fraction in hundredths.

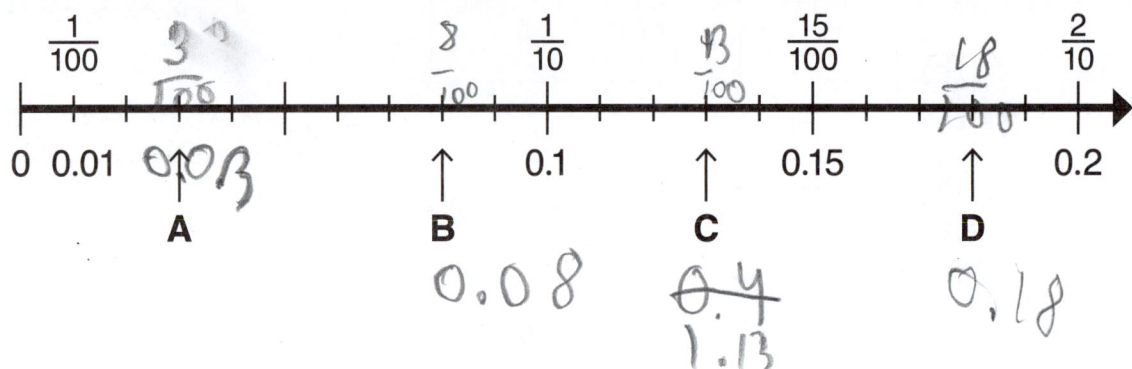

[Number line with marks: 1/100, 3/100 (written), 8/100 (written), 1/10, 13/100 (written), 15/100, 18/100 (written), 2/10; labels 0, 0.01, 0.03 (A written), 0.1, 0.15, 0.2]

A — 0.03
B — 0.08
C — 0.4 / 1.13
D — 0.18

4. Complete the number patterns.

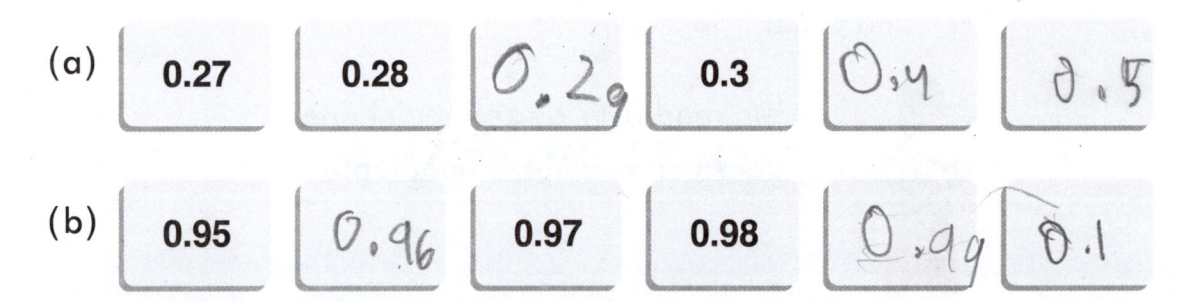

(a) | 0.27 | 0.28 | 0.29 | 0.3 | 0.4 | 0.5 |

(b) | 0.95 | 0.96 | 0.97 | 0.98 | 0.99 | 0.1 |

5. Express each fraction as a decimal.

(a) $\frac{5}{100}$ 0.05

(b) $\frac{69}{100}$ 0.69

(c) $\frac{70}{100}$ 0.70

6. (a) 0.08 + 0.02 = 0.1

(b) 0.1 − 0.05 = 0.05

7. A ribbon is 35 cm long. Express the length of the ribbon in meters as a decimal.

100 cm = 1 m

Exercise 3 • page 56

Lesson 4
Hundredths — Part 2

Think

The table below shows the amount of water Emma's pets require each day.

Animal	Water Needed Each Day in Liters
Dog	1
Rabbit	0.3
Guinea Pig	0.05

How much water does she need to give to her pets altogether in one day? Express the amount as a decimal.

$1 + \frac{3}{10} + \frac{5}{100} = ?$

Learn

Method 1

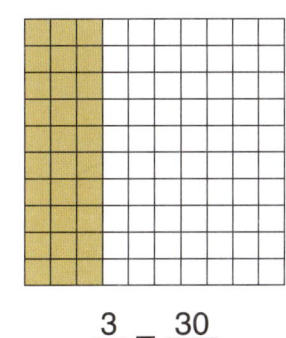

1 $\frac{3}{10} = \frac{30}{100}$ $\frac{5}{100}$

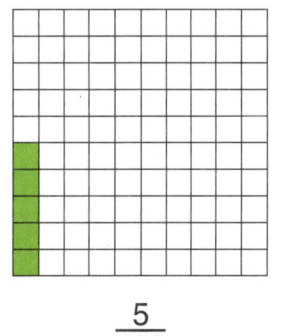

$1 + \frac{3}{10} + \frac{5}{100} = 1 + \frac{30}{100} + \frac{5}{100} = 1\frac{35}{100} = 1.35$

Method 2

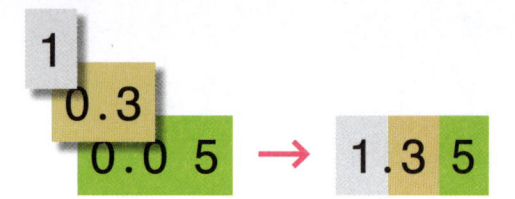

1.35 is read as **one point three five** or **one and thirty-five hundredths**.

1 + 0.3 + 0.05 = 1.35

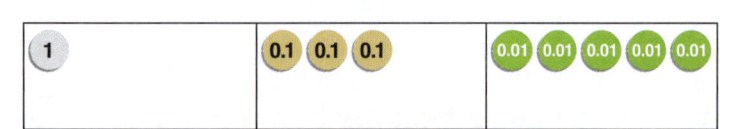

Emma gives her pets ⬚ L of water each day.

Ones	Tenths	Hundredths
1 .	3	5

The digit 1 in 1.35 is in the **ones** place. Its value is 1.

The digit 3 in 1.35 is in the _____ place. Its value is 3 tenths or 0.3.

The digit 5 in 1.35 is in the _____ place. Its value is ⬚ hundredths or 0.05.

1.35 = 1 + 0.3 + 0.05

1 + 0.3 + 0.05 is 1.35 expressed in expanded form.

78   12-4 Hundredths — Part 2

Do

1. (a)

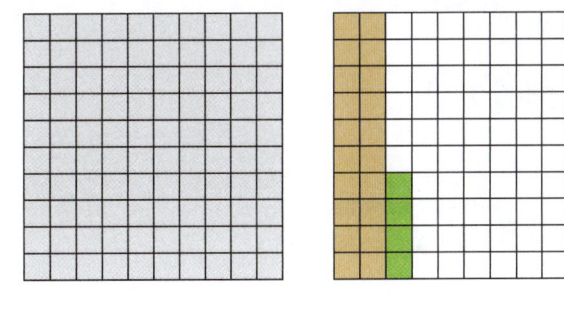

$$\frac{124}{100} = \frac{100}{100} + \frac{20}{100} + \frac{4}{100} = 1 + \frac{\square}{10} + \frac{\square}{100}$$

Ones	Tenths	Hundredths

(b)

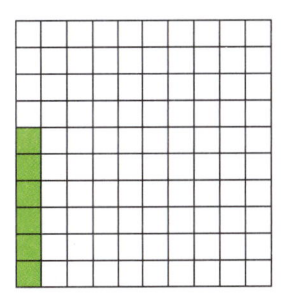

$$2\frac{6}{100} = 2 + \frac{6}{100}$$

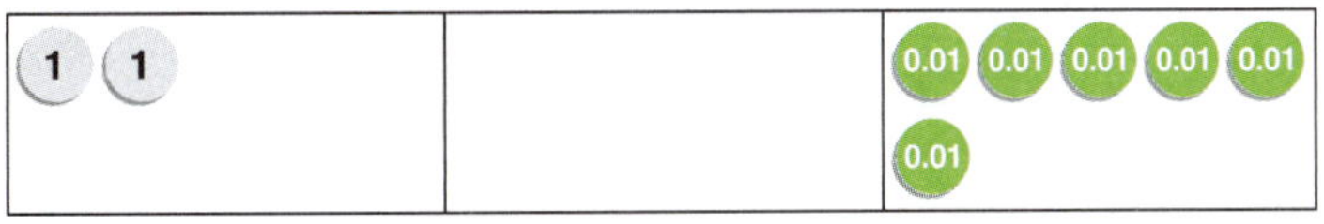

Ones	Tenths	Hundredths

2 ones + 0 tenths + 6 hundredths

12-4 Hundredths — Part 2

2 What is the value of each digit in 4.82?

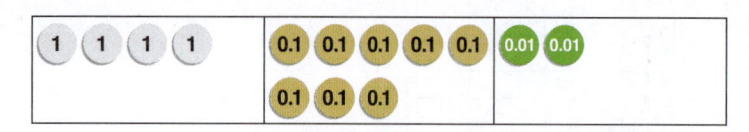

Ones	Tenths	Hundredths

The digit 4 is in the _____ place. Its value is 4.

The digit 8 is in the _____ place. Its value is ☐ tenths or 0.8.

The digit 2 is in the _____ place. Its value is ☐ hundredths or 0.☐☐.

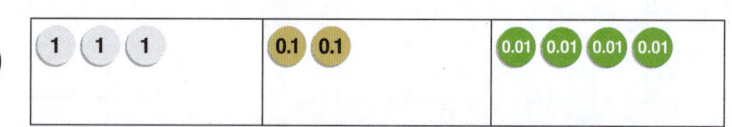

4.82 = 4 + ☐ + ☐

3 (a)

Ones	Tenths	Hundredths

3 + 0.2 + 0.04 = ☐

(b)

Tens	Ones	Tenths	Hundredths

30 + 4 + 0.5 + 0.02 = ☐

12-4 Hundredths — Part 2

(c)

Tens	Ones	Tenths	Hundredths

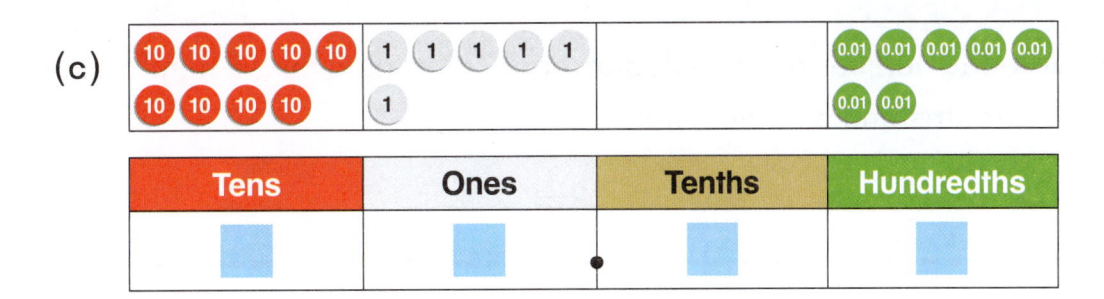

90 + 6 + 0.07 =

4. Write the numbers shown by the place-value cards in numerals and in expanded form.

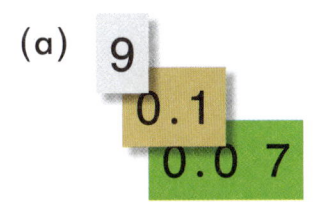

(a) 9, 0.1, 0.07

(b) 30, 0.4, 0.08

(c) 6, 0.05

(d) 100, 2, 0.1, 0.02

5 Write the number represented by each letter as a mixed number in hundredths and as a decimal.

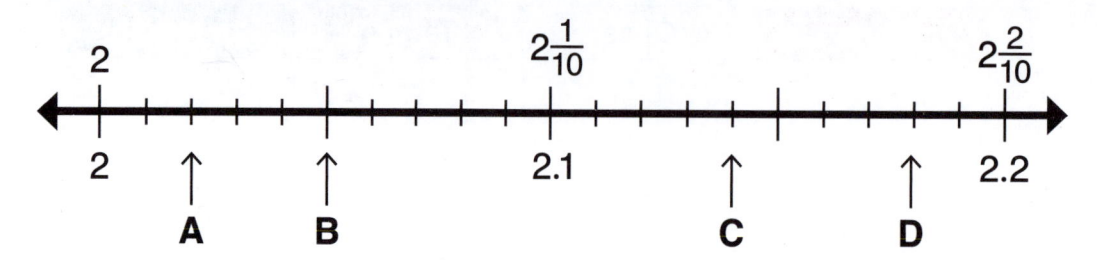

6 Express each mixed number as a decimal.

(a) $2\frac{9}{100}$

(b) $4\frac{25}{100}$

(c) $30\frac{40}{100}$

7 (a) 50 + 0.07 = ☐

(b) 4.68 = 4 + ☐ + ☐

(c) 29.05 = 20 + 9 + ☐

(d) 4.73 − 0.7 = ☐

(e) 39.75 − 0.75 = ☐

(f) 892.05 − 90 = ☐

8 Sofia had 2.75 m of ribbon. She used 0.7 m of ribbon to wrap a present. How much ribbon does she have left?

Exercise 4 • page 59

Lesson 5
Expressing Decimals as Fractions in Simplest Form

Think

A foam football is 0.75 ft long.

(a) Express the length of the football in feet as a fraction in simplest form.

(b) Express the length of the football in inches.

Learn

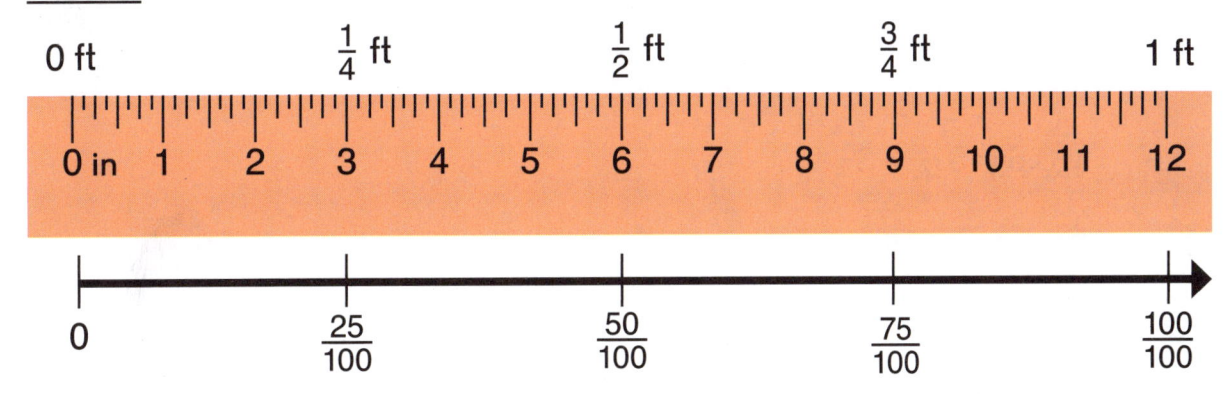

(a) $0.75 = \dfrac{75}{100} = \dfrac{3}{4}$ (× 4)

The football is _____ ft long.

(b) $0.75 \times 12 = \dfrac{3}{4} \times 12 = 9$

$\dfrac{75}{100} \times 12 = \dfrac{3}{4} \times 12$

The football is _____ in long.

12-5 Expressing Decimals as Fractions in Simplest Form

Do

1 (a) Express 0.6 as a fraction in simplest form.

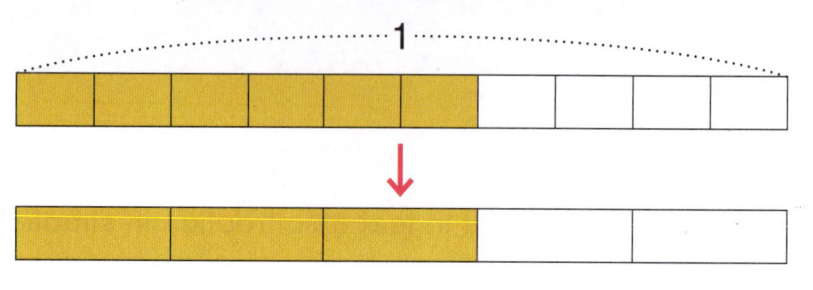

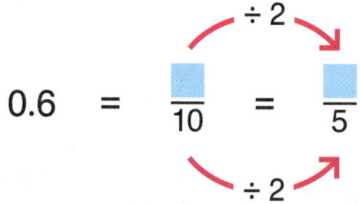

$$0.6 = \frac{\square}{10} = \frac{\square}{5}$$

with ÷2 applied to numerator and denominator.

$\frac{6}{10} = \frac{3}{5}$

(b) Express 3.6 as a mixed number in simplest form.

$$3.6 = 3\frac{\square}{10} = 3\frac{\square}{5}$$

2 (a) Express 0.05 as a fraction in simplest form.

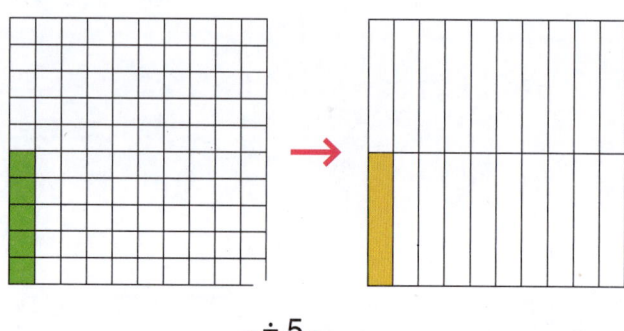

$$0.05 = \frac{\square}{100} = \frac{\square}{\square}$$

with ÷5 applied to numerator and denominator.

(b) Express 4.05 as a mixed number in simplest form.

$$4.05 = 4\frac{\square}{100} = 4\frac{\square}{\square}$$

12-5 Expressing Decimals as Fractions in Simplest Form

③ (a) Express 0.84 as a fraction in simplest form.

$$0.84 = \frac{84}{100} = \frac{\square}{\square}$$

with ÷4 applied to numerator and denominator.

(b) Express 8.84 as a mixed number in simplest form.

$$8.84 = 8\frac{\square}{100} = 8\frac{\square}{\square}$$

④ Express each decimal as a fraction or as a mixed number in simplest form.

(a) 0.25   (b) 0.5

(c) 0.75   (d) 0.2

(e) 0.8   (f) 0.08

(g) 0.64   (h) 5.04

(i) 11.36   (j) 50.02

⑤

A book weighs 0.25 lb.

(a) Express the weight of the book in pounds as a fraction in simplest form.

(b) Express the weight of the book in ounces.

Exercise 5 • page 63

Lesson 6
Expressing Fractions as Decimals

Think

Mei has a $\frac{3}{5}$ L bottle of water. Express the amount of water in liters as a decimal.

Learn

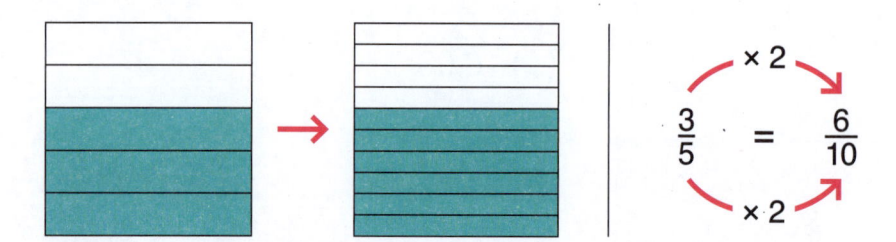

$\frac{3}{5} \xrightarrow{\times 2} \frac{6}{10}$

$\frac{3}{5}$ can be expressed as an equivalent fraction with a denominator of 10.

$\frac{3}{5} = \frac{6}{10} = 0.6$

The amount of water expressed as a decimal is ____ L.

Do

1 Express $\frac{7}{20}$ as a decimal.

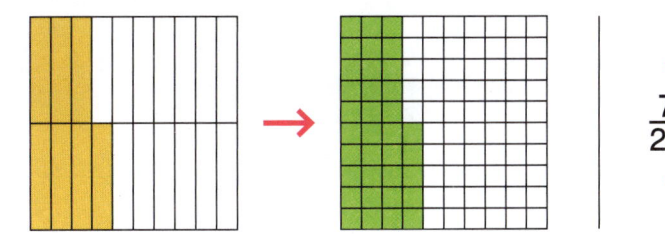

$\frac{7}{20} = \frac{\boxed{}}{100} = \boxed{}$

$\frac{7}{20}$ = ? ×5 → $\frac{\boxed{}}{100}$ ×5

$\frac{7}{20}$ can be expressed as an equivalent fraction with a denominator of 100.

2 Express $\frac{3}{4}$ as a decimal.

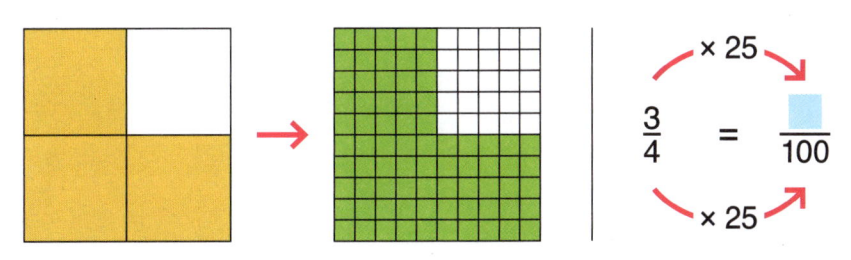

$\frac{3}{4} = \frac{\boxed{}}{100} = \boxed{}$

$\frac{3}{4}$ ×25 = $\frac{\boxed{}}{100}$ ×25

$\frac{1}{4} = \frac{25}{100}$ so $\frac{3}{4} = ?$

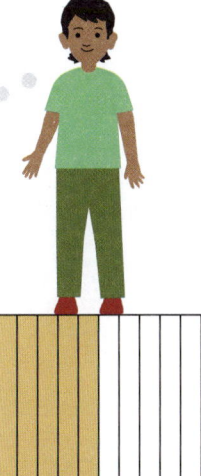

3 Express $1\frac{1}{2}$ as a decimal.

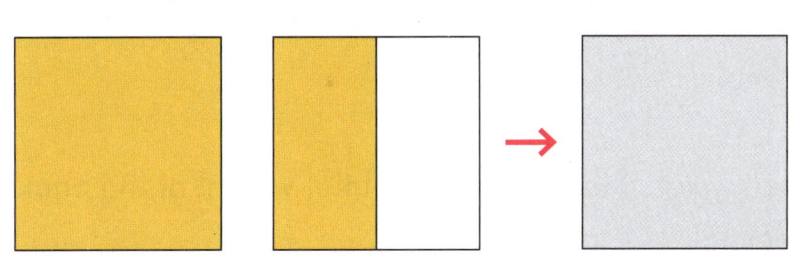

$1\frac{1}{2} = 1\frac{\boxed{}}{10} = \boxed{}$

12-6 Expressing Fractions as Decimals   87

4. Express $\frac{7}{5}$ as a decimal.

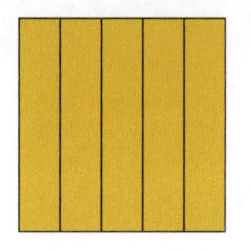

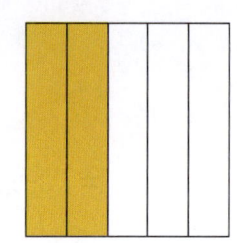

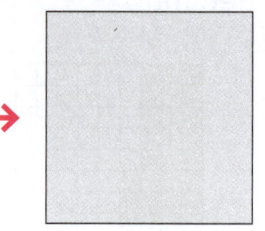

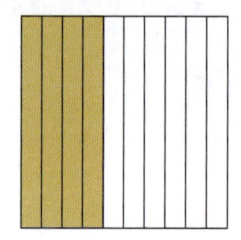

$\frac{7}{5} = 1\frac{\square}{5} = 1\frac{\square}{10} = \square$

5. Express each fraction as a decimal.

(a) $\frac{1}{2}$ (b) $\frac{1}{4}$ (c) $\frac{1}{5}$

(d) $\frac{1}{20}$ (e) $\frac{1}{25}$ (f) $\frac{1}{50}$

6. Express each fraction or mixed number as a decimal.

(a) $\frac{9}{25}$ (b) $\frac{13}{20}$ (c) $\frac{4}{5}$

(d) $\frac{28}{50}$ (e) $\frac{7}{4}$ (f) $\frac{3}{2}$

(g) $1\frac{3}{4}$ (h) $2\frac{4}{5}$ (i) $5\frac{17}{20}$

7. Two packages each weigh $\frac{4}{5}$ lb. Express the total weight of the packages in pounds as a decimal.

Exercise 6 • page 66

88 12-6 Expressing Fractions as Decimals

Lesson 7
Practice A

1 Express each decimal as a fraction or as a mixed number.

(a) 4.7 (b) 3.9 (c) 0.03

(d) 3.23 (e) 40.19 (f) 100.01

2 Express each fraction or mixed number as a decimal.

(a) $\frac{3}{10}$ (b) $\frac{17}{100}$ (c) $15\frac{8}{10}$

(d) $2\frac{5}{100}$ (e) $9\frac{12}{100}$ (f) $\frac{12}{10}$

3 (a) 9 + 0.5 + 0.03 = ☐   (b) 3 + 0.02 = ☐

(c) 60 + ☐ = 60.15   (d) 2.8 = 2 + ☐

(e) 3.24 = 3 + ☐ + 0.04   (f) 45.76 = 45.7 + ☐

(g) 2.8 + 3 + 0.07 = ☐   (h) 43 + 6.04 + 0.5 = ☐

4 What is the value of the digit 3 in each number?

(a) 3.06   (b) 4.13

(c) 30.01   (d) 0.35

5 (a) 0.2 and ▭ make 1.   (b) ▭ and 0.6 make 1.

6 Express each value as a whole number or as a decimal.

(a) 32 tenths

(b) 56 hundredths

(c) 200 hundredths

(d) 10 tenths 4 hundredths

7 Express each decimal as a mixed number in simplest form.

(a) 1.6

(b) 4.5

(c) 9.08

(d) 6.25

(e) 24.14

(f) 50.05

8 Express each fraction or mixed number as a whole number or as a decimal.

(a) $\frac{12}{50}$

(b) $3\frac{1}{2}$

(c) $7\frac{2}{5}$

(d) $\frac{7}{20}$

(e) $\frac{7}{4}$

(f) $\frac{75}{25}$

9 Jason ran in the morning and in the afternoon. He ran a total distance of 1 mile. If he ran $\frac{2}{5}$ miles in the morning, how far did he run in the afternoon? Express the answer as a decimal.

10 A melon weighs 2 lb, an apple weighs 0.3 lb, and a grape weighs 0.02 lb. How much do the three fruits weigh altogether? Express the answer as a mixed number in simplest form.

Exercise 7 • page 68

Lesson 8
Comparing and Ordering Decimals

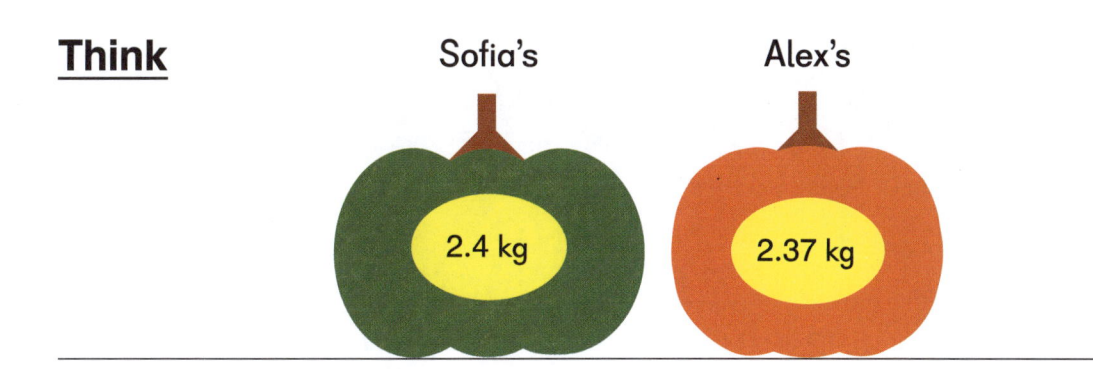

Think

Sofia's 2.4 kg   Alex's 2.37 kg

Sofia and Alex picked their own pumpkins and weighed them. Whose pumpkin weighs more?

Learn

Start by comparing the digits in the highest place first.

Ones	Tenths	Hundredths
2	4	

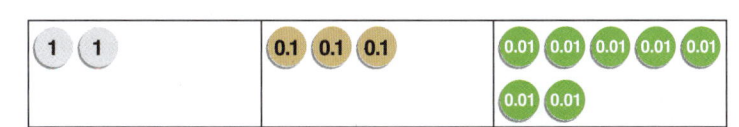

The ones are the same so compare the tenths next.

Ones	Tenths	Hundredths
2	3	7

2.4 > 2.37

2.4 = 2.40

_____'s pumpkin weighs more.

Do

1 (a) Which is greater, 0.15 or 0.2?

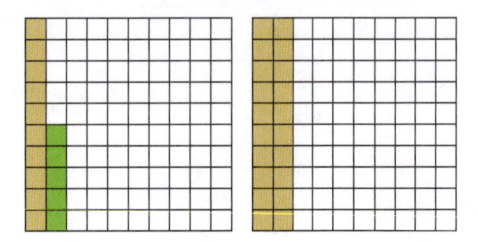

(b) Which is less, 0.92 or 0.9?

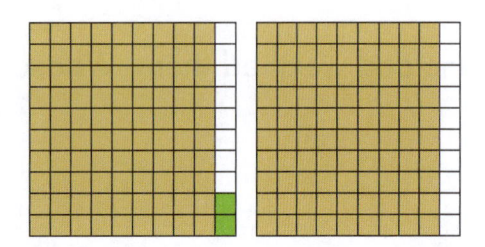

2 (a) Compare 0.48 and 0.52.

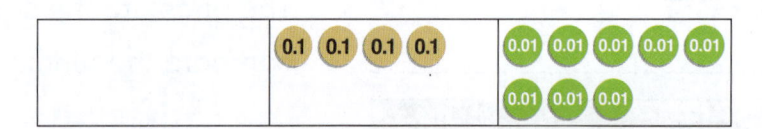

Ones	Tenths	Hundredths
0 .	4	8

Ones	Tenths	Hundredths
0 .	5	2

0.48 ◯ 0.52

The ones are the same, so compare the tenths.

(b) Compare 1.09 and 1.08.

Ones	Tenths	Hundredths
1 .	0	9

Ones	Tenths	Hundredths
1 .	0	8

1.09 ◯ 1.08

(c) Compare 32.5 and 32.51.

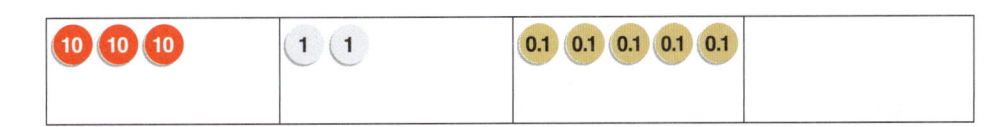

Tens	Ones	Tenths	Hundredths
3	2 .	5	

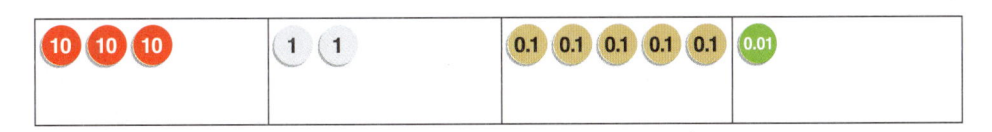

Tens	Ones	Tenths	Hundredths
3	2 .	5	1

32.5 ◯ 32.51

12-8 Comparing and Ordering Decimals

3

Ones	Tenths	Hundredths
0 .	5	4

(a) What number is 0.1 more than 0.54?

(b) What number is 0.01 less than 0.54?

(c) What number should be added to 0.54 to get 0.6?

(d) What number should be added to 0.54 to get 1?

54 hundredths + ? hundredths = 100 hundredths

4 What sign, > or <, goes in each ◯?

(a) 0.74 ◯ 0.69

(b) 0.86 ◯ 0.88

(c) 0.3 ◯ 0.28

(d) 3.4 ◯ 0.92

(e) 4.01 ◯ 4

(f) 75.6 ◯ 75.58

(g) 16.9 ◯ 4.87

(h) 4.35 ◯ 43.5

5 Order the numbers from least to greatest.

(a) 132, 1.32, 13.2

(b) 28.84, 28.34, 28.05, 28.3

(c) 1.8, 1.75, 1.9, 1.81

(d) 10.84, 108.4, 10.09, 100.9

6 Compare $\frac{2}{5}$ and 0.38.

$\frac{2}{5} = \frac{4}{10} = 0.4$

0.4 ? 0.38

$\frac{2}{5} = \frac{4}{10} = \frac{40}{100}$

$0.38 = \frac{38}{100}$

$\frac{40}{100}$? $\frac{38}{100}$

$\frac{2}{5}$ ◯ 0.38

7 Order the numbers from least to greatest.

(a) $\frac{1}{2}$, 0.4, 0.75, $\frac{3}{5}$

(b) 4.34, $4\frac{3}{4}$, $3\frac{45}{50}$, 3.6

(c) 0.99, $\frac{93}{100}$, 0.94, $\frac{19}{20}$

(d) $\frac{4}{5}$, 4.5, $\frac{5}{4}$, 5.4

8 Alex ran $\frac{3}{5}$ km. Sofia ran 0.8 km. Who ran farther?

Exercise 8 • page 70

Lesson 9
Rounding Decimals

Think

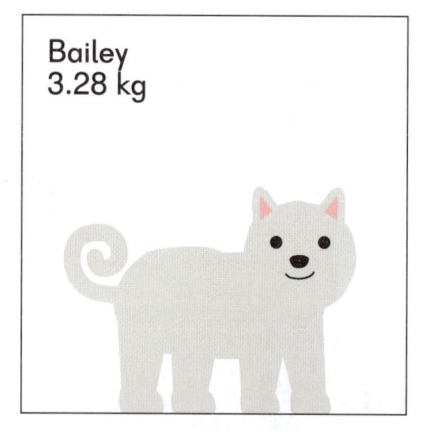

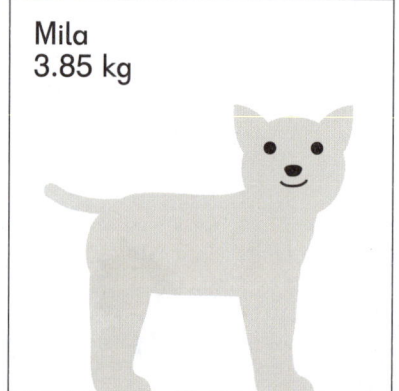

Bailey
3.28 kg

Mila
3.85 kg

Sheriff
3.54 kg

A veterinarian weighed three dogs. Round the weight of each dog to the nearest whole number of kilograms, and to the nearest tenth of a kilogram.

Learn

All the weights are between 3 kg and 4 kg.

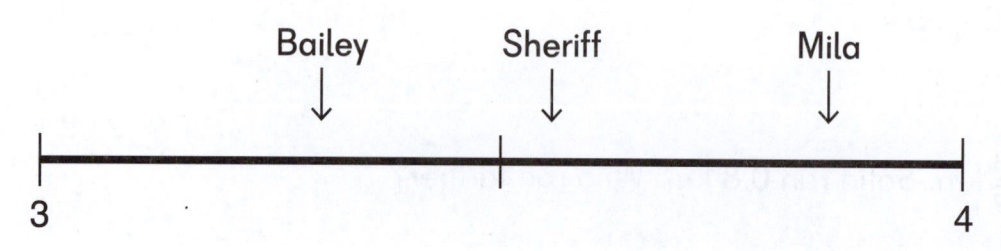

Bailey ↓   Sheriff ↓   Mila ↓

3 ———————————————— 4

Bailey

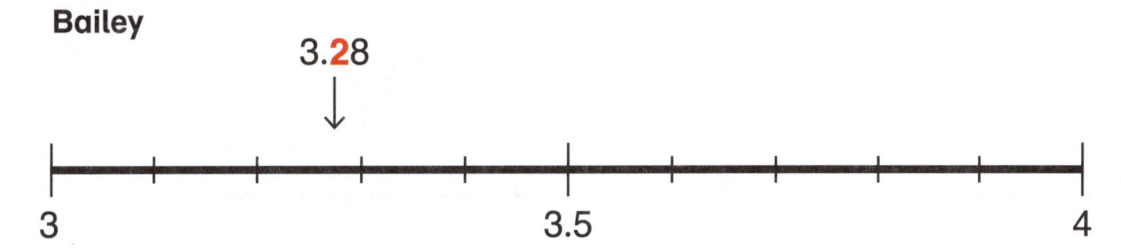

3.**2**8

3 — 3.5 — 4

> The digit in the tenths place tells us which whole number the decimal is closest to. 3.28 kg is closer to 3 kg than to 4 kg.

3.28 kg is 3 kg when rounded to the nearest whole number of kilograms.

> Rounding to the nearest whole number means we are rounding to the ones place.

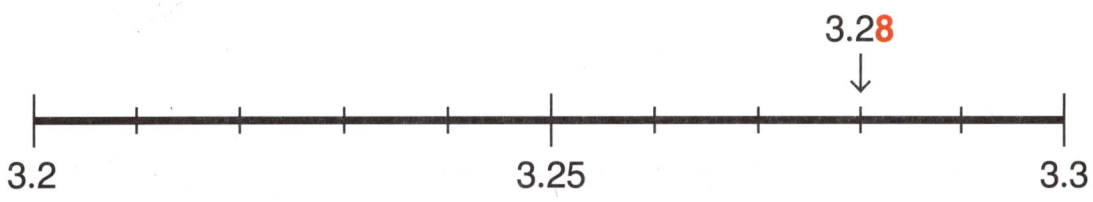

3.2**8**

3.2 — 3.25 — 3.3

> The digit in the hundredths place tells us which tenth the decimal is closest to. 3.28 kg is closer to 3.3 kg than to 3.2 kg.

3.28 kg is 3.3 kg when rounded to the nearest tenth of a kilogram.

> Rounding to the nearest tenth is the same as rounding to 1 decimal place.

12-9 Rounding Decimals

Mila

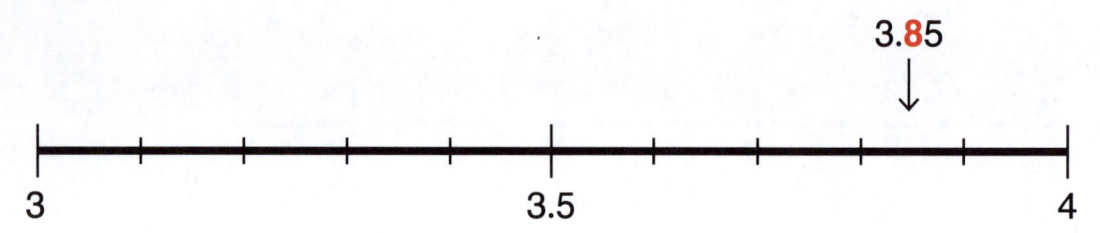

3.85 kg is 4 kg when rounded to the nearest whole number of kilograms.

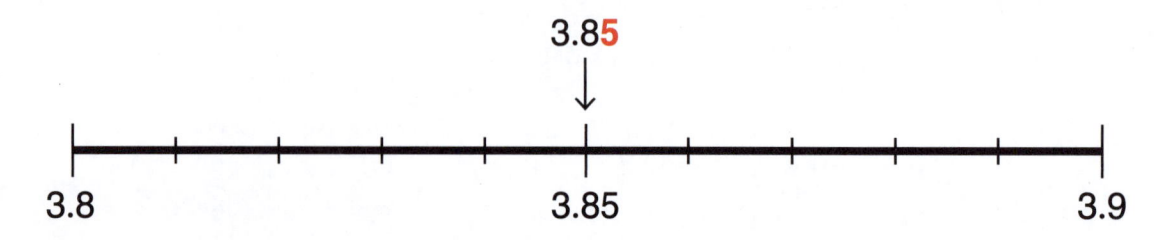

3.85 kg is halfway between 3.8 kg and 3.9 kg, so we round up.
3.85 kg is 3.9 kg when rounded to the nearest tenth of a kilogram.

Sheriff

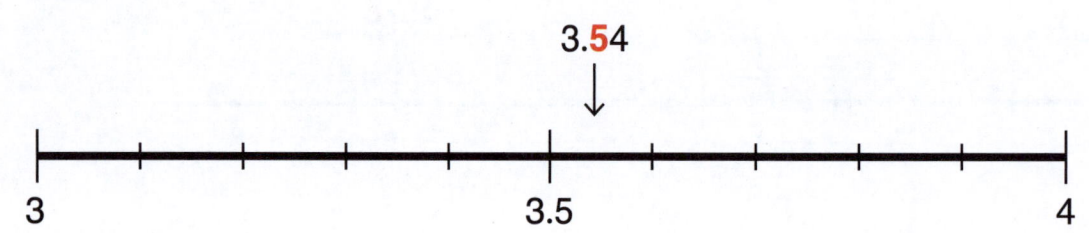

3.54 kg is 4 kg when rounded to the nearest whole number of kilograms.

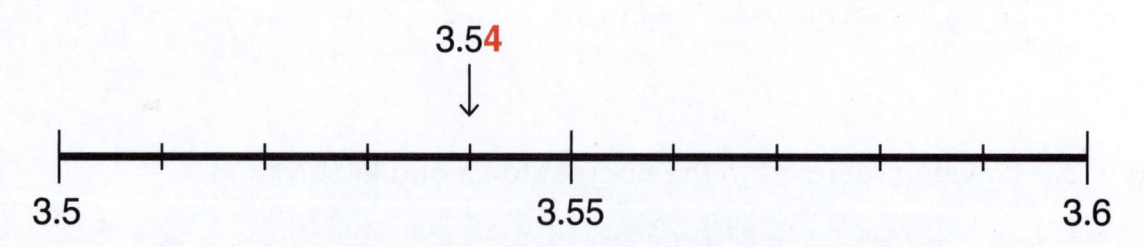

3.54 kg is 3.5 kg when rounded to 1 decimal place.

Do

① A leaf is 12.37 cm long.

(a) Round the length of the leaf to the nearest centimeter.

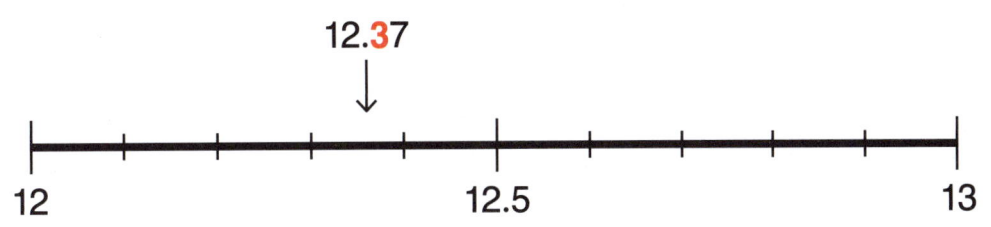

12.**3**7
↓

|————|————|————|————|————|————|————|————|————|————|
12   12.5   13

The leaf is ⬜ cm when rounded to the nearest centimeter.

(b) Round the length of the leaf to 1 decimal place.

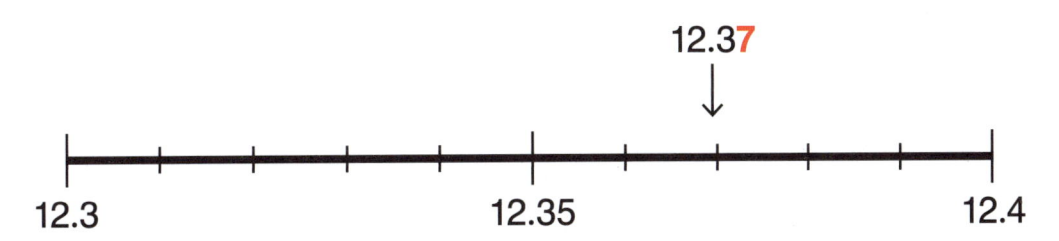

12.3**7**
↓

|————|————|————|————|————|————|————|————|————|————|
12.3   12.35   12.4

The leaf is ⬜ cm when rounded to 1 decimal place.

② A horse weighs 840.5 lb. Round the weight of the horse to the nearest pound.

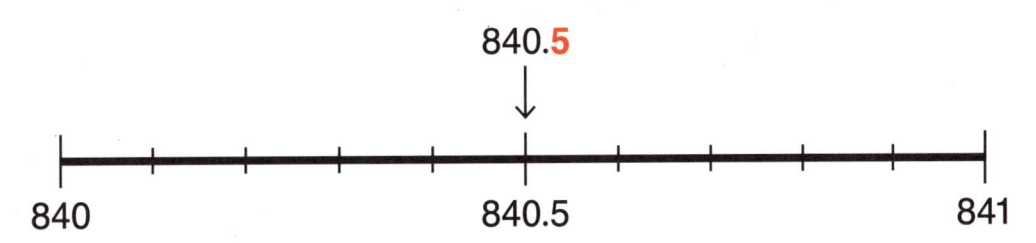

840.**5**
↓

|————|————|————|————|————|————|————|————|————|————|
840   840.5   841

The weight of the horse is ⬜ lb when rounded to the nearest pound.

12-9 Rounding Decimals

3. Round each number to 1 decimal place.

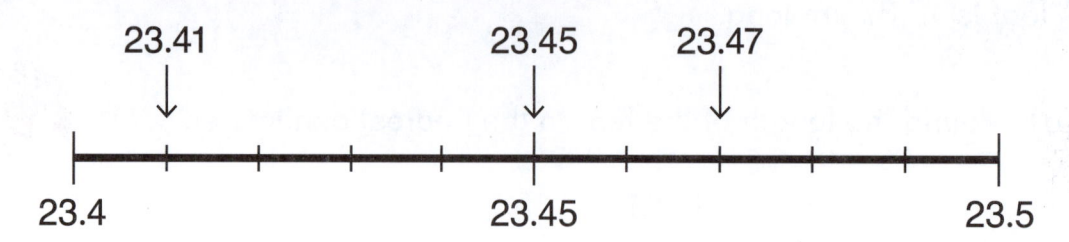

(a) 23.41 is ▭ when rounded to 1 decimal place.

(b) 23.45 is ▭ when rounded to 1 decimal place.

(c) 23.47 is ▭ when rounded to 1 decimal place.

4. Round 10.02 to 1 decimal place.

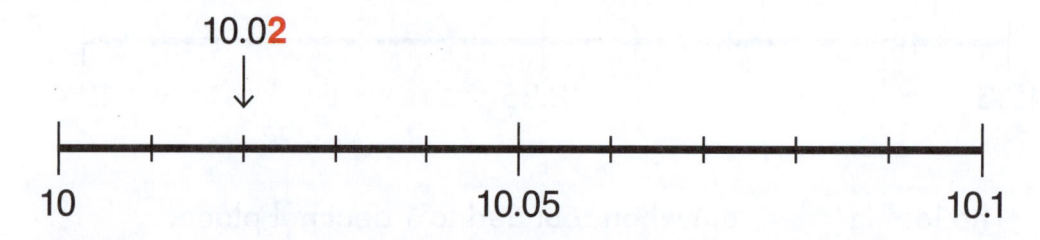

When we round to 1 decimal place, we include a digit in the first decimal place in the answer, even if it is 0.

10.02 is ▭ when rounded to 1 decimal place.

5. (a) Round 4.2**5** to 1 decimal place.

(b) Round 4.**2**5 to a whole number.

6 Round each decimal to a whole number.

(a) 0.6

(b) 4.5

(c) 17.6

(d) 0.19

(e) 3.52

(f) 60.93

7 Round each decimal to 1 decimal place.

(a) 0.82

(b) 2.34

(c) 7.07

(d) 5.55

(e) 15.63

(f) 172.03

8

McTOWNSVILLEBURGH
CITY LIMIT
POP 1.7 MILLION   ELEV 52 FT

There are 1.7 million people in a city. Which is a closer estimate of the number of people in the city, 1 million or 2 million people?

9 Alex rounded a number with 2 decimal places to 1 decimal place and got 2.3. What are the possible numbers Alex could have rounded?

Exercise 9 • page 73

Lesson 10
Practice B

1 (a) What number is 0.1 less than 0.85?

(b) What number is 0.01 more than 0.85?

(c) What number should be added to 0.85 to get 1?

2 What sign, >, <, or =, goes in each ◯?

(a) 8.09 ◯ 8.9   (b) 3.4 ◯ 3.40

(c) 64.3 ◯ 21.28   (d) 100 ◯ 1.00

3 Order the numbers from least to greatest.

(a) 0.4, $\frac{3}{10}$, 0.7, $\frac{8}{10}$

(b) 1, 0.45, 0, 0.09

(c) 4, 0.4, 0.04, 0.44

(d) $3\frac{7}{10}$, 2.9, $2\frac{5}{10}$, 3.3

(e) $5\frac{3}{100}$, 5.3, 3.5, $3\frac{5}{100}$

(f) $3\frac{1}{2}$, $\frac{3}{2}$, $2\frac{3}{5}$, 2.35

4 Round each decimal to a whole number.

(a) 0.2

(b) 0.7

(c) 4.5

(d) 19.4

(e) 58.5

(f) 1.62

(g) 45.08

(h) 100.51

5 Round each number to 1 decimal place.

(a) 0.53

(b) 0.47

(c) 0.25

(d) 1.09

(e) 3.47

(f) 93.93

(g) 6.95

(h) 38.97

6 A watermelon weighs 5.8 kg. About how much does the watermelon weigh to the nearest kilogram?

7 Usain ran the 100 m dash in 10.49 seconds.

(a) Express his time to the nearest tenth of a second.

(b) Express his time to the nearest second.

8 Dion, Sofia, and Emma each swam 200 m. Their times in minutes are shown here.

Dion	2.78 min
Sofia	2.73 min
Emma	2.75 min

(a) Who swam the fastest?

(b) Express each time to 1 decimal point.

9 A flagpole is 4.98 m tall.

(a) Express the height of the flagpole to the nearest tenth of a meter.

(b) Express the height of the flagpole to the nearest meter.

10 Mei played tennis for 0.5 hours.

(a) Express this time in hours as a fraction in simplest form.

(b) Express this time in minutes.

11 Alice is 4.25 ft tall.

(a) Express her height in feet as a mixed number in simplest form.

(b) Express her height in feet and inches.

Exercise 10 • page 76

Chapter 13

Addition and Subtraction of Decimals

Chicken Rice

—Chicken
—Cucumber
—Cilantro
—Ginger garlic paste
—Chili dipping sauce
—Soy sauce
—Rice
—Chicken broth

CHICKEN $9.50

GINGER GARLIC PASTE $4.99

CHILI SAUCE $3.89

CILANTRO $2.75 PER BUNCH

RICE $5.69 5 LB BAG

SOY SAUCE $2.69

CHICKEN BROTH $1.99

CUCUMBER $1.25 EACH

How much will I pay for all of this food?

105

Lesson 1
Adding and Subtracting Tenths

Think

Sofia drank 0.5 L of juice. Alex drank 0.3 L of juice.

(a) How much juice did they drink altogether?

(b) How much more juice did Sofia drink than Alex?

Learn

(a) 0.5 + 0.3

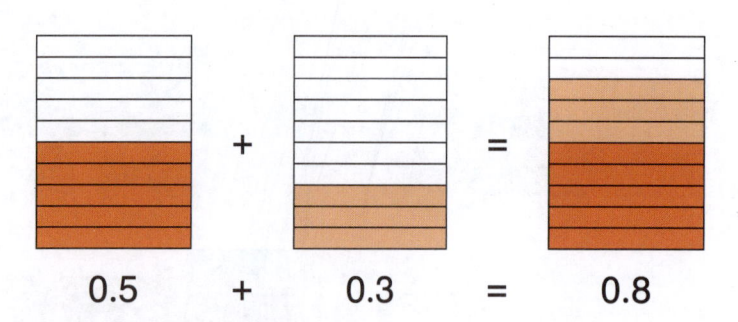

5 tenths + 3 tenths

0.5 + 0.3 = 0.8

They drank _0.8_ L of juice altogether.

(b) 0.5 − 0.3

0.5 − 0.3 = 0.2

Sofia drank _0.2_ L more juice than Alex.

Do

① Add 0.4 and 0.2.

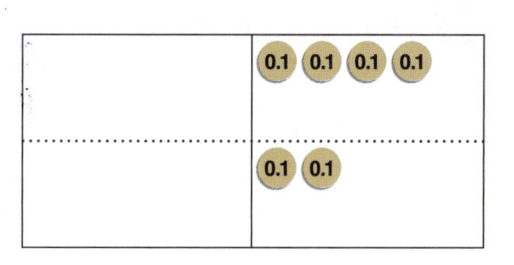

4 tenths + 2 tenths = ▭ tenths

0.4 + 0.2 = ▭

② Subtract 0.2 from 0.4.

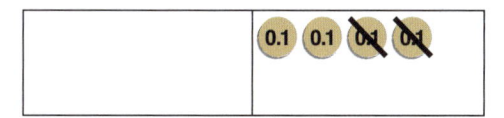

4 tenths − 2 tenths = ▭ tenths

0.4 − 0.2 = ▭

③ Add 0.7 and 0.3.

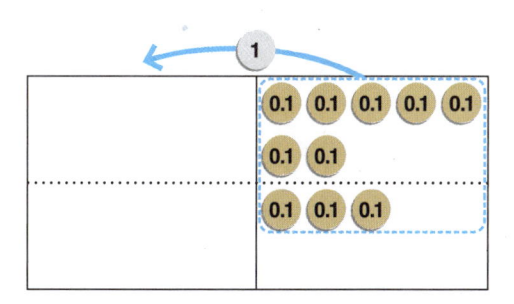

7 tenths + 3 tenths = 10 tenths

= ▭ one

0.7 + 0.3 = ▭

④ Subtract 0.3 from 1.

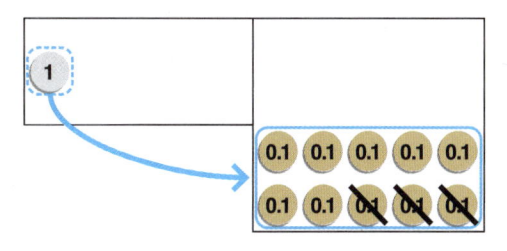

1 one − 3 tenths = 10 tenths − 3 tenths

= ▭ tenths

1 − 0.3 = ▭

13-1 Adding and Subtracting Tenths

5. Add 0.8 and 0.5.

   8 tenths + 5 tenths = 13 tenths
   = ☐ one ☐ tenths

   0.8 + 0.5 = ☐

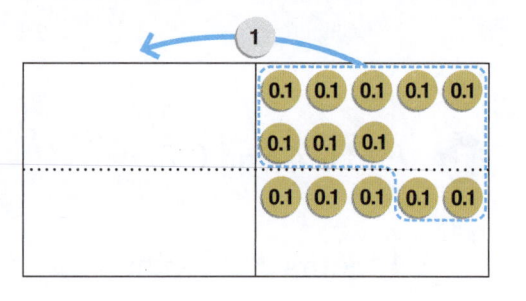

6. Subtract 0.7 from 1.3.

   1 one 3 tenths − 7 tenths = 13 tenths − 7 tenths
   = ☐ tenths

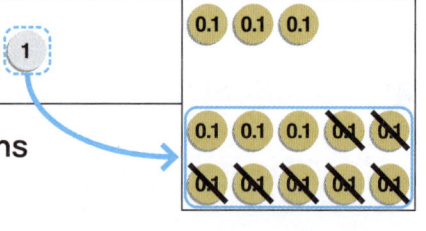

   1.3 − 0.7 = ☐

7. Add or subtract.

   (a) 0.5 + 0.9

   (b) 0.5 + 0.6

   (c) 1 − 0.8

   (d) 1.7 − 0.5

   (e) 1.4 − 0.8

   (f) 2.7 − 2

8. Sam's house, the school, the library, and the museum are on the same road. What is the distance between the library and the museum?

   Sam's house —0.4 km— School —0.3 km— Library —?— Museum

   1.5 km

Exercise 1 • page 79

108   13-1 Adding and Subtracting Tenths

Lesson 2
Adding Tenths with Regrouping

Think

A bucket contains 2.7 L of water. A bottle contains 1.5 L of water. How much water is in both containers altogether?

2.7 ≈ 3 and 1.5 ≈ 2 so it should be less than…

Learn

Method 1

2.7 + 1.5 = 27 tenths + 15 tenths

= 42 tenths

= 4.2

Method 2

2.7 + 1.5

Add the tenths.

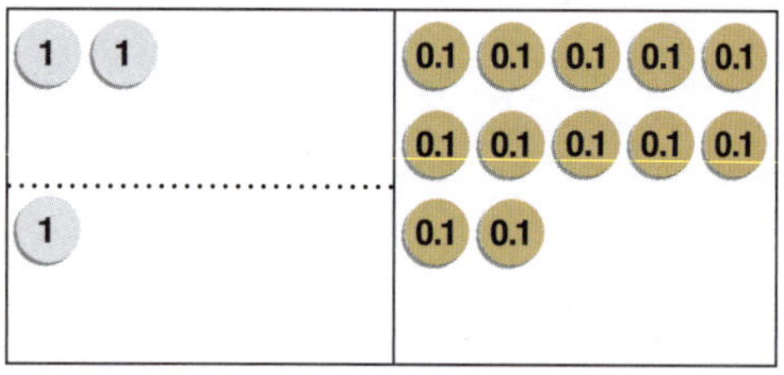

7 tenths + 5 tenths = 12 tenths

Regroup the tenths.

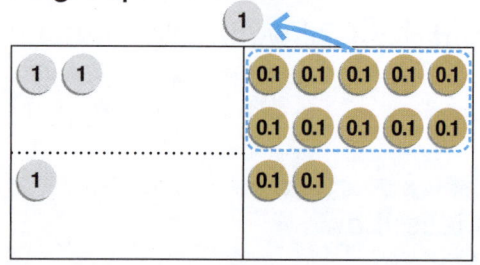

$$\begin{array}{r} \overset{1}{}2.7 \\ +\ 1.5 \\ \hline .2 \end{array}$$

12 tenths = 1 one 2 tenths

Add the ones.

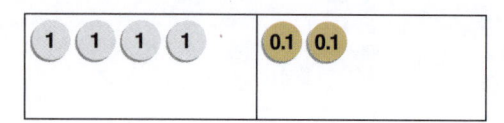

$$\begin{array}{r} \overset{1}{}2.7 \\ +\ 1.5 \\ \hline 4.2 \end{array}$$

1 one + 2 ones + 1 one = 4 ones

There are _____ L of water in both containers.

Add decimals the same way as whole numbers. Line up the digits in each place and the decimal points. Put a decimal point between the ones place and the tenths place in the answer.

$$\begin{array}{r} 2.7 \\ +\ 1.5 \\ \hline 4.2 \end{array}$$

13-2 Adding Tenths with Regrouping

Do

1 4.9 and 3.6.

> 4.9 + 3.6 ≈ 5 + 4 = 9
> I rounded both numbers up, so the answer will be less than 9.

```
   4.9
 + 3.6
 -----
```

2 Add 15.8 and 6.7.

```
   15.8
 +  6.7
 ------
```

3 Add 27 and 4.6.

```
   27.0
 +  4.6
 ------
```

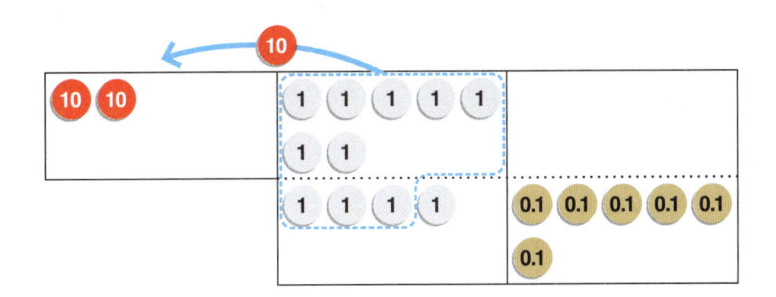

> 27 = 27.0

13-2 Adding Tenths with Regrouping

4. Find the sum of 4.5, 8.5, and 13.2.

   4.5
   8.5
   +13.2
   ____

   I added all the tenths first, then the ones, then the tens.

5. Estimate, and then add.

   (a) 3.7 + 1.2

   (b) 2.9 + 4

   (c) 5.8 + 6.5

   (d) 13.5 + 1.5

   (e) 18.8 + 5.9

   (f) 54 + 8.7

   (g) 75.2 + 24.8

   (h) 7.5 + 16.6 + 5.7

6. 10.6 kg   4.5 kg   4.9 kg

   How much do the peanuts weigh altogether?

Exercise 2 • page 81

Lesson 3
Subtracting Tenths with Regrouping

Think

Sofia had 3.5 m of twine. She used 1.8 m to tie up some tomato plants. How many meters of twine does she have left?

3.5 ≈ 4 and 1.8 ≈ 2
so it should be about…

Learn

Method 1

3.5 − 1.8 = 35 tenths − 18 tenths

= 17 tenths

= 1.7

Method 2

3.5 − 1.8

Regroup 1 one and subtract the tenths.

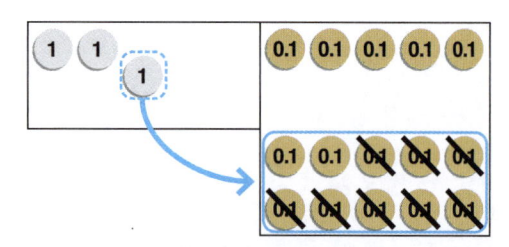

3 ones 5 tenths = 2 ones 15 tenths
15 tenths − 8 tenths = 7 tenths

Subtract the ones.

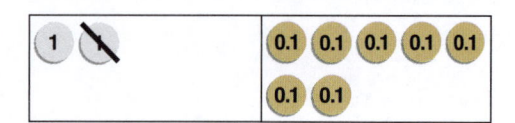

She has _____ m of twine left.

> Subtract decimals the same way as whole numbers. Line up the digits in each place and the decimal points. Write the decimal point in the answer.

> There are not enough tenths to subtract 8 tenths.

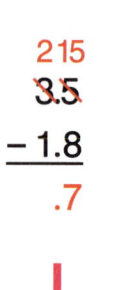

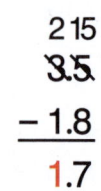

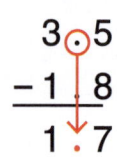

```
  2 15
  3.5
− 1.8
─────
   .7
```

```
  2 15
  3.5
− 1.8
─────
  1.7
```

```
  3.5
− 1.8
─────
  1.7
```

Add to check answers.

```
   3.5          ☐
 − 1.8    ✕   + 1.8
  ───         ─────
   ☐           3.5
```

13-3 Subtracting Tenths with Regrouping

Do

1 Subtract 1.6 from 3.4.

3.4 − 1.6 ≈ 3 − 2 = 1, so the answer will be between 1 and 2.

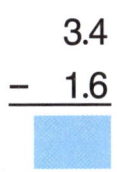

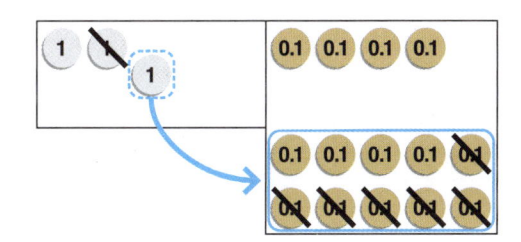

```
  3.4
−　1.6
```

2 Subtract 7.8 from 12.3.

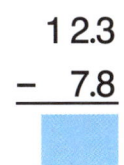

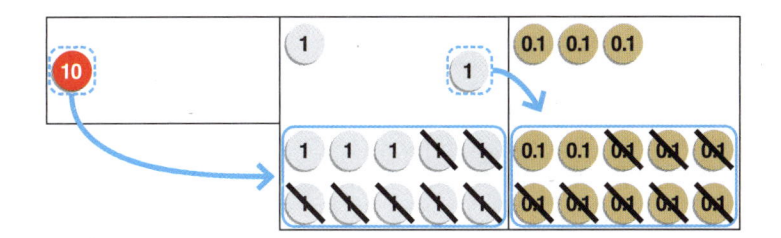

```
  1 2.3
−   7.8
```

3 Subtract 4.5 from 8.

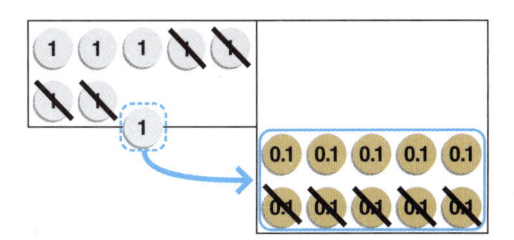

```
  8.0
− 4.5
```

8 = 8.0

13-3 Subtracting Tenths with Regrouping

4 Find the value of 13.2 − 0.6 − 4.8.

13.2 − 0.6 − 4.8 = ☐

> I subtracted 0.6 from 13.2 first, then subtracted 4.8 from that answer.

5 Estimate and then subtract.

(a) 3.8 − 1.4

(b) 5.2 − 1.2

(c) 4.1 − 0.3

(d) 5.2 − 2.8

(e) 14.3 − 3.5

(f) 48.4 − 6.9

(g) 83.7 − 58.8

(h) 117.2 − 85.6

(i) 3 − 2.2

(j) 25 − 0.8 − 5.1

6 The soccer field, the skateboard park, and the tennis club are on the same road. What is the distance between the skateboard park and the tennis club?

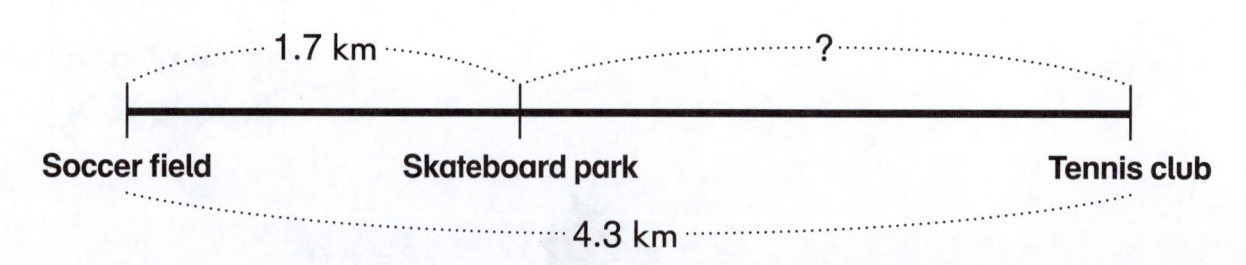

1.7 km — ?

Soccer field   Skateboard park   Tennis club

4.3 km

Exercise 3 • page 83

Lesson 4
Practice A

1 Find the values

(a) 0.3 + 0.5

(b) 0.6 + 0.4

(c) 0.9 + 0.6

(d) 72.5 + 14.8

(e) 59.6 + 48.7

(f) 0.2 + 0.7 + 0.8

(g) 37.5 − 18.4

(h) 1.3 − 0.6

(i) 45.3 − 26.7

(j) 9 − 2.4

(k) 20 − 0.5 − 9.5

(l) 7.5 + 3.1 + 2.9

(m) 85.6 + 348.7

(n) 648 − 42.9

2 Imaini had 10 m of string. She used 3.5 m to wrap a package and 4.8 m to make wind chimes. How many meters of string does she have left?

3 A flagpole is buried in the ground to a depth of 1.8 m. The top of the pole is 6.2 m above ground.

(a) What is the total length of the pole?

(b) The pole is pounded farther into the ground another half meter. How much of the pole is now above ground?

4 The pharmacy, the music store, and the farmers market are on the same street.

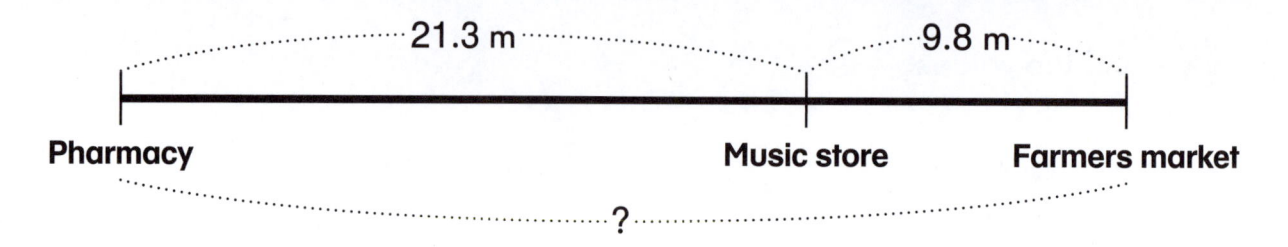

Pharmacy — 21.3 m — Music store — 9.8 m — Farmers market
?

(a) How far is the pharmacy from the farmers market?

(b) How much farther is the music store from the pharmacy than it is from the farmers market?

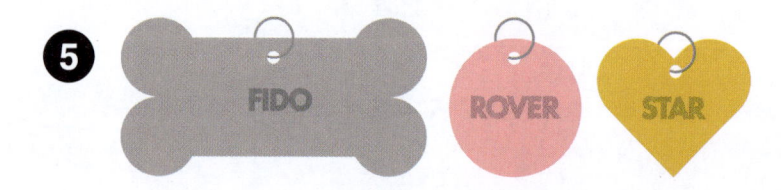

5 Fido weighs 12.8 lb. Rover weighs 12.5 lb more than Fido. Fido weighs 62.2 lb less than Star.

(a) How much more does Star weigh than Rover?

(b) What is the total weight of all three dogs?

6 One rod is 3.8 m long and the other rod is 5.2 m long. They are bound together with part of each rod overlapping. The total length is 8.1 m. How many meters is the overlap?

Exercise 4 • page 86

Lesson 5
Adding Hundredths

Think

3 green apples weigh 0.47 kg and 3 red apples weigh 0.35 kg. How many kilograms do the apples weigh altogether?

0.47 ≈ 0.5 and 0.35 ≈ 0.4 so it should be about…

Learn

Method 1

0.47 + 0.35 = 47 hundredths + 35 hundredths

= 82 hundredths

= 0.82

Method 2

0.47 + 0.35

Add the hundredths and regroup.

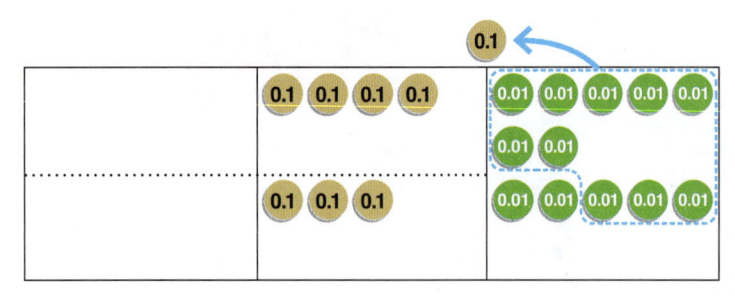

7 hundredths + 5 hundredths
= 12 hundredths
= 1 tenth 2 hundredths

```
  1
  0.4 7
+ 0.3 5
      2
```

Add the tenths.

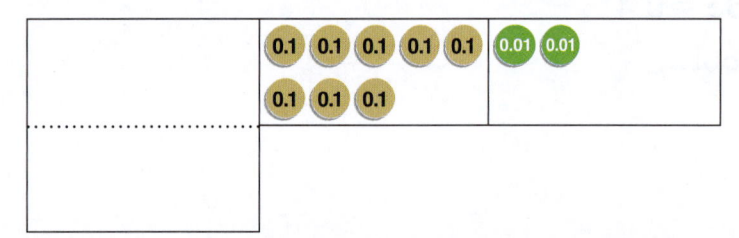

1 tenth + 4 tenths + 3 tenths = 8 tenths

```
  1
  0.4 7
+ 0.3 5
  .8 2
```

Add the ones.

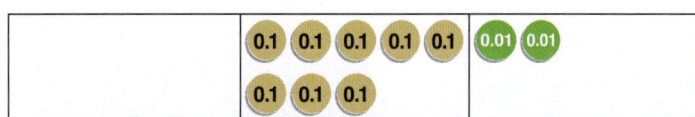

0 ones + 0 ones = 0 ones

```
  1
  0.4 7
+ 0.3 5
  0.8 2
```

The apples weigh _____ kg altogether.

Remember to write the decimal point in the answer.

120   13-5 Adding Hundredths

Do

1. Add 0.79 and 0.16. Estimate first. Will the answer be less than or greater than 1?

    0.79
   + 0.16
   _____

2. Add 1.56 and 0.45.

    1.56
   + 0.45
   _____

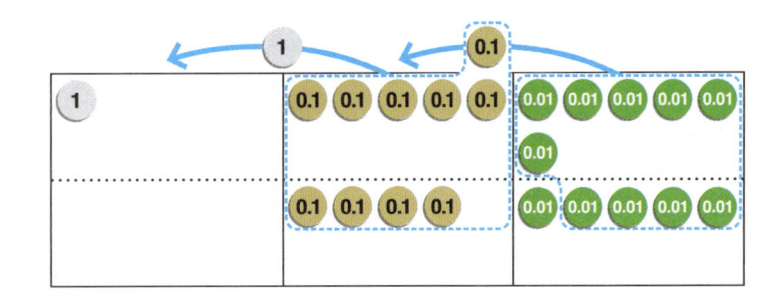

3. Add 3.45 and 2.8.

    3.45
   + 2.80
   _____

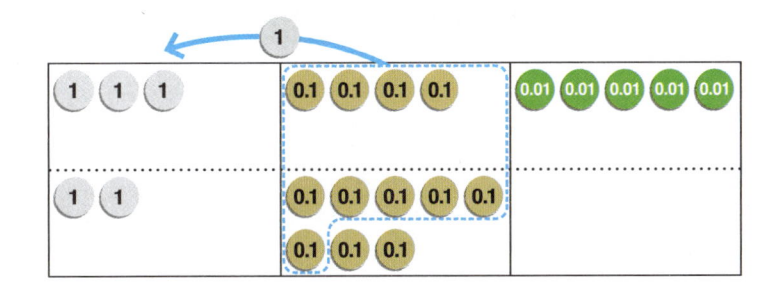

2.8 = 2.80

From my estimate, I knew that the answer would be a little more than 6.

4 Add 48.63 and 27.87.

76.50 = 76.5

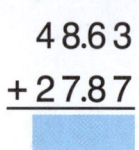

```
   48.63
 + 27.87
 -------
```

5 Estimate and then add.

(a) 0.05 + 0.04

(b) 0.36 + 0.25

(c) 5.72 + 1.63

(d) 8 + 6.75

(e) 18.39 + 2.61

(f) 1.43 + 0.9

(g) 12.4 + 0.53

(h) 43.01 + 6.9

6

Swimmer	Time (min)
Mei	1.08
Alex	0.59
Dion	1.76
Emma	0.53

Mei, Alex, Dion, and Emma each swam one length of the pool in a relay race. Their individual times in minutes are shown in the table. What is their total combined time in minutes for the race?

Exercise 5 • page 88

Lesson 6
Subtracting from 1 and 0.1

Think

Mei has 1 kg of colored sand. She uses 0.68 kg of it for an art project. How many kilograms of sand does she have left?

Learn

Method 1

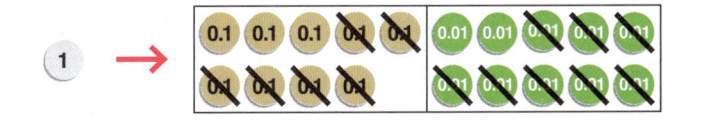

1 one = 9 tenths 10 hundredths

```
   9 tenths   10 hundredths
-  6 tenths    8 hundredths
   3 tenths    2 hundredths
```

1 − 0.68 = 0.32

Method 2

1 one = 100 hundredths

100 hundredths − 68 hundredths = 32 hundredths = 0.32

She has _____ kg of sand left.

Do

1 Subtract 0.07 from 0.1.

0.1 − 0.07 = ☐

10 hundredths − 7 hundredths = ? hundredths

2 Find pairs of numbers that make 0.1.

| 0.06 | 0.02 | 0.01 | 0.08 | 0.09 | 0.04 |

3 Subtract 0.07 from 1.

1 − 0.07 = ☐

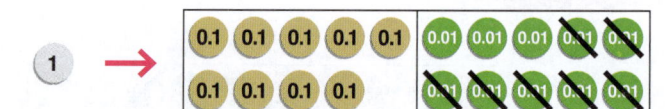

4 Subtract 0.45 from 1.

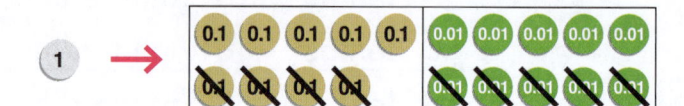

1 − 0.45 = ☐

5 Find pairs of numbers that make 1.

| 0.76 | 0.57 | 0.92 | 0.84 | 0.08 |

| 0.45 | 0.16 | 0.24 | 0.43 | 0.55 |

13-6 Subtracting from 1 and 0.1

6 Subtract 0.05 from 0.2.

0.2 − 0.05 = ☐

0.2 − 0.05
 / \
0.1 0.1

7 Subtract 0.35 from 3.

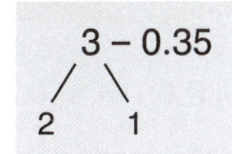

3 − 0.35 = ☐

3 − 0.35
 / \
2   1

8 Subtract.

(a) 0.1 − 0.02 (b) 0.1 − 0.05

(c) 1 − 0.09 (d) 1 − 0.33

(e) 1 − 0.27 (f) 1 − 0.99

(g) 0.5 − 0.05 (h) 5 − 0.05

(i) 4 − 0.40 (j) 10 − 0.65

9 Emma has 2 L of milk. She uses 0.85 L to make biscuits. How much milk does she have left in liters?

Exercise 6 • page 90

13-6 Subtracting from 1 and 0.1

Lesson 7
Subtracting Hundredths

Think

Mei has 4.62 m of rope. She uses 2.65 m to make a swing. How much rope does she have left?

4.62 ≈ 5 and 2.65 ≈ 3 so it should be about…

Learn

4.62 − 2.65

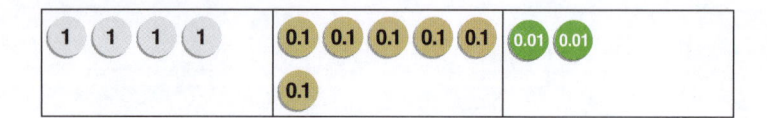

$$\begin{array}{r} 4.6\,2 \\ -\,2.6\,5 \\ \hline \end{array}$$

There are not enough hundredths to subtract 5 hundredths.

Regroup 1 tenth.
Subtract the hundredths.

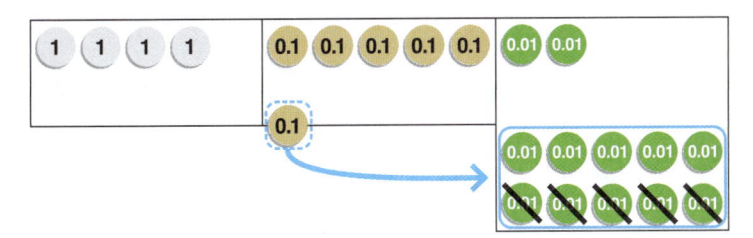

6 tenths 2 hundredths = 5 tenths 12 hundredths
12 hundredths − 5 hundredths = 7 hundredths

$$\begin{array}{r} ^{5\ 12}\\ 4.\cancel{6}\cancel{2} \\ -\ 2.6\ 5 \\ \hline 7 \end{array}$$

Regroup 1 one.
Subtract the tenths.

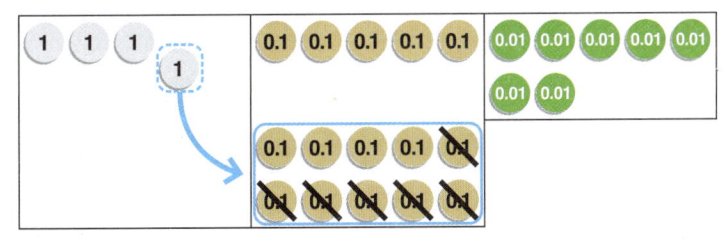

4 ones 5 tenths = 3 ones 15 tenths
15 tenths − 6 tenths = 9 tenths

$$\begin{array}{r} ^{3\ 15\ 12}\\ \cancel{4}.\cancel{6}\cancel{2} \\ -\ 2.6\ 5 \\ \hline .9\ 7 \end{array}$$

Subtract the ones.

3 ones − 2 ones = 1 one

$$\begin{array}{r} ^{3\ 15\ 12}\\ \cancel{4}.\cancel{6}\cancel{2} \\ -\ 2.6\ 5 \\ \hline 1.9\ 7 \end{array}$$

He has _____ m of rope left.

Check your answer.

4.6 2
− 2.6 5
☐

+ 2.6 5
4.6 2

13-7 Subtracting Hundredths

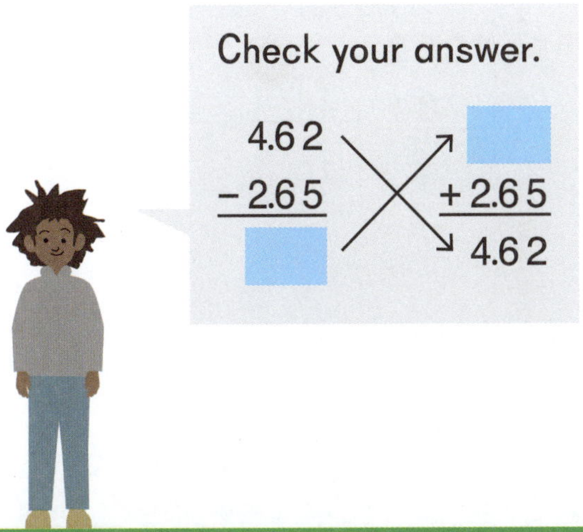

Do

1. Subtract 0.82 from 3.06. Estimate first. The answer will be between which two whole numbers?

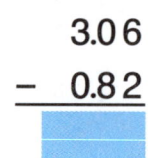

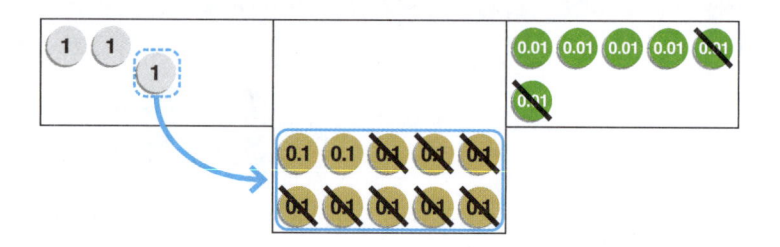

    3.06
  − 0.82
  ──────

2. Subtract 1.19 from 4.1.

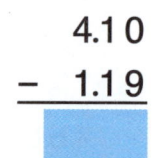

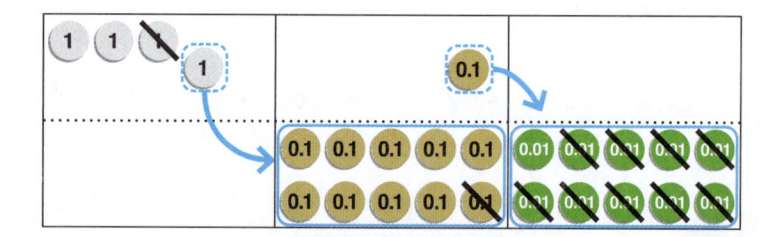

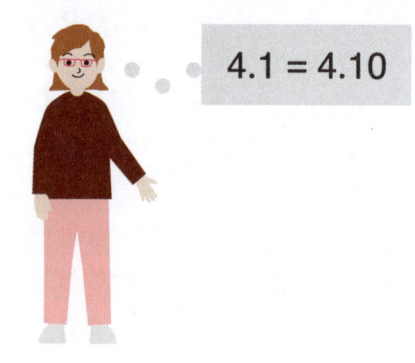

    4.10
  − 1.19
  ──────

   4.1 = 4.10

   I knew from my estimate that the answer would be close to 3.

3. Subtract 7.31 from 10.

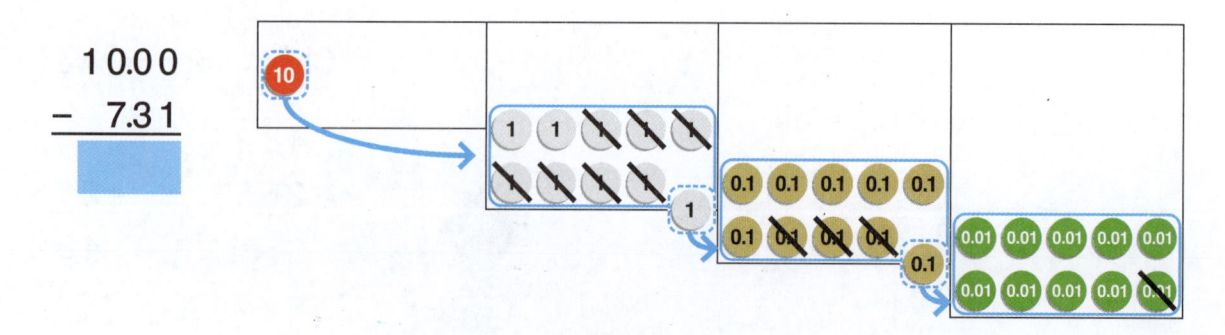

    10.00
  − 7.31
  ──────

128   13-7 Subtracting Hundredths

4 Subtract 19 from 32.71.

19 = 19.00

```
  32.71
- 19.00
```

5 Estimate and then subtract.

(a) 5.35 − 1.04

(b) 7.82 − 0.65

(c) 8.07 − 5.25

(d) 3.05 − 1.49

(e) 11.44 − 3

(f) 8.16 − 5.8

(g) 9 − 2.06

(h) 12.27 − 0.5

6 The mall, the pet shop, and the market are on the same road. How much greater is the distance between the pet shop and the mall than between the pet shop and the market?

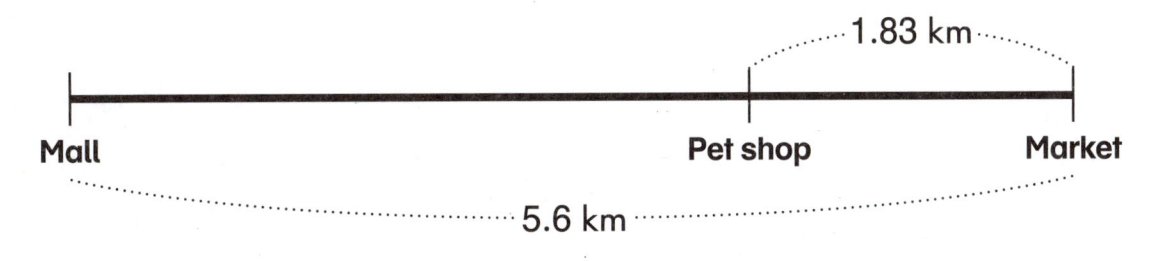

Mall — Pet shop — Market
Pet shop to Market: 1.83 km
Mall to Market: 5.6 km

Exercise 7 • page 92

Lesson 8
Money, Decimals, and Fractions

Think

Alex's money

Emma's money

(a) What fraction of $1 is 1 penny?

(b) What fraction of $1 is 1 dime?

(c) How much money do Alex and Emma have altogether?

Learn

(a) There are 100 pennies in 1 dollar.

1 penny = $0.01

1 penny is $\frac{1}{100}$ of $1.

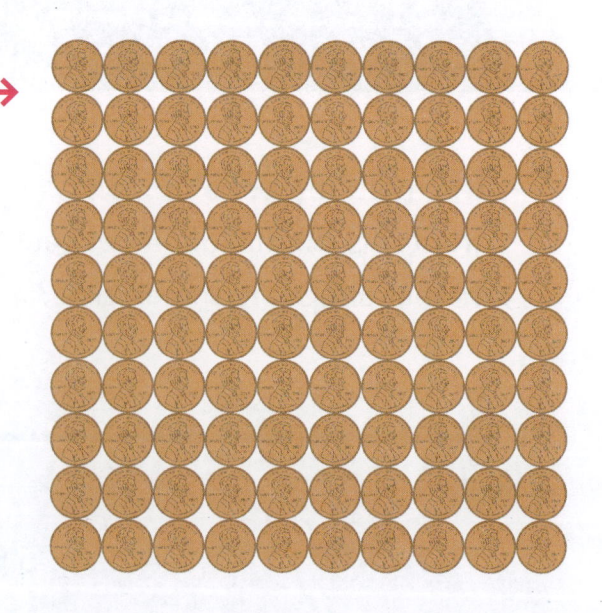

(b) There are 10 dimes in $1.

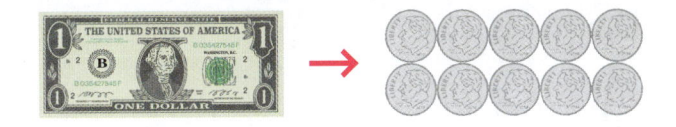

1 dime = $0.10

1 dime is $\frac{1}{10}$ of $1.

1 dime is $\frac{10}{100}$ of $1.

We write amounts in dollars and cents with 2 decimal places. We write 10 cents as $0.10, not $0.1.

(c) Add $3.78 and $2.65.

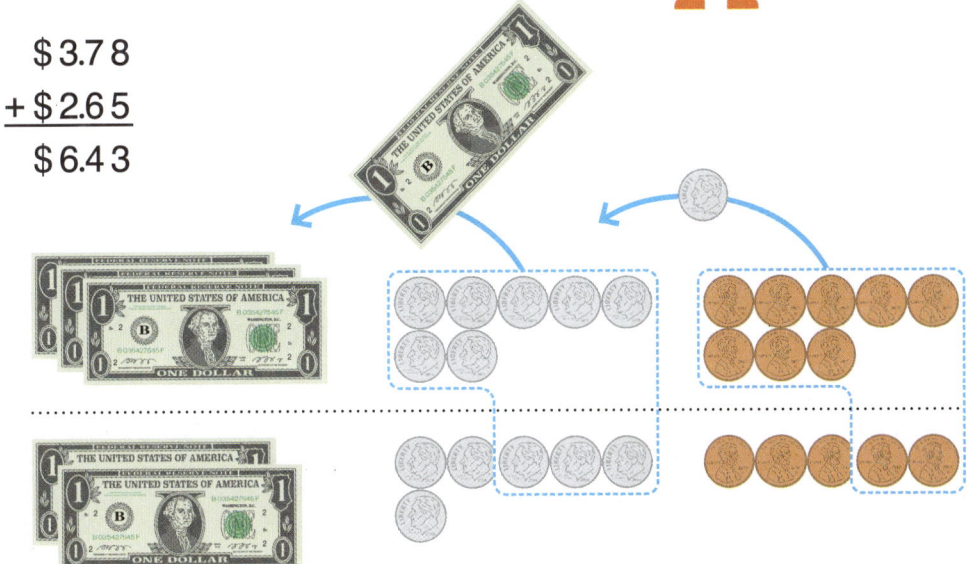

$$\begin{array}{r} \$3.78 \\ +\$2.65 \\ \hline \$6.43 \end{array}$$

They have $_____ altogether.

We add and subtract money the same way we add and subtract decimals.

13-8 Money, Decimals, and Fractions

Do

1. What fraction of $1 is 17¢?

   $0.17 = \dfrac{\square}{100}$

   $0.17 is \dfrac{\square}{100}$ of $1.

2. Express 25¢ as a fraction of $1 in simplest form.

   $0.25 = \dfrac{\square}{100} = \dfrac{\square}{4}$

   $0.25 is \dfrac{\square}{4}$ of $1.

   There are 4 quarters in $1.

3. Express 5¢ as a fraction of $1 in simplest form.

   $0.05 = \dfrac{\square}{100} = \dfrac{\square}{\square}$

   $0.05 is \dfrac{\square}{\square}$ of $1.

   How many nickels make $1?

4. Subtract 27 cents from 61 cents. Express the answer in dollars.

   $\$0.61$
   $-\$0.27$
   _____

   Estimate first: 61 − 27 ≈ 60 − 30

5 Add $5.63 and $3.96.

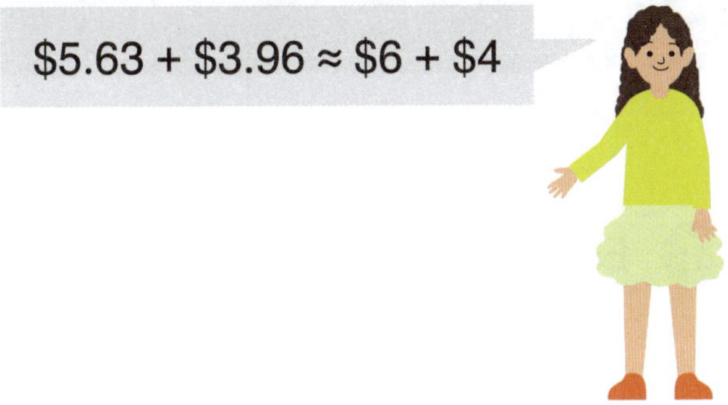

$5.63 + $3.96 ≈ $6 + $4

$5.63
+ $3.96

6 Subtract $2.43 from $5

$5 = $5.00

$5.00
− $2.43

7 Estimate and then find the values.

(a) $0.98 + $0.47

(b) $0.58 − $0.39

(c) $4.87 + $8.55

(d) $9.60 − $5.71

(e) $27.46 + $15.54

(f) $45.10 − $26.50

(g) $8 + $0.42

(h) $10 − $1.28

8 $8.75 $12.99

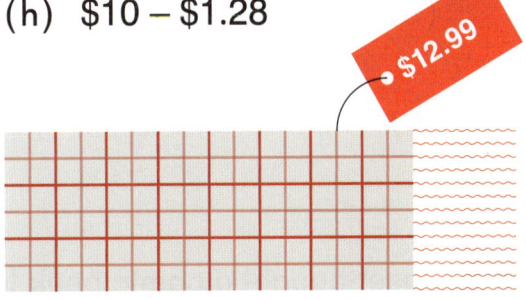

Mei had $25. She bought the hat and the scarf. How much money does she have left?

Exercise 8 · page 95

13-8 Money, Decimals, and Fractions

Lesson 9
Practice B

1 Estimate and then find the values.

(a) 2.63 + 1.34

(b) 0.68 + 0.56

(c) 0.4 + 0.97

(d) 6.07 + 2.16

(e) 85.79 + 26.28

(f) 36.78 + 0.6 + 7

(g) 50.34 − 6.13

(h) 30.01 − 12.34

(i) 1 − 0.92

(j) 5 − 2.03

(k) 1.45 − 0.57

(l) 9.6 − 3.28

(m) 72 − 8.09

(n) 10.3 − 2.05 − 6.8

2 (a) Express 50¢ as a fraction of $1 in simplest form.

(b) Express 8 nickels as a fraction of $1 in simplest form.

(c) Express 45¢ as a fraction of $1 in simplest form.

3 Josef bought a comic book for $7.95 and a picture book for $15.28. How much did he spend?

4 Daniel had $100. He bought some shoes for $46.80 and a hat for $12.75. How much money does he have left?

5 Dana had $47.32. She spent $32.07. Then she earned another $8. How much money does she have now?

6 Brianna says she has six and four-fifths dollars. How much money does she have?

7 A baker had 20 lb of flour. He used 4.25 lb to make a cake, 3.6 lb to make muffins, and 3.75 lb to make bread. How many pounds of flour does he have left?

8 A basket of apples weighed 8.12 kg more than a basket of pears. After 4.65 kg of apples were removed from the basket of apples, it weighed 12 kg. How much does the basket of pears weigh?

9 String A is 5.62 m shorter than String B and 1.2 m longer than String C. String C is 6 m long. How long are the three strings altogether?

Exercise 9 • page 98

Review 3

1 | 32,574 | 450,096 | 632.57 | 40.25 |

What does the digit 5 stand for in each number?

Write each number in expanded form.

2 Write each value as a whole number or a decimal.

(a) 60 hundreds

(b) 60 hundredths

(c) 200 tens

(d) 200 tenths

3 Estimate and then find the values.

(a) 86,956 + 7,872

(b) 103,424 − 63,527

(c) 2,052 × 30

(d) 302 ÷ 7

(e) 87 × 652

(f) 2,014 ÷ 4

(g) 0.7 + 0.5

(h) 2.4 − 1.9

(i) 43.7 + 2.31

(j) 20.02 − 11.45

(k) 45.87 + 54.13

(l) 100 − 0.7

4 (a) Find the first four common multiples of 3, 4, and 6.

(b) Find the common factors of 18, 24, and 30.

(c) Find all the prime numbers less than 30.

5 Express the values as a fraction or mixed number in simplest form.

(a) $\frac{3}{4} + \frac{7}{12}$

(b) $6\frac{1}{3} - \frac{7}{9}$

(c) $4\frac{3}{5} - 1\frac{1}{10}$

(d) $\frac{5}{6} \times 18$

(e) $8 \times \frac{7}{20}$

(f) $\frac{5}{12} \times 20$

6 Find the area and perimeter of each shape.

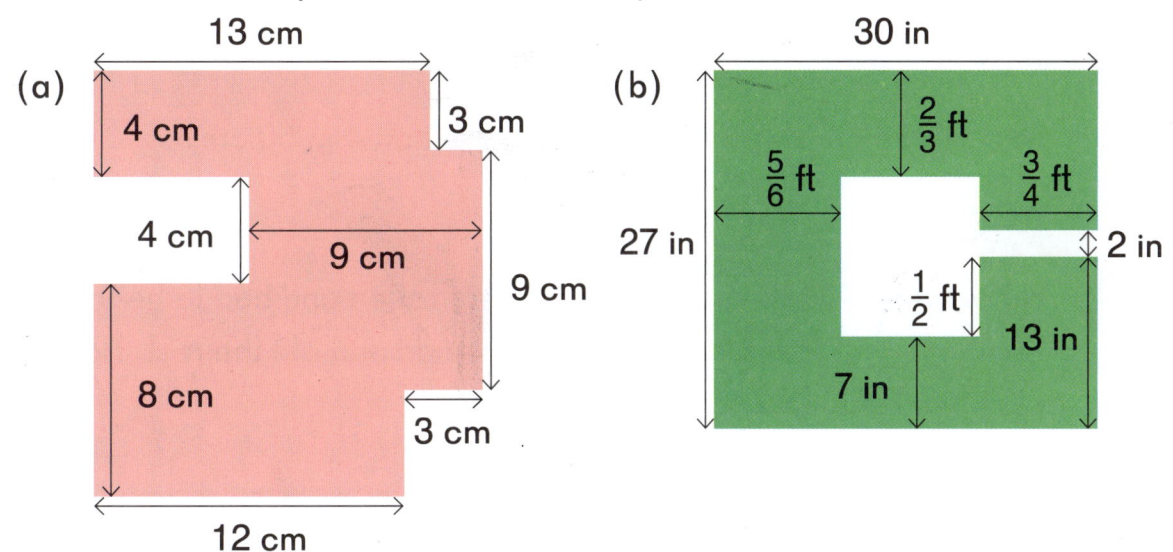

(a) 13 cm, 4 cm, 3 cm, 4 cm, 9 cm, 9 cm, 8 cm, 3 cm, 12 cm

(b) 30 in, $\frac{2}{3}$ ft, $\frac{5}{6}$ ft, $\frac{3}{4}$ ft, 27 in, 2 in, $\frac{1}{2}$ ft, 13 in, 7 in

7 The perimeter of a rectangular painting is 30 ft. The width of the painting is $2\frac{1}{3}$ ft. What is the area of the painting in square inches?

8 Express each decimal as a mixed number in simplest form and each mixed number as a decimal.

(a) 2.4 (b) 40.08 (c) 6.35

(d) $2\frac{9}{100}$ (e) $3\frac{3}{25}$ (f) $10\frac{1}{5}$

9 Some students recorded the distance their paper airplanes traveled and then shared their data.

4 m 30 cm	$4\frac{2}{5}$ m	5.04 m	385 cm
$5\frac{3}{4}$ m	4 m 3 cm	$3\frac{3}{4}$ m	5.8 m

(a) What is the difference in meters between the shortest and longest distance?

(b) How many airplanes traveled less than 4 m 50 cm?

10 Natasha had 24 plums. $\frac{1}{3}$ of them were rotten and had to be thrown away. She gave $\frac{3}{4}$ of the remainder to her friends and ate the rest. How many plums did she eat?

11 There are two baskets of plums. Basket A weighs 4.6 kg less than Basket B. 1.62 kg of plums was transferred from Basket B to Basket A. How much more does Basket B now weigh than Basket A?

Exercise 10 • page 101

Chapter 14

Multiplication and Division of Decimals

BANANAS — $1.50 PER LB — PRODUCT OF GUATEMALA

PEARS — PRODUCT OF OREGON — $3.25 PER LB

KIWIS — $3.10 PER LB — PRODUCT OF MEXICO

ORANGES — $2.50 PER LB — PRODUCT OF ECUADOR

I need 3 pounds of each kind of fruit to make a fruit salad. How much will I pay?

Lesson 1
Multiplying Tenths and Hundredths

Think

The capacity of a bottle is 0.4 L. The capacity of a glass vial is 0.04 L.

(a) What is the capacity of 3 bottles in liters?

(b) What is the capacity of 3 vials in liters?

Learn

(a) Multiply 0.4 by 3.

4 tenths × 3 = 12 tenths
= 1 one 2 tenths

0.4 × 3 = 1.2

The capacity of 3 bottles is _____ L.

(b) Multiply 0.04 by 3.

4 hundredths × 3 = 12 hundredths
= 1 tenth 2 hundredths

0.04 × 3 = 0.12

The capacity of 3 vials is _____ L.

Do

1 (a) Multiply 0.2 by 3.

2 tenths × 3 = [ ] tenths

0.2 × 3 = [ ]

(b) Multiply 0.02 by 3.

2 hundredths × 3 = [ ] hundredths

0.02 × 3 = [ ]

2 (a) Multiply 0.5 by 4.

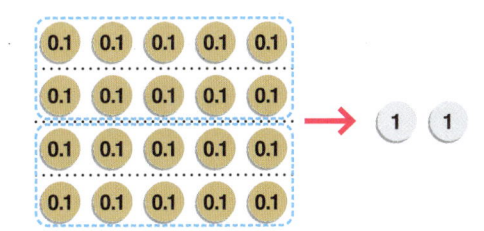

5 tenths × 4 = 20 tenths
= [ ] ones

0.5 × 4 = [ ]

(b) Multiply 0.05 by 4.

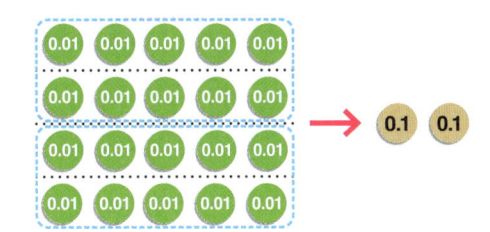

5 hundredths × 4 = 20 hundredths
= [ ] tenths

0.05 × 4 = [ ]

3 Multiply 0.09 by 4.

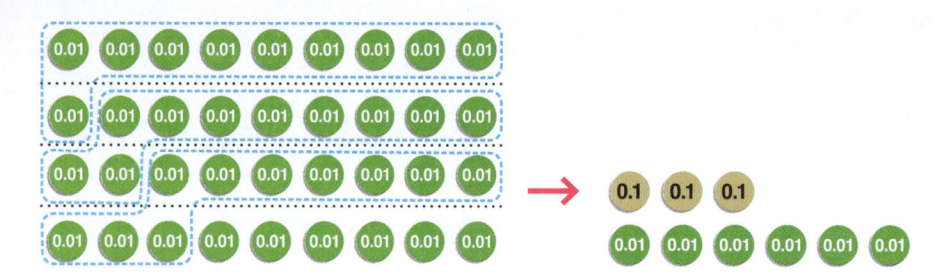

9 hundredths × 4 = ☐ hundredths = ☐ tenths ☐ hundredths

0.09 × 4 = ☐

4 (a) 6 × 4 = ☐   0.6 × 4 = ☐   0.06 × 4 = ☐

(b) 7 × 7 = ☐   0.7 × 7 = ☐   0.07 × 7 = ☐

(c) 8 × 5 = ☐   0.8 × 5 = ☐   0.08 × 5 = ☐

5 Multiply.

(a) 0.4 × 7   (b) 0.6 × 5   (c) 0.3 × 9

(d) 0.07 × 6   (e) 0.08 × 7   (f) 0.05 × 9

6 A paper clip weighs 0.8 g. How many grams do 9 paper clips weigh?

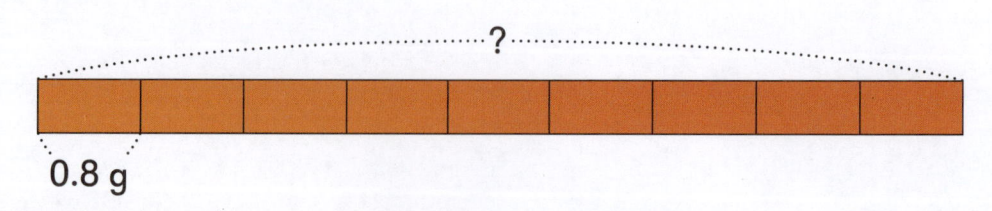

0.8 g

Exercise 1 • page 107

Lesson 2
Multiplying Decimals by a Whole Number — Part 1

Think

Three packages each weigh 2.4 kg. How many kilograms do they weigh altogether?

> 2.4 × 3 is greater than 2 × 3 and less than 3 × 3. The product will be between 6 and 9.

Learn

Method 1

2.4 × 3 = 24 tenths × 3

= 72 tenths

= 7.2

Method 2

Multiply the tenths and regroup them.

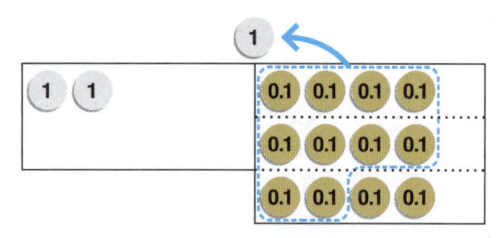

4 tenths × 3 = 12 tenths
= 1 one 2 tenths

Multiply the ones.

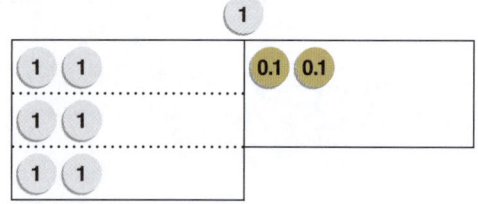

2 ones × 3 = 6 ones

Add in the regrouped 1.

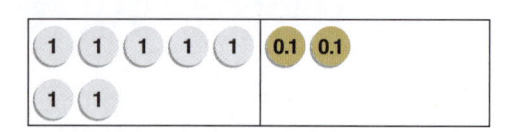

6 ones + 1 one = 7 ones

The packages weigh _____ kg altogether.

$$\begin{array}{r} 2.4 \\ \times\ \ 3 \\ \hline \end{array}$$

$$\begin{array}{r} 1\ \ \ \\ 2.4 \\ \times\ \ 3 \\ \hline .2 \end{array}$$

The digit 2 in the product is in the tenths place, so write a decimal point in front of it.

$$\begin{array}{r} 1\ \ \ \\ 2.4 \\ \times\ \ 3 \\ \hline 7.2 \end{array}$$

↑ (2 ones × 3) + 1 one

Multiply decimals the same way as whole numbers. Put a decimal point between the ones and the tenths.

14-2 Multiplying Decimals by a Whole Number — Part 1

Do

① Multiply 6.8 by 3.

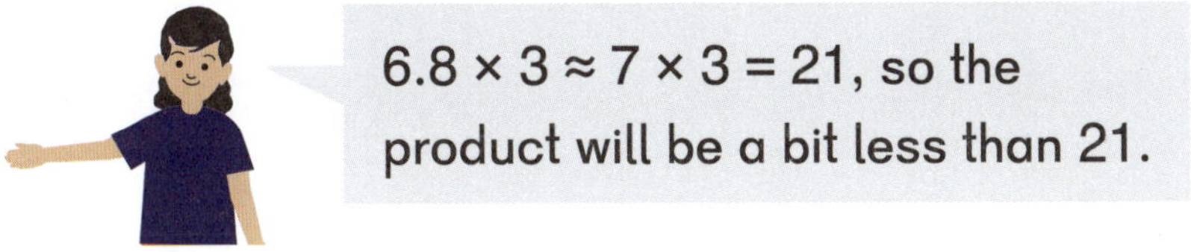

> 6.8 × 3 ≈ 7 × 3 = 21, so the product will be a bit less than 21.

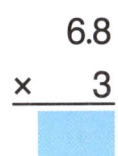

```
   6.8
 ×   3
 ─────
```

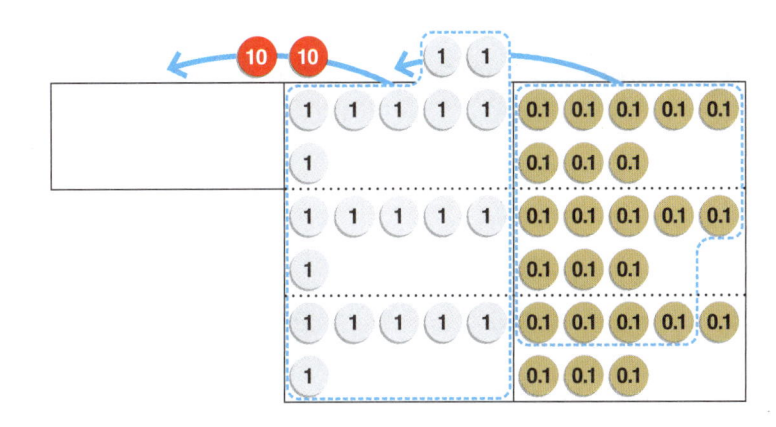

② Multiply 32.4 by 4.

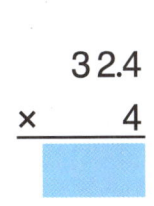

```
  32.4
 ×   4
 ─────
```

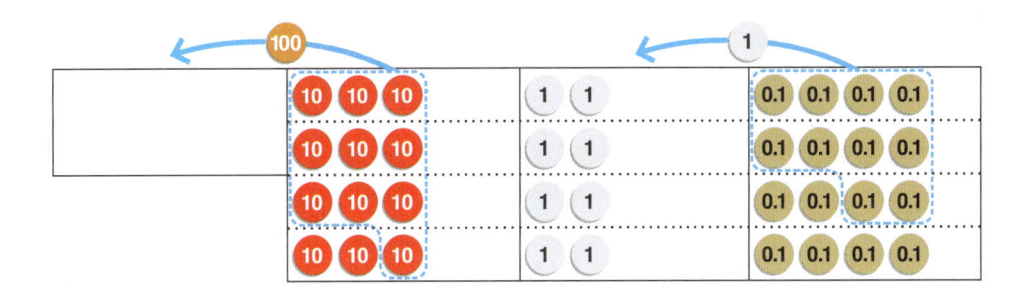

③ Multiply 3.4 by 5.

```
   3.4
 ×   5
 ─────
```

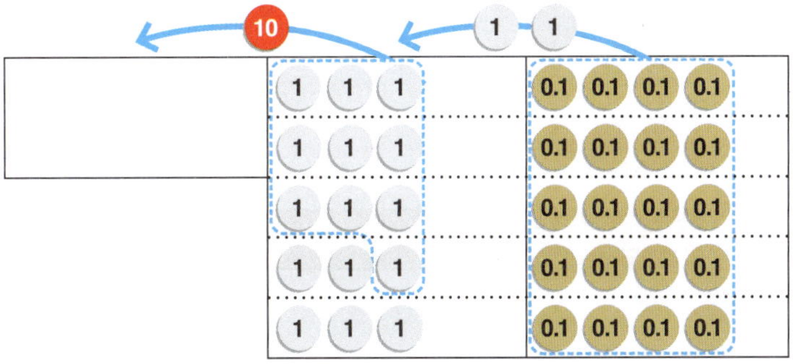

17.0 = 17

14-2 Multiplying Decimals by a Whole Number — Part 1

4 Find the product of 9 and 236.7.

```
   236.7
×      9
────────
```

5 Estimate and then find the actual values.

(a) 3.2 × 3   (b) 4.7 × 2

(c) 9.7 × 6   (d) 7.5 × 8

(e) 13.4 × 2   (f) 10.7 × 9

(g) 25.6 × 3   (h) 84.9 × 7

(i) 803.5 × 4 (j) 360.9 × 6

6 Dion's first paper airplane flew 2.5 m. He changed the design and made another paper airplane that flew 7 times as far. How much farther did his second airplane fly than his first airplane?

Exercise 2 • page 109

Lesson 3
Multiplying Decimals by a Whole Number — Part 2

Think

A tub of cottage cheese weighs 0.45 kg. How many kilograms do 3 tubs weigh?

> 0.45 × 3 ≈ 0.5 × 3, so the answer will be between 1 and 2.

Learn

Method 1

0.45 × 3 = 45 hundredths × 3

= 135 hundredths

= 1.35

Method 2

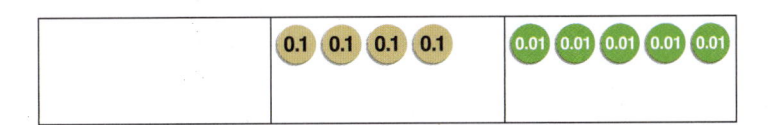

0.4 5
×   3

Multiply the hundredths and regroup them.

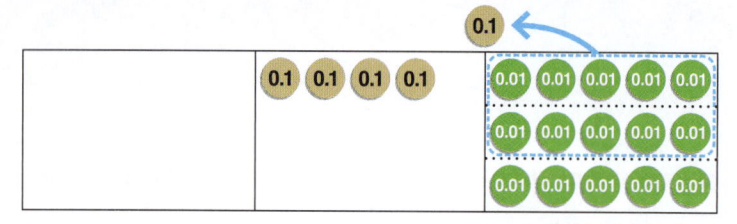

5 hundredths × 3 = 15 hundredths
= 1 tenth 5 hundredths

$$\begin{array}{r} 1 \\ 0.45 \\ \times3 \\ \hline 5 \end{array}$$

Multiply the tenths.

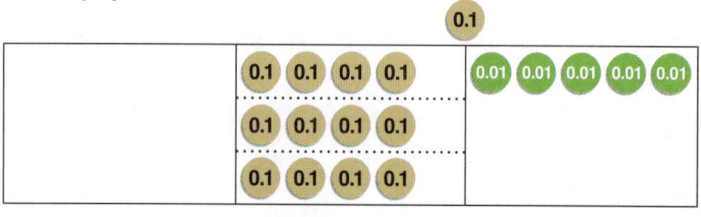

4 tenths × 3 = 12 tenths

Add in the regrouped tenth. Regroup the total tenths.

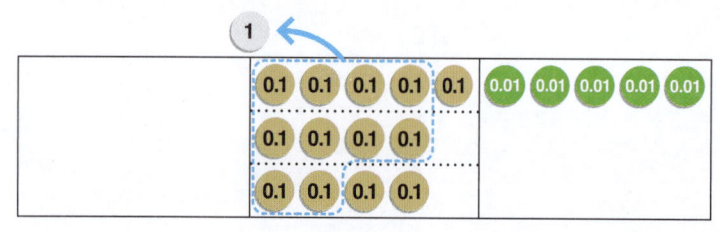

12 tenths + 1 tenth = 13 tenths
= 1 one 3 tenths

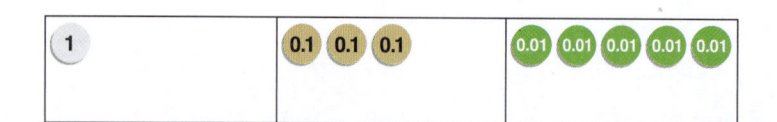

$$\begin{array}{r} 1\,1 \\ 0.45 \\ \times3 \\ \hline 1.35 \end{array}$$

Three tubs of cottage cheese weigh _____ kg.

The decimal point in the answer goes between the ones and the tenths.

Do

① Multiply 6.48 by 3.

The product will be between 6 × 3 = 18 and 7 × 3 = 21.

```
  6.4 8
×     3
───────
```

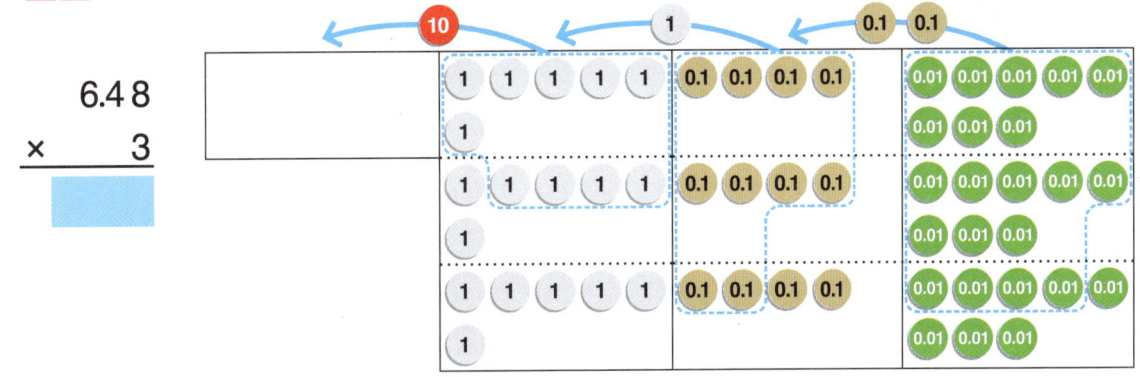

② Multiply 1.05 by 2.

```
  1.0 5
×     2
───────
```

2.10 = 2.1

③ Multiply 2.25 by 4.

```
  2.2 5
×     4
───────
```

9.00 = 9

14-3 Multiplying Decimals by a Whole Number — Part 2   149

4 1 ping pong paddle costs $2.95. How much will 4 ping pong paddles cost?

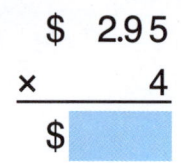

$ 2.95
× 4
$ ☐

$2.95 × 4 ≈ $3 × 4

Answers given in dollars and cents always have 2 decimal places.

5 Estimate and then find the actual values.

(a) 0.71 × 6

(b) 0.44 × 5

(c) 3.12 × 2

(d) 9.07 × 3

(e) 45.07 × 7

(f) 70.06 × 8

(g) 9.99 × 8

(h) 8.45 × 6

(i) 29.86 × 5

(j) 345.12 × 5

6 How much do 6 basketballs cost?

$19.50

Exercise 3 • page 112

Lesson 4
Practice A

P 4

1 Find the product.

(a) 0.7 × 8

(b) 0.4 × 6

(c) 0.07 × 9

(d) 0.07 × 4

(e) 0.02 × 5

(f) 0.1 × 20

2 Estimate and then find the actual values.

(a) 6.9 × 4

(b) 8.4 × 7

(c) 54.9 × 5

(d) 2.84 × 6

(e) 60.09 × 7

(f) 82.94 × 9

(g) 223.4 × 5

(h) 132.06 × 6

3 A bag of apples weighs 3.5 lb.

(a) Estimate the weight of 8 bags of apples.

(b) Find the actual weight of 8 bags of apples.

4. A bag of flour costs $5.65 and a bag of sugar costs $4.58. A bakery buys 5 bags of flour and 5 bags of sugar.

   (a) Estimate the total cost.

   (b) Find the actual total cost.

5. Emma wants to buy 4 boxes of cookies and 5 bottles of juice for a birthday party. A box of cookies costs $6.89 and a bottle of juice costs $5.30. She has $40.

   (a) Does she have enough money?

   (b) Determine how much money she will have left over, or how much more money she will need.

6. Last week, Camilla ran 2.5 miles a day for 5 days. This week, she ran 3.75 miles a day for 4 days.

   (a) In which week did she run farther?

   (b) How much farther did she run?

7. A bottle of shampoo costs $6.85. A bottle of conditioner costs 90¢ more than the bottle of shampoo. Elena bought 2 of each. How much did she spend?

Exercise 4 • page 115

Lesson 5
Dividing Tenths and Hundredths

Think

(a) Dion divided 1.2 liters of water equally into 3 containers for a science experiment. How much water is in each container?

(b) Alex divided 0.12 liters of water equally into 3 test tubes. How much water is in each test tube?

Learn

(a) Divide 1.2 by 3.

1.2 = 12 tenths

12 tenths ÷ 3 = 4 tenths

1.2 ÷ 3 = 0.4   0.4 × ? = 1.2

Each container will have _____ L of water.

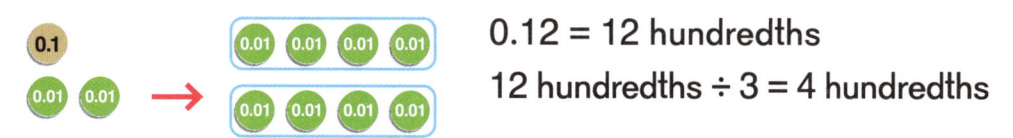

(b) Divide 0.12 by 3.

0.12 = 12 hundredths

12 hundredths ÷ 3 = 4 hundredths

0.12 ÷ 3 = 0.04   0.04 × ? = 0.12

Each test tube will have _____ L of water.

Do

1 (a) Divide 0.6 by 2.

6 tenths ÷ 2 = [ ] tenths

0.6 ÷ 2 = [ ]

(b) Divide 0.06 by 2.

6 hundredths ÷ 2 = [ ] hundredths

0.06 ÷ 2 = [ ]

2 (a) Divide 2 by 4.

2 = 20 tenths

20 tenths ÷ 4 = [ ] tenths

2 ÷ 4 = 2.0 ÷ 4 = [ ]

(b) Divide 0.2 by 4.

0.2 = 20 hundredths

20 hundredths ÷ 4 = [ ] hundredths

0.2 ÷ 4 = 0.20 ÷ 4 = [ ]

3. Divide 4.5 by 5.

   45 tenths ÷ 5 = ?

   4.5 ÷ 5 = ☐

4. 0.45 ÷ 5 = ☐   45 hundredths ÷ 5 = ?

5. (a) 72 ÷ 9 = ☐   7.2 ÷ 9 = ☐   0.72 ÷ 9 = ☐

   (b) 28 ÷ 7 = ☐   2.8 ÷ 7 = ☐   0.28 ÷ 7 = ☐

   (c) 40 ÷ 8 = ☐   4 ÷ 8 = ☐   0.4 ÷ 8 = ☐

6. Divide.

   (a) 4.2 ÷ 7   (b) 6.4 ÷ 8   (c) 0.63 ÷ 9

   (d) 0.36 ÷ 4   (e) 2 ÷ 5   (f) 0.3 ÷ 6

7. Mei spent $3.20 on 8 donuts. How much did 1 donut cost?

Exercise 5 • page 117

14-5 Dividing Tenths and Hundredths   155

Lesson 6
Dividing Decimals by a Whole Number — Part 1

Think

Alex has 7.2 m of ribbon. He wants to cut it into 3 pieces of the same length. How long should he cut each piece in meters?

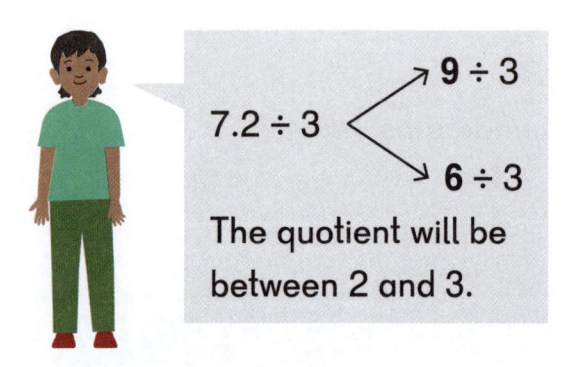

7.2 ÷ 3
- 9 ÷ 3
- 6 ÷ 3

The quotient will be between 2 and 3.

Learn

Method 1

7.2 = 72 tenths

72 tenths ÷ 3 = 24 tenths

= 2.4

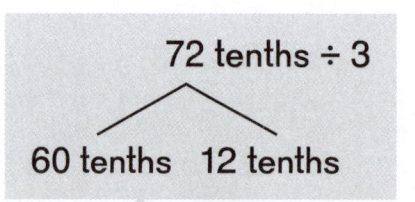

72 tenths ÷ 3
- 60 tenths
- 12 tenths

Method 2

$7.2 \div 3$

Divide the ones by 3.

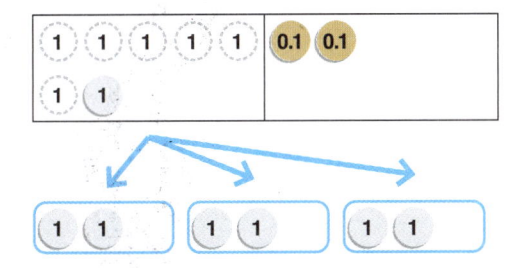

$$3\overline{)7.2}$$

$$\begin{array}{r} 2 \\ 3\overline{)7.2} \\ 6 \\ \hline 1 \end{array}$$

← 2 ones in each group
← 2 ones × 3
← ones still to divide

Regroup the remaining ones.
Divide the tenths by 3.

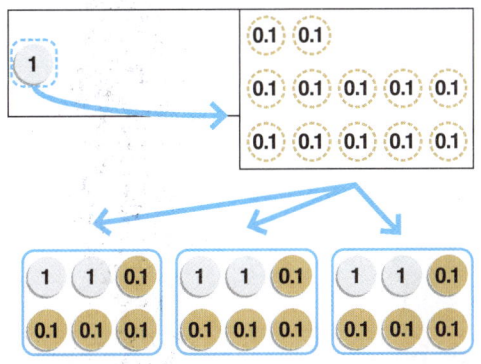

$$\begin{array}{r} 2.4 \\ 3\overline{)7.2} \\ 6 \\ \hline 1\,2 \\ 1\,2 \\ \hline 0 \end{array}$$

← 4 tenths in each group
← 12 tenths
← 4 tenths × 3

Divide decimals the same way as whole numbers. Write the decimal point between the ones and the tenths in the quotient.

$$3\overline{)7.2} \quad \begin{array}{c} 2.4 \end{array}$$

Check the answer. Does 2.4 × 3 = 7.2?

Each piece should be _____ m long.

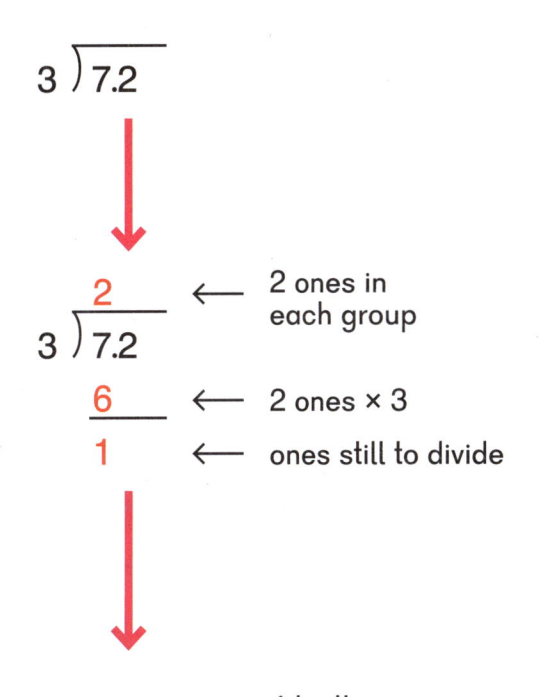

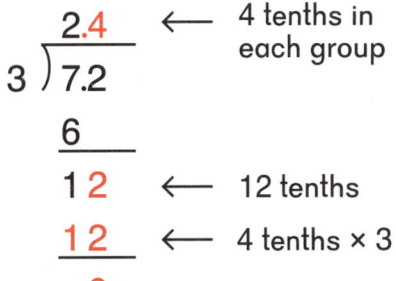

14-6 Dividing Decimals by a Whole Number — Part 1

Do

1 Divide 3.6 by 2.

3.6 ÷ 2 ≈ 4 ÷ 2, so the quotient will be a little less than 2.

2)3.6

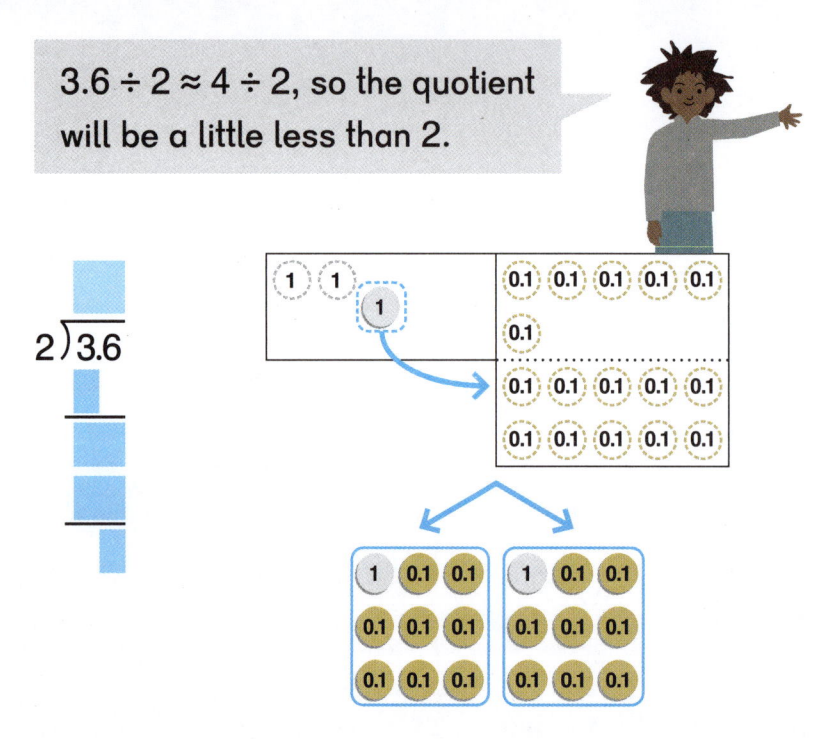

2 Divide 35.4 by 2.

35.4 ÷ 2 ≈ 40 ÷ 2, so the quotient will be a little less than 20.

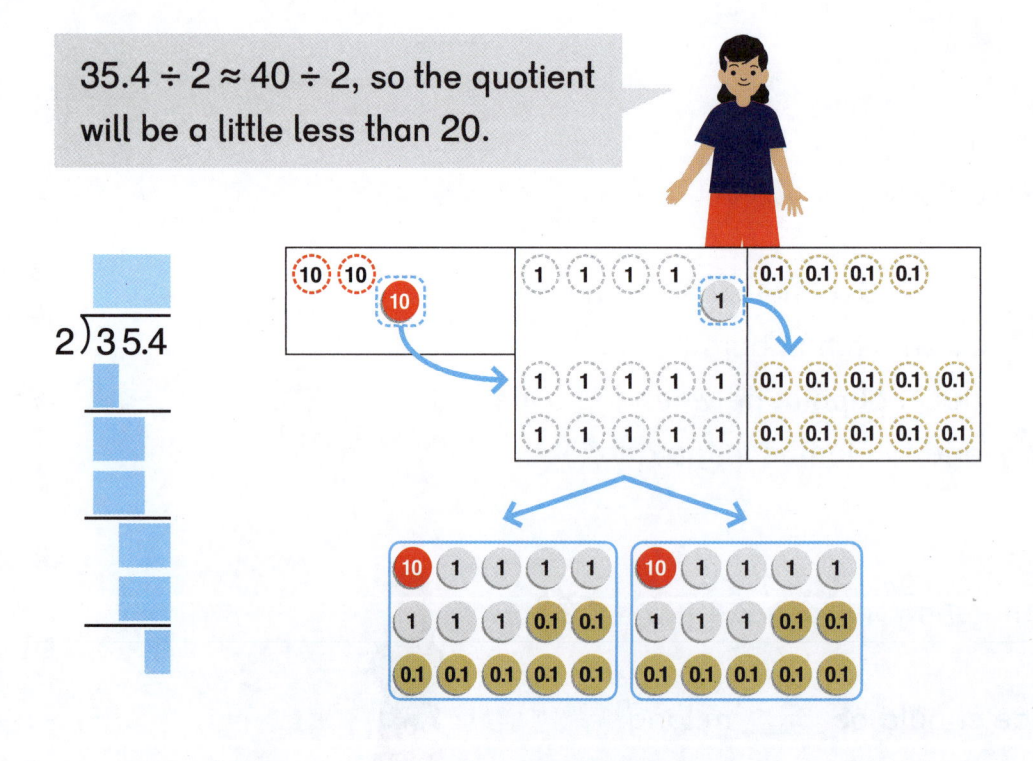

2)35.4

14-6 Dividing Decimals by a Whole Number — Part 1

3 Divide 23.4 by 3.

3)23.4

23.4 ÷ 3 ≈ 24 ÷ 3, so the quotient will be a little less than 8.

4 Estimate and then find the actual values.

(a) 8.4 ÷ 2

(b) 4.8 ÷ 4

(c) 6.5 ÷ 5

(d) 7.8 ÷ 6

(e) 43.4 ÷ 7

(f) 83.2 ÷ 8

(g) 78.3 ÷ 9

(h) 136.5 ÷ 5

5 Dion ran 10.8 miles this week. He ran 3 times as far this week as he did last week. How many miles did he run last week?

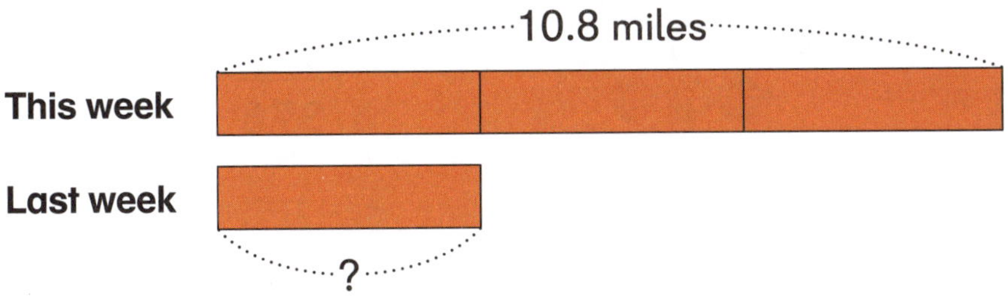

This week — 10.8 miles

Last week — ?

Exercise 6 • page 119

14-6 Dividing Decimals by a Whole Number — Part 1   159

Lesson 7
Dividing Decimals by a Whole Number — Part 2

Think

Alex wants to divide 3.78 kg of fertilizer equally to mix with dirt in 3 trays for a science experiment. How many kilograms of fertilizer does each tray get?

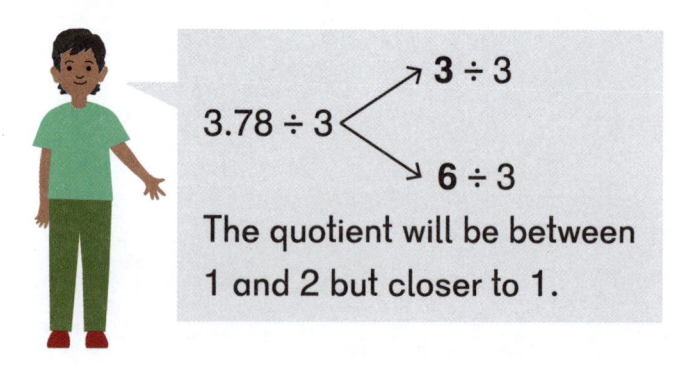

3.78 ÷ 3
- 3 ÷ 3
- 6 ÷ 3

The quotient will be between 1 and 2 but closer to 1.

Learn

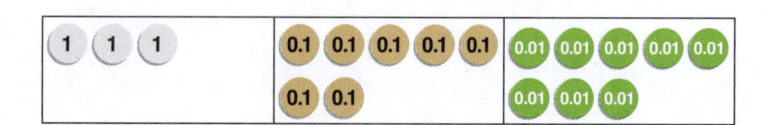

3.78 ÷ 3

Divide the ones by 3.

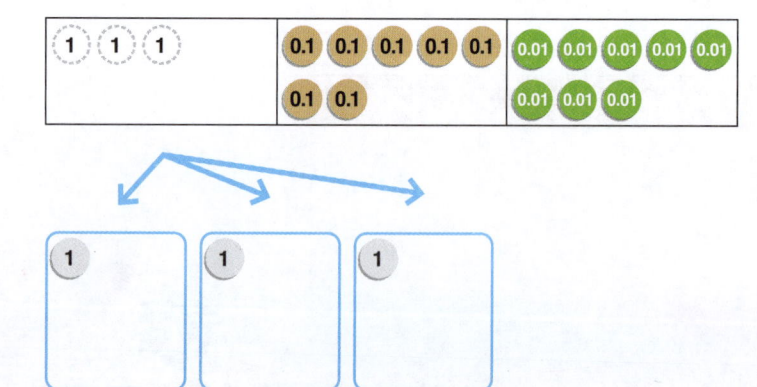

$3\overline{)3.78}$

$3\overline{)3.78}$ → 1 one in each group
$\underline{3}$ ← 1 one × 3

Divide the tenths by 3.

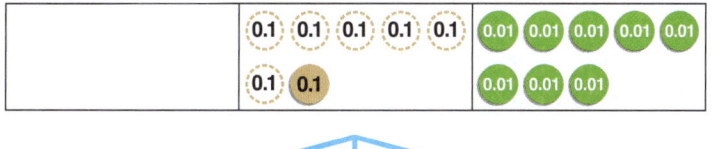

$\begin{array}{r} 1.2 \\ 3\overline{)3.78} \\ \underline{3} \\ 7 \\ \underline{6} \\ 1 \end{array}$ ← 2 tenths in each group

← tenths to divide

← 2 tenths × 3

← tenths still to divide

Write the decimal point between the ones and the tenths in the quotient.

Regroup the remaining tenth.
Divide the hundredths by 3.

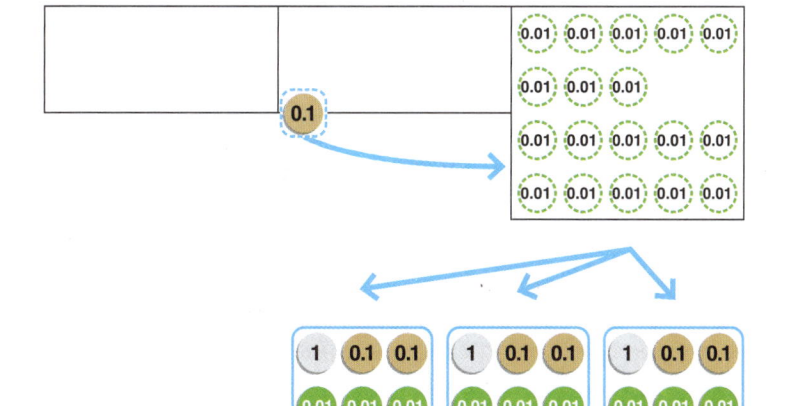

$\begin{array}{r} 1.26 \\ 3\overline{)3.78} \\ \underline{3} \\ 7 \\ \underline{6} \\ 18 \\ \underline{18} \\ 0 \end{array}$ ← 6 hundredths in each group

← hundredths to divide

← 6 hundredths × 3

Each tray gets _____ kg of fertilizer.

Check the answer. Does 1.26 × 3 = 3.78?

14-7 Dividing Decimals by a Whole Number — Part 2

Do

1 Divide 0.68 by 4.

0.68 ÷ 4 is between 0.4 ÷ 4 and 0.8 ÷ 4, so the quotient will be between 0.1 and 0.2.

2 Divide 6.24 by 3.

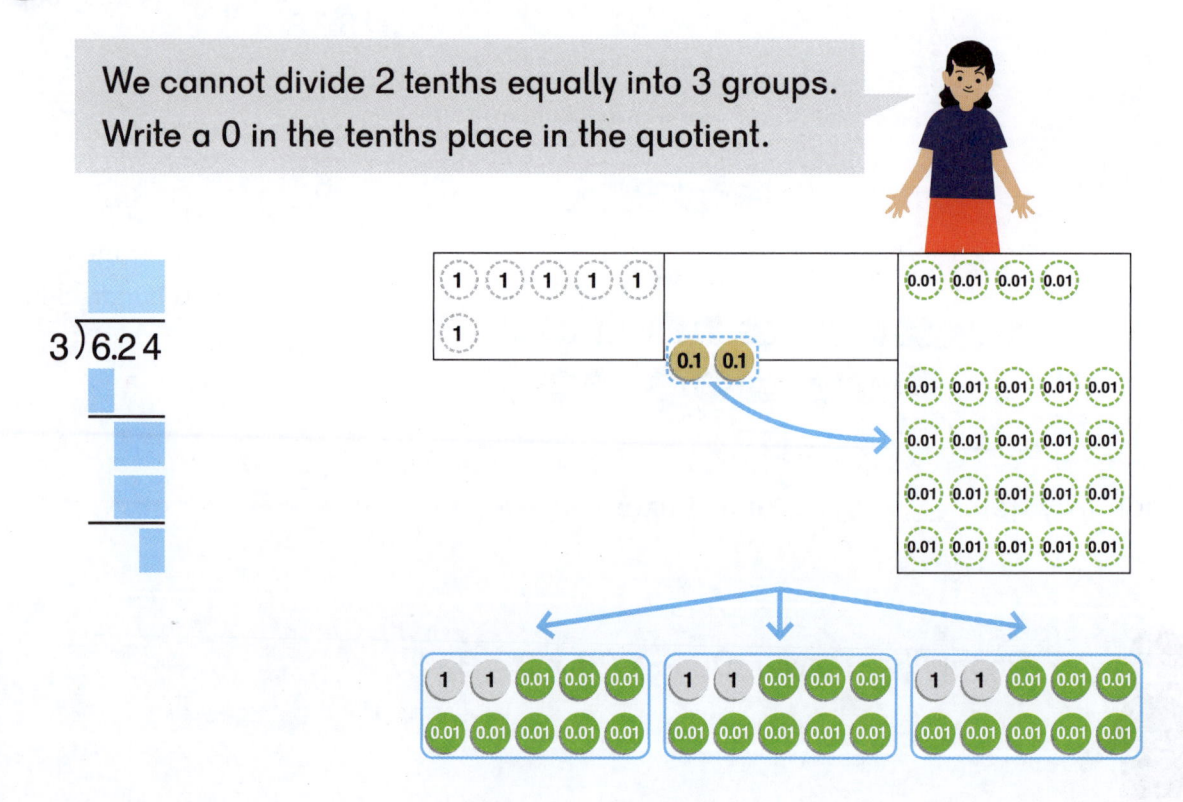

We cannot divide 2 tenths equally into 3 groups. Write a 0 in the tenths place in the quotient.

③ Divide 2.15 by 5.

5)2.15

20 tenths ÷ 5 = 4 tenths, so the quotient will be a little more than 4 tenths.

④ Estimate and then find the actual values.

(a) 0.92 ÷ 4

(b) 8.31 ÷ 3

(c) 5.04 ÷ 9

(d) 9.48 ÷ 4

(e) 83.15 ÷ 5

(f) 144.24 ÷ 8

⑤ A painting easel costs 3 times as much as a painting canvas. Jack bought 1 easel and 4 canvases for $17.92. How much does 1 canvas cost?

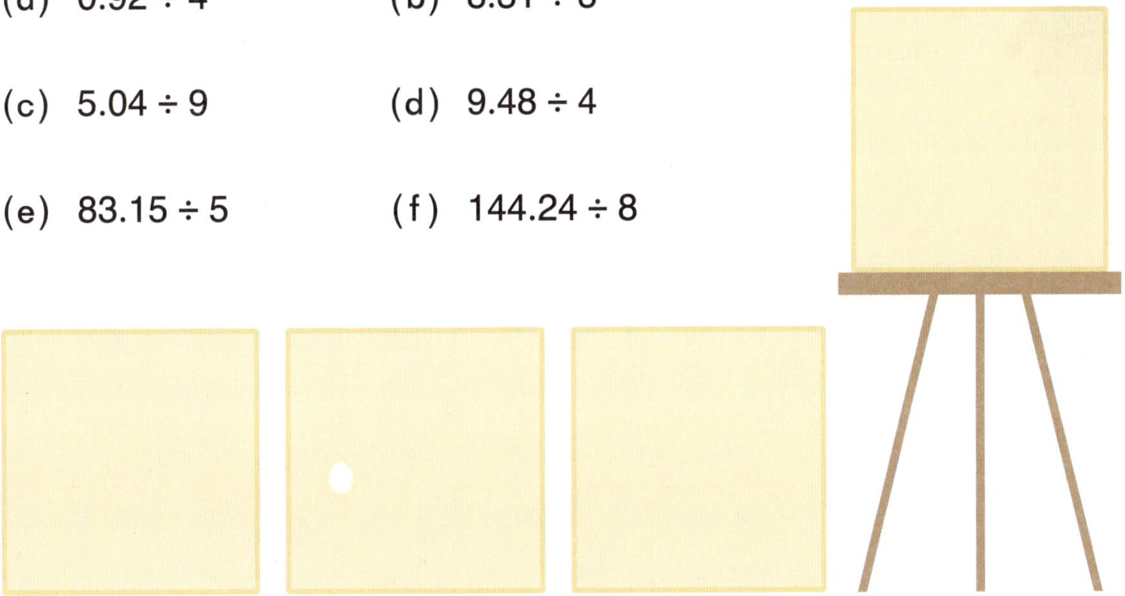

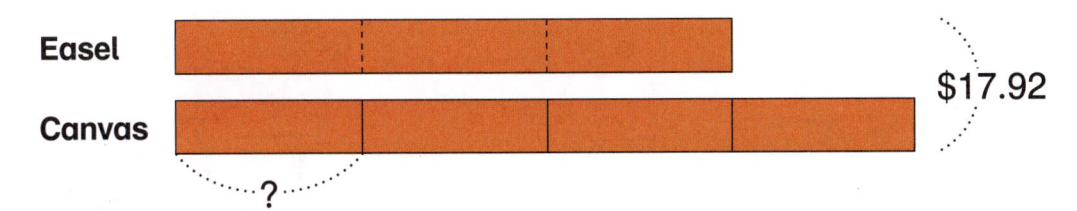

Easel

Canvas

?

$17.92

Exercise 7 • page 122

14-7 Dividing Decimals by a Whole Number — Part 2

Lesson 8
Dividing Decimals by a Whole Number — Part 3

Think

Emma has a piece of fabric 5 meters long. She wants to cut it into 4 equal pieces. How long should each piece be in meters?

$5 \div 4 \approx 4 \div 4$
Each piece will be a little more than 1 m long.

Learn

$5 \div 4$

Divide the ones by 4.

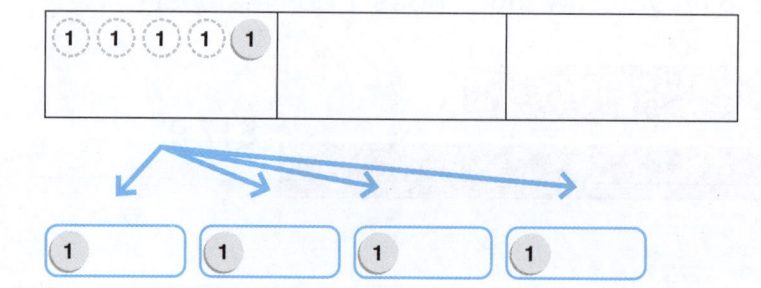

1 ← 1 one in each group
4)5
4 ← 1 one × 4
1 ← remainder

When we divide the remaining tenths and then hundredths, we can write a 0 in the tenths place and then hundredths place of the dividend to help align the digits.

Regroup the remaining one as tenths.
Divide the tenths by 4.

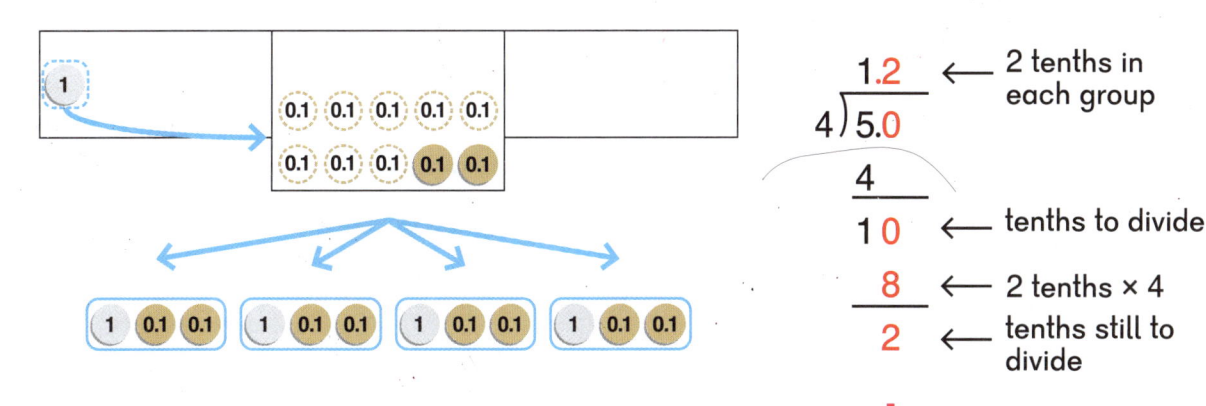

```
     1.2    ← 2 tenths in each group
  4 ) 5.0
      4
      1 0   ← tenths to divide
        8   ← 2 tenths × 4
        2   ← tenths still to divide
```

Regroup the remaining tenths as hundredths.
Divide the hundredths by 4.

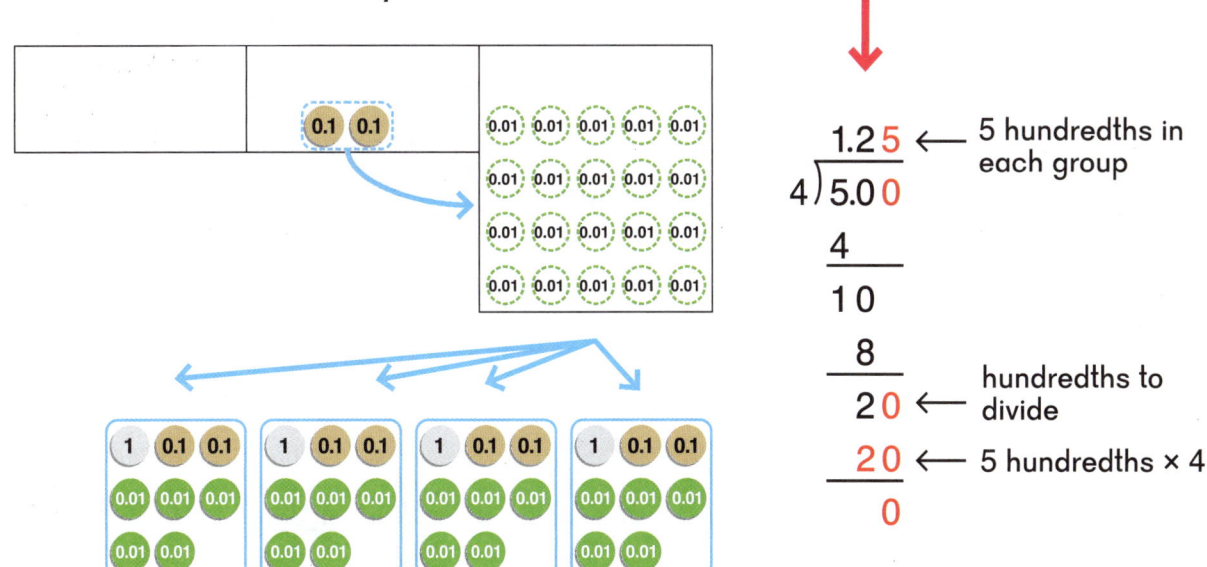

```
     1.2 5   ← 5 hundredths in each group
  4 ) 5.0 0
      4
      1 0
        8
        2 0 ← hundredths to divide
        2 0 ← 5 hundredths × 4
          0
```

Each piece should be _____ m long.

14-8 Dividing Decimals by a Whole Number — Part 3

Do

1 Divide 0.9 by 2.

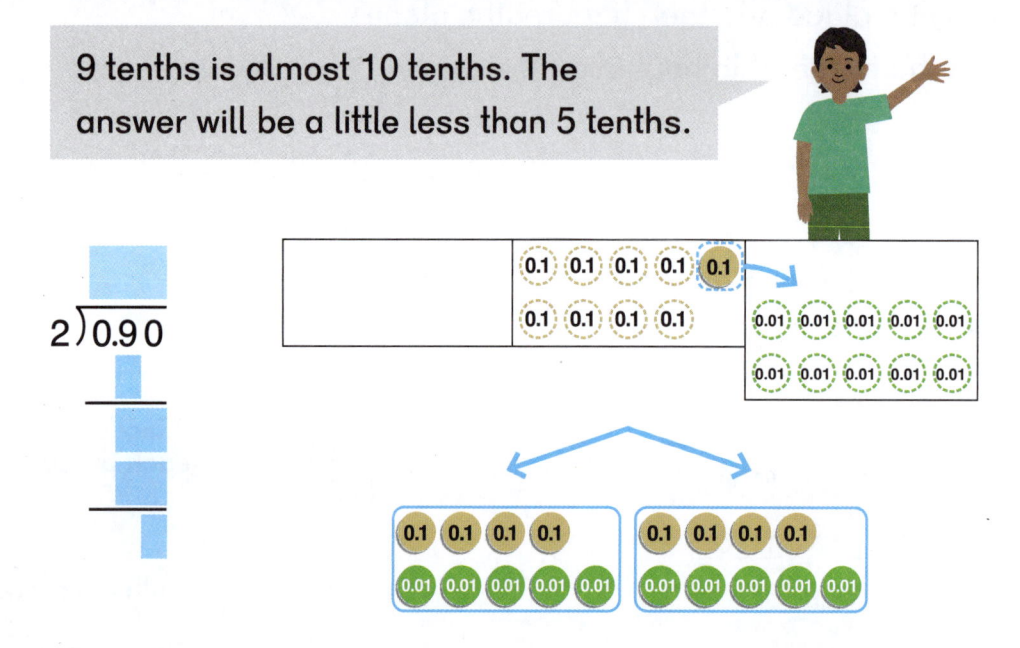

9 tenths is almost 10 tenths. The answer will be a little less than 5 tenths.

2) 0.9 0

2 Divide 8.1 by 6.

8.1 ÷ 6 ≈ 6 ÷ 6, so the answer will be a little more than 1.

Divide the ones.   Divide the tenths.   Regroup the remaining tenths as hundredths and divide the hundredths.

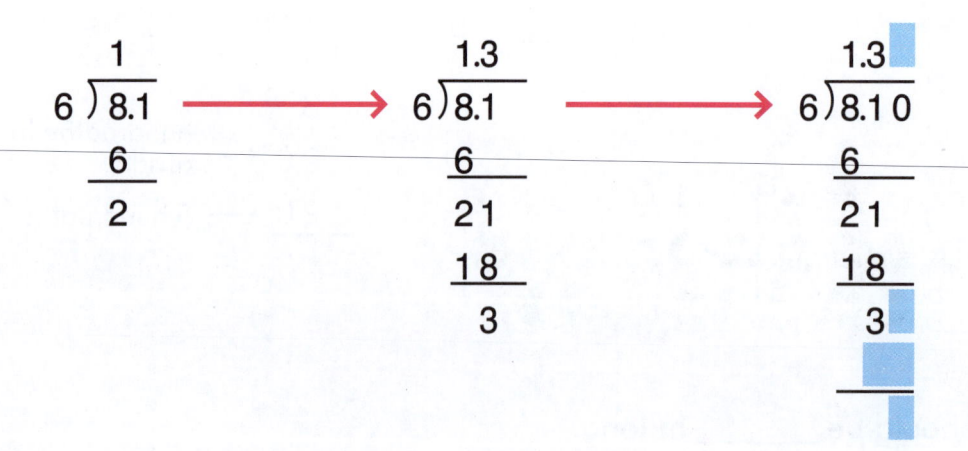

```
    1              1.3              1.3
6 ) 8.1    →    6 ) 8.1     →    6 ) 8.1 0
    6              6                6
    2              2 1              2 1
                   1 8              1 8
                     3                3
```

166   14-8 Dividing Decimals by a Whole Number — Part 3

3 Divide 22 by 8.

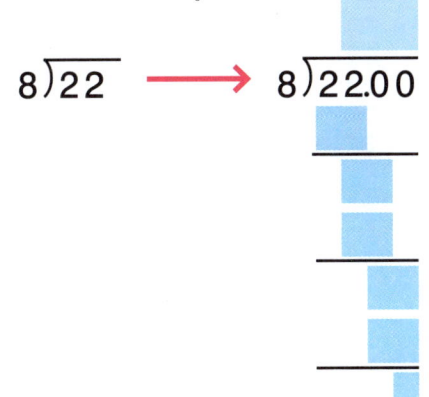

8)22 ⟶ 8)22.00

> 22 ÷ 8 ≈ 24 ÷ 8, so the quotient will be a little less than...

4 Estimate and then find the actual values.

(a) 10 ÷ 4
(b) 4.3 ÷ 2
(c) 25.5 ÷ 6

(d) 46 ÷ 4
(e) 30.4 ÷ 5
(f) 100 ÷ 8

5 Five friends shared the cost of a meal equally. The meal cost $113. How much did each friend spend?

6 A laboratory technician is putting 70 g of sodium chloride equally into 4 test tubes. How many grams of sodium chloride need to be put into each test tube?

Exercise 8 • page 125

Lesson 9
Practice B

1 Find the quotient. Express the answers as decimals.

(a) 1.8 ÷ 3   (b) 0.36 ÷ 9   (c) 5.6 ÷ 8

(d) 1 ÷ 2   (e) 3 ÷ 5   (f) 0.4 ÷ 8

2 Estimate and then find the actual values. Express the answers as decimals.

(a) 4.8 ÷ 2   (b) 8.7 ÷ 3   (c) 41.6 ÷ 8

(d) 5 ÷ 2   (e) 7.8 ÷ 4   (f) 17 ÷ 5

(g) 41.6 ÷ 8   (h) 36.48 ÷ 8   (i) 14.2 ÷ 4

(j) 136.8 ÷ 6   (k) 15.05 ÷ 7   (l) 568.2 ÷ 5

3 Alex bought two puzzles that cost the same amount of money. He paid $7.70. How much did each puzzle cost?

4. An employee put 6 lb of coffee equally into 4 bags. How much coffee is in each bag?

5. In a walkathon, 5 students walked a combined distance of 34 miles. If they each walked the same distance, how far did each student walk?

6. Store A sells 5 bottles of juice for $11.75. Store B sells 6 bottles of the same juice for $15.12.

   (a) Estimate to determine which store has a better deal.

   (b) How much does one bottle of juice cost at each store?

7. Harrison added some plant food to water. He has 15.5 gal of this mixture. He used 10.8 gal to water his plants and poured the rest equally into 5 bottles. How much mixture is in each bottle?

8. The perimeter of a square garden is 33.2 m. How many meters long is each side of the garden?

9 The area of a rectangle is 65.7 cm². The length of the rectangle is 9 cm. What is the perimeter of the rectangle?

10 Aisha raised $25.50 a week for 3 weeks for charity. She gave the money equally to 5 animal shelters. How much money did each shelter receive?

11

4 stools cost $76.96. How much do 6 stools cost?

12 Jerry worked for 4 hours. He then spent $12.50 of the money he earned and had $50.90 left. How much was he paid per hour?

13

Sharon sells necklaces for $2.50 each. She sold 5 necklaces. She also sold 8 bracelets. Each bracelet had the same price. She received $27.30. How much did she sell each bracelet for?

Exercise 9 • page 127

Chapter 15

Angles

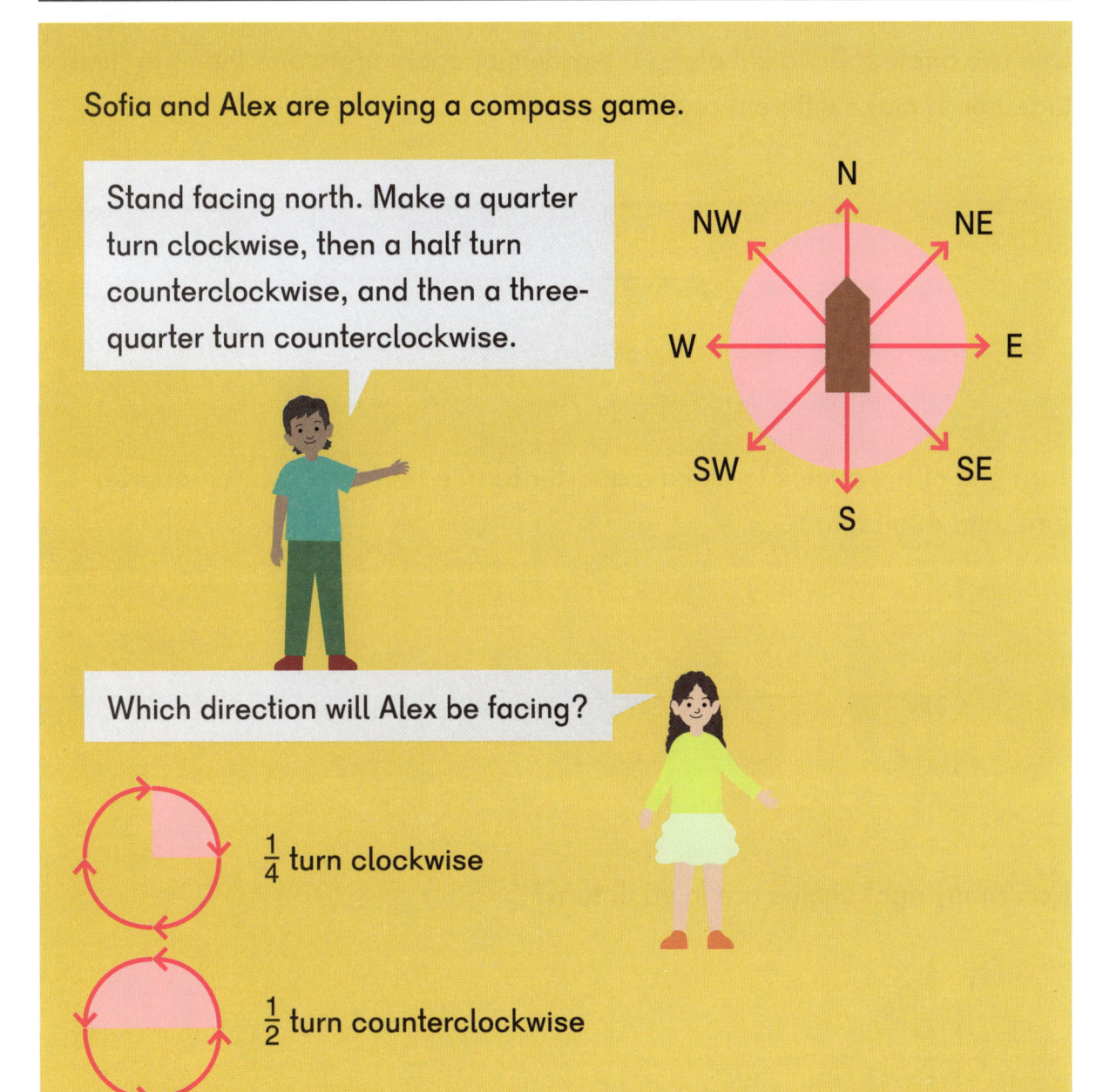

Sofia and Alex are playing a compass game.

Stand facing north. Make a quarter turn clockwise, then a half turn counterclockwise, and then a three-quarter turn counterclockwise.

Which direction will Alex be facing?

$\frac{1}{4}$ turn clockwise

$\frac{1}{2}$ turn counterclockwise

$\frac{3}{4}$ turn counterclockwise

171

Lesson 1
The Size of Angles

1

Think

Use two circles. Cut a slit along the radius of each circle and then put them together to make different angles.

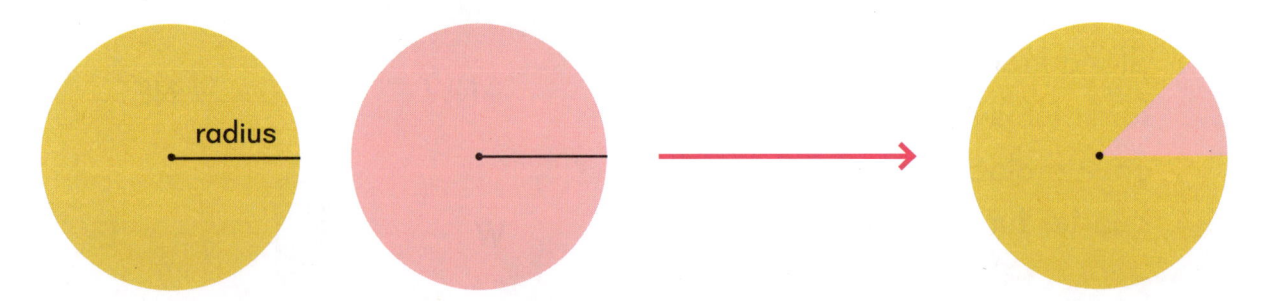

Turn one of the circles to make a quarter turn, a half turn, a three-quarter turn, and a full turn.

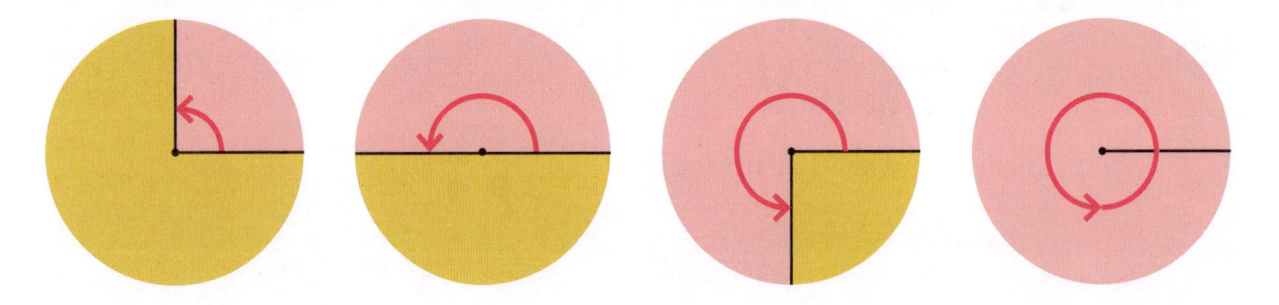

How many right angles are in each turn?

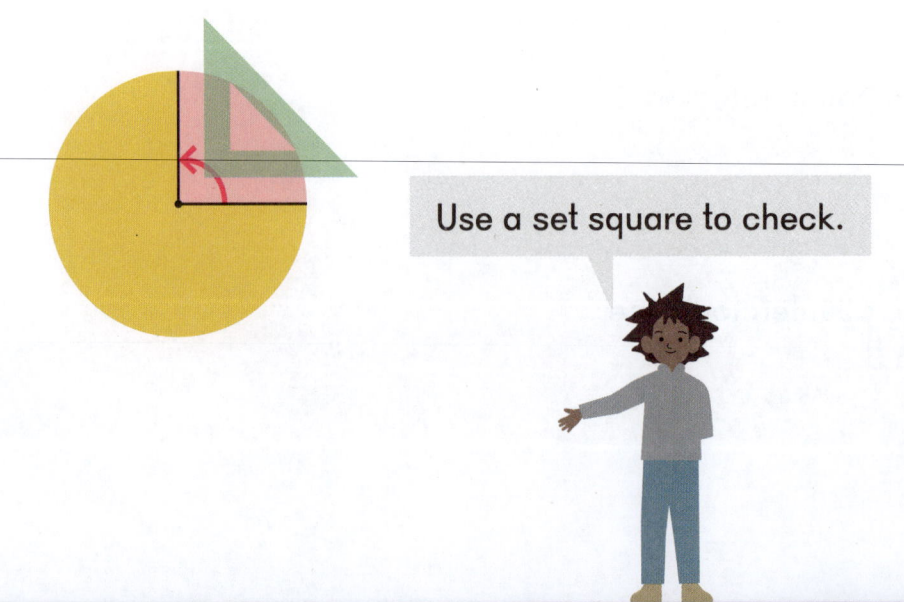

Use a set square to check.

172   15-1 The Size of Angles

Learn

We measure angles in degrees. When a circle is divided into 360 equal size angles, the size of one angle is 1 degree. We write 1 degree as 1°.

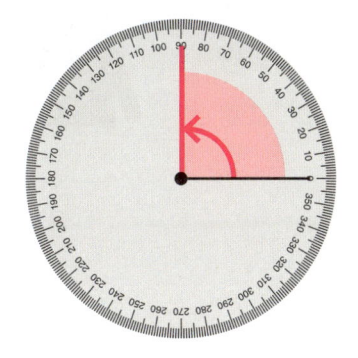

A quarter turn is 90°. A 90° angle is a right angle. Angles that measure between 0° and 90° are called **acute angles**.

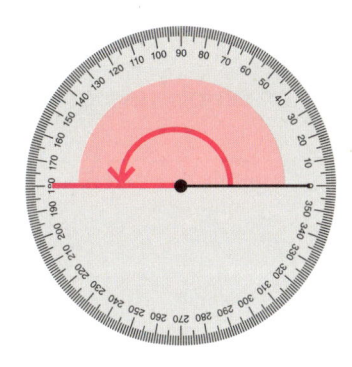

A half turn is 2 × 90° = 180°. A 180° angle makes a straight line. Angles that measure between 90° and 180° are called **obtuse angles**. A 180° angle is called a **straight angle**.

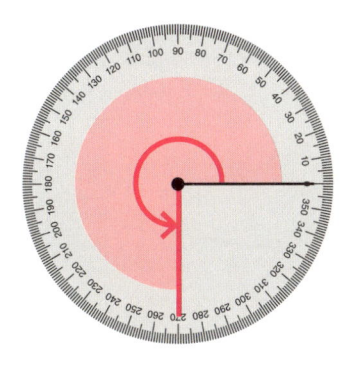

A three-quarter turn is 3 × 90° = 270°. Angles that measure between 180° and 360° are called **reflex angles**.

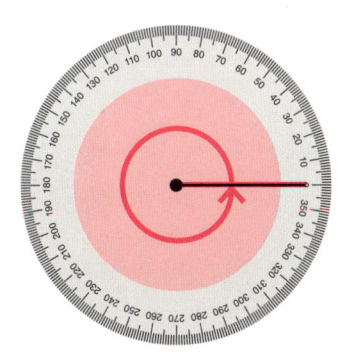

A full turn is 4 × 90° = 360°.

Do

1 Use a set square to find obtuse angles and acute angles.

When I open the scissors this much it forms an acute angle.

2 Tell whether each angle is a right angle, an acute angle, or an obtuse angle.

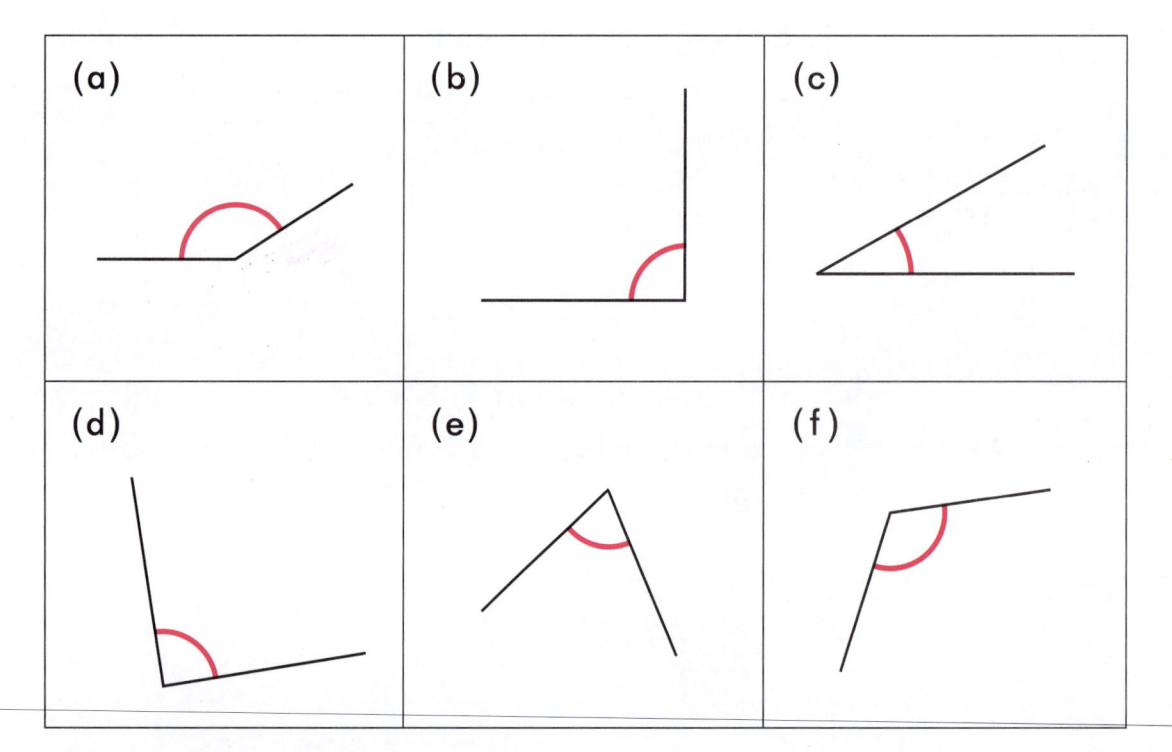

(a)

(b)

(c)

(d)

(e)

(f)

Use a set square to check.

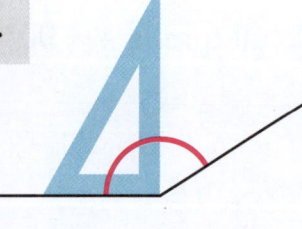

174   15-1 The Size of Angles

3 (a) Examine the angles of set squares. Which angles are right angles? Which angles are acute angles?

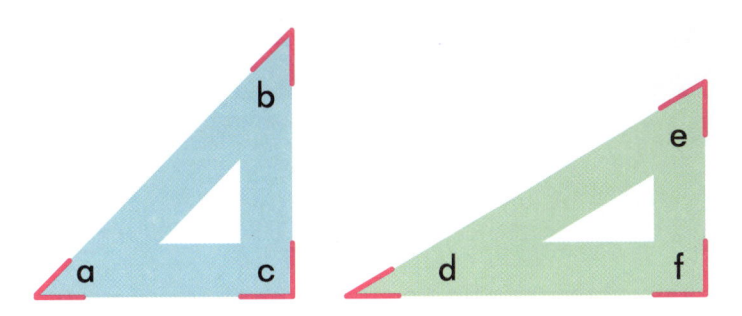

(b) Put two similar set squares together to form a right angle.

$\frac{1}{2} \times 90° = ?$

Angle a = ☐ °

(c) Put three similar set squares together to form a right angle.

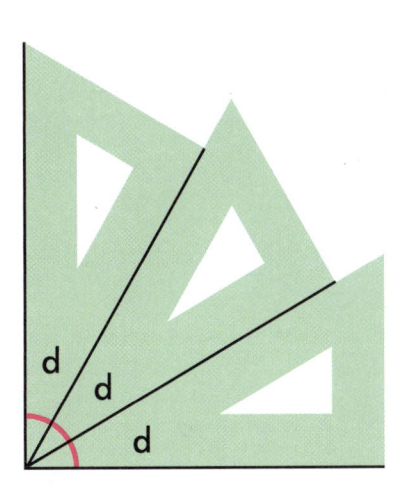

Angle d = ☐ °

15-1 The Size of Angles

(d) Put three similar set squares together to form a straight line.

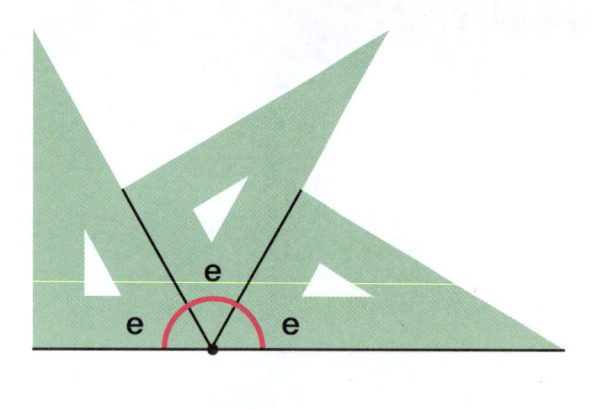

Angle e = ☐°

4. Use the set squares to find the measure of each angle.

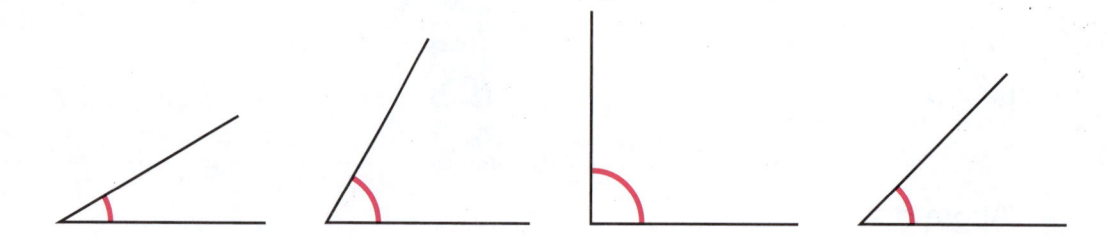

5. The compass shows a circle divided into 8 equal sized angles. Dion is facing east. He makes a $\frac{5}{8}$ turn counterclockwise. How many degrees did he turn?

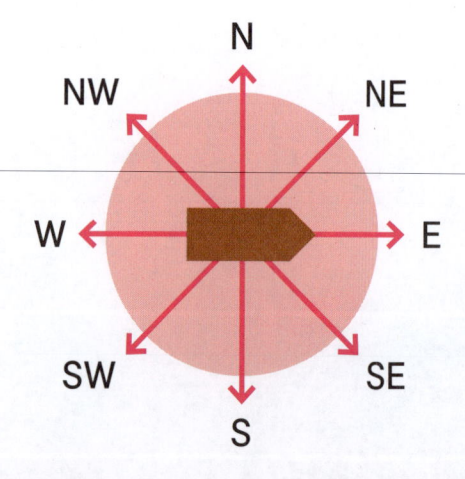

Exercise 1 • page 131

15-1 The Size of Angles

Lesson 2
Measuring Angles

(2)

Think

We use a protractor to measure angles.

(a) Examine a protractor. What do you notice?

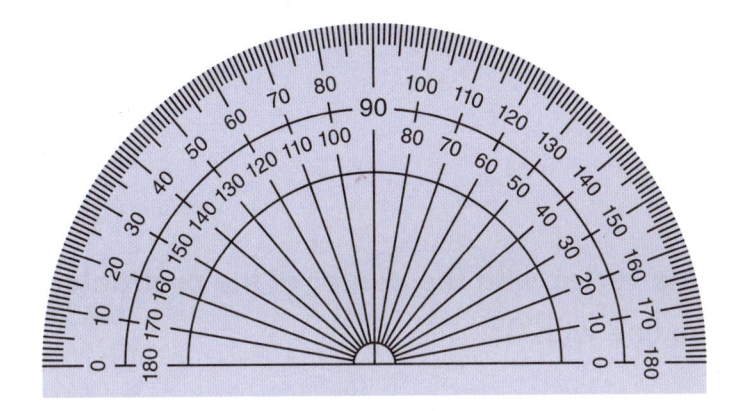

(b) Use the protractor to measure each angle in degrees. Which angle is greater and by how much?

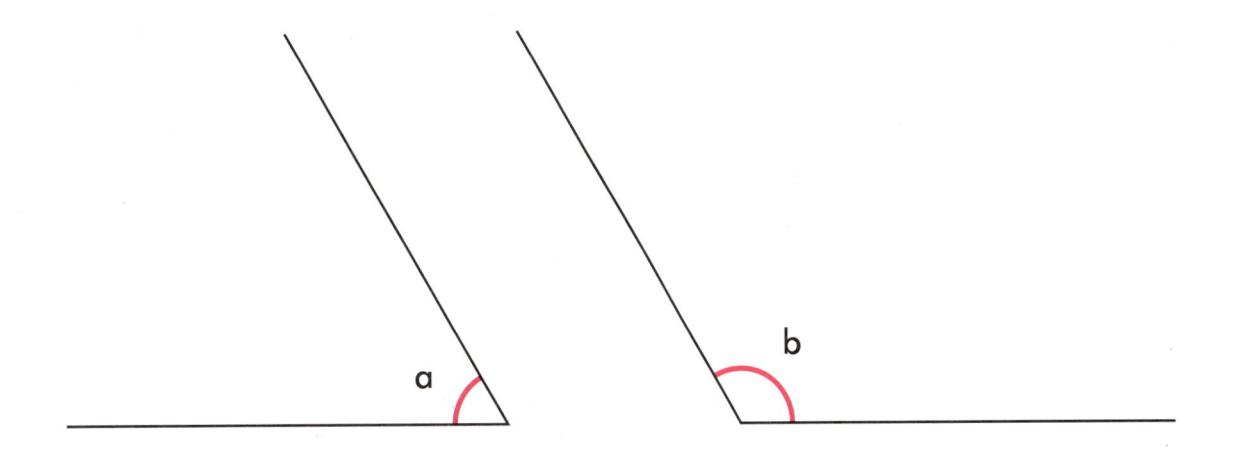

Which angle is an acute angle?
Which one is an obtuse angle?

15-2 Measuring Angles 177

Learn

A protractor is shaped like a half-circle. It has two 180-degree scales, a center and a base line.

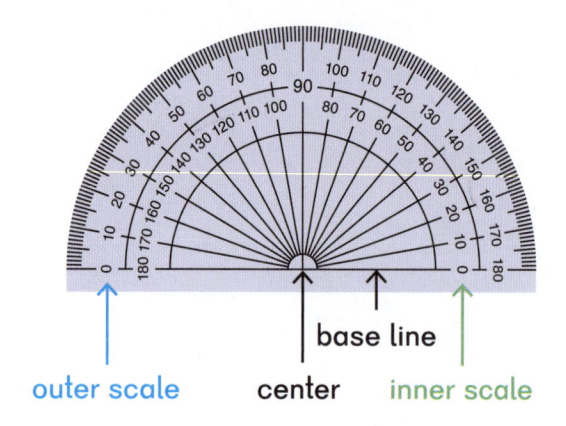

outer scale — center — base line — inner scale

To measure an angle, line up the vertex with the center of the protractor and one of the sides along the base line with 0°.

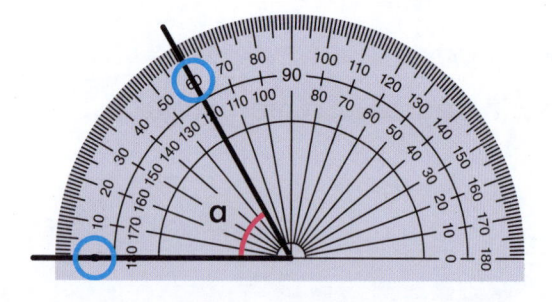

Angle a is an acute angle. It is less than 90°.

∠a = 60°

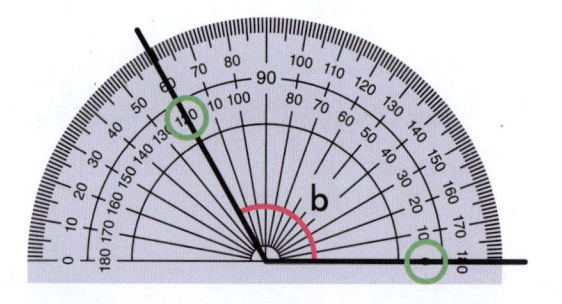

Angle b is an obtuse angle. It is greater than 90°.

∠b = 120°

∠ means angle.
∠a is read as "angle a."

Which scale did you use to measure each angle?

178 15-2 Measuring Angles

Do

1 What is the size of each angle?

> Before measuring, think about whether the angle is greater than or less than 90°.

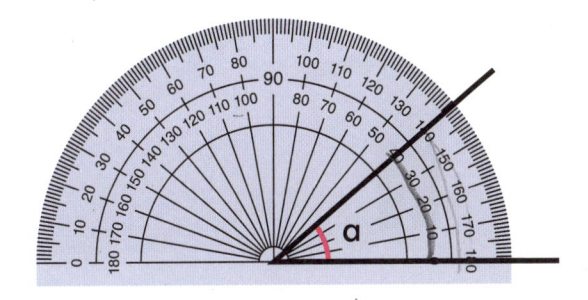

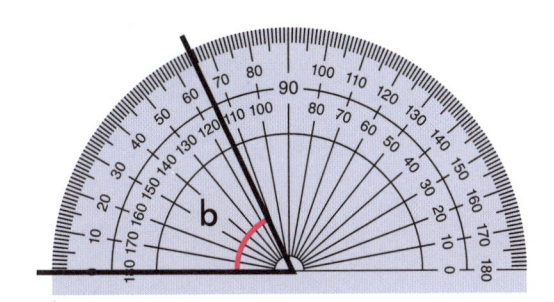

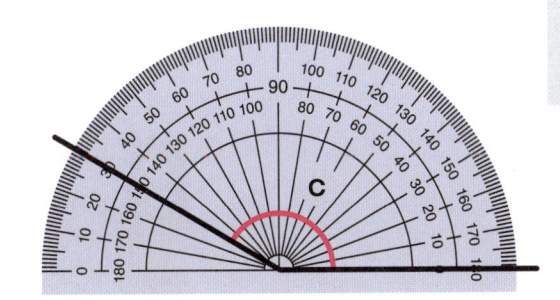

(a) ∠a = 40°

(b) ∠b = 65°

(c) ∠c = 150°

> Make sure you are reading the correct scale on the protractor.

15-2 Measuring Angles

(d) ∠d = 110°

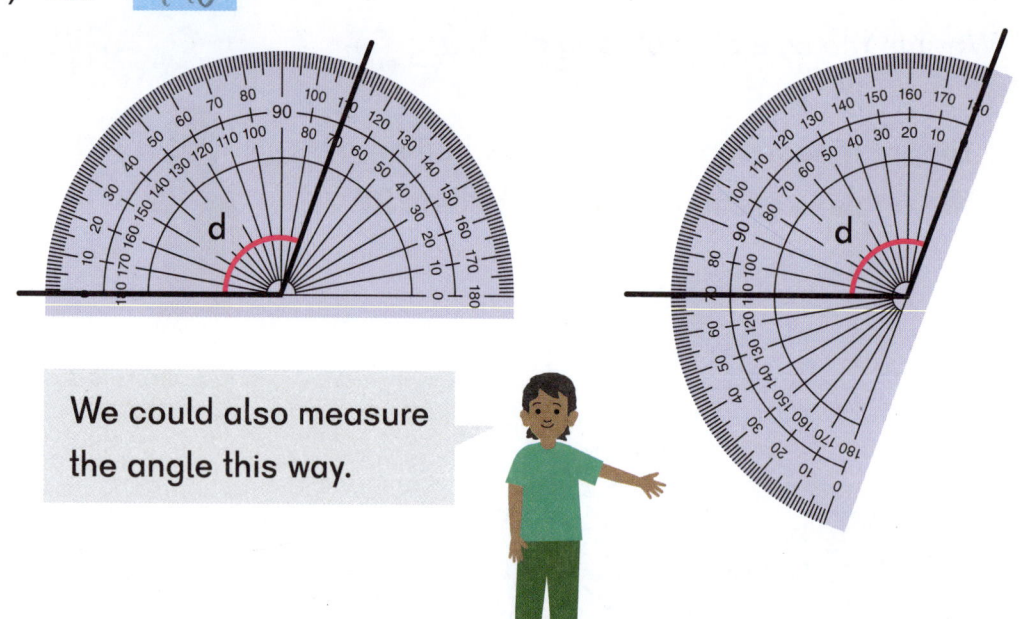

We could also measure the angle this way.

② Use a protractor to measure the angles on the set squares.

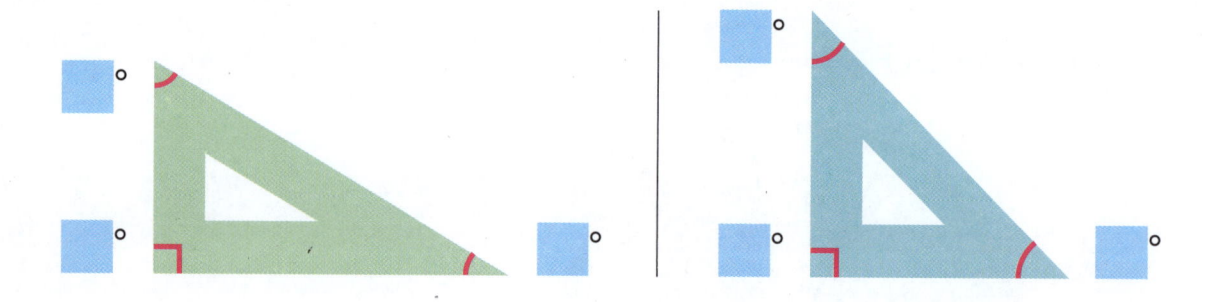

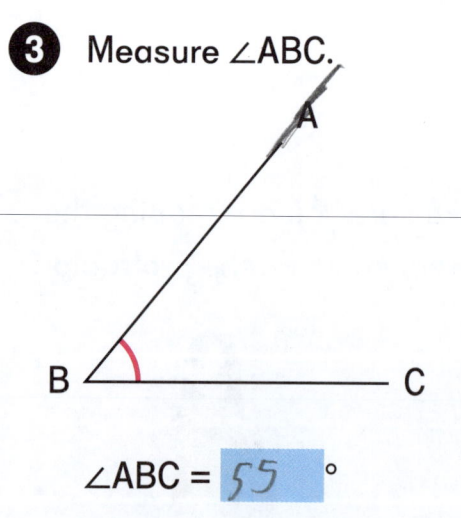

③ Measure ∠ABC.

If we label the vertex and a point on each line, we can use the letters to name the angle. We can name the angle ∠ABC or ∠CBA.

∠ABC = 55°

4. Estimate the size of each angle. Then measure each angle with a protractor.

(a) ∠DEF = 20°

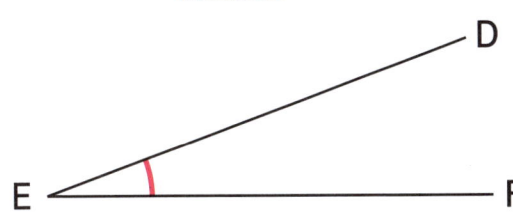

I know what 30°, 45°, 60°, 90°, and 180° angles look like.

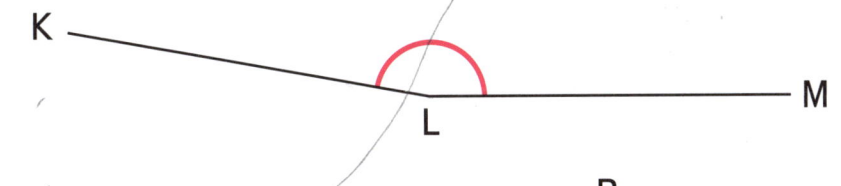

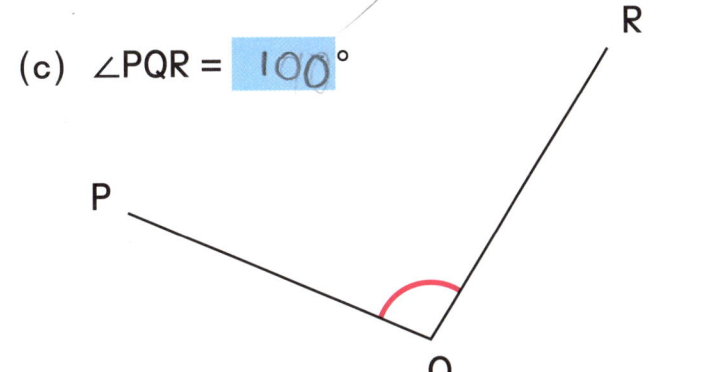

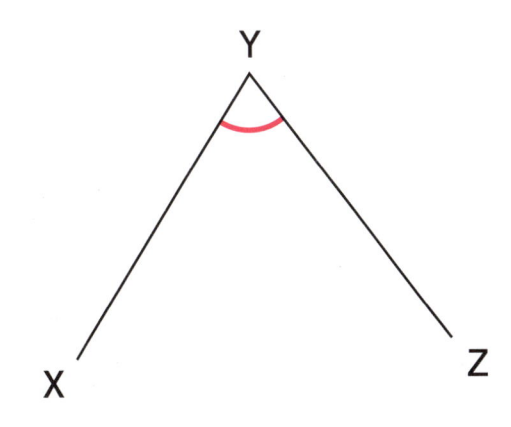

(b) ∠KLM = 170°

(c) ∠PQR = 100°

(d) ∠XYZ = 70°

Make sure you line up one side of the angle with the 0° base line.

Exercise 2 • page 135

Lesson 3
Drawing Angles

Think

Use a protractor to draw an angle between 0° and 180°. Have a friend estimate the size of your angle and then measure it.

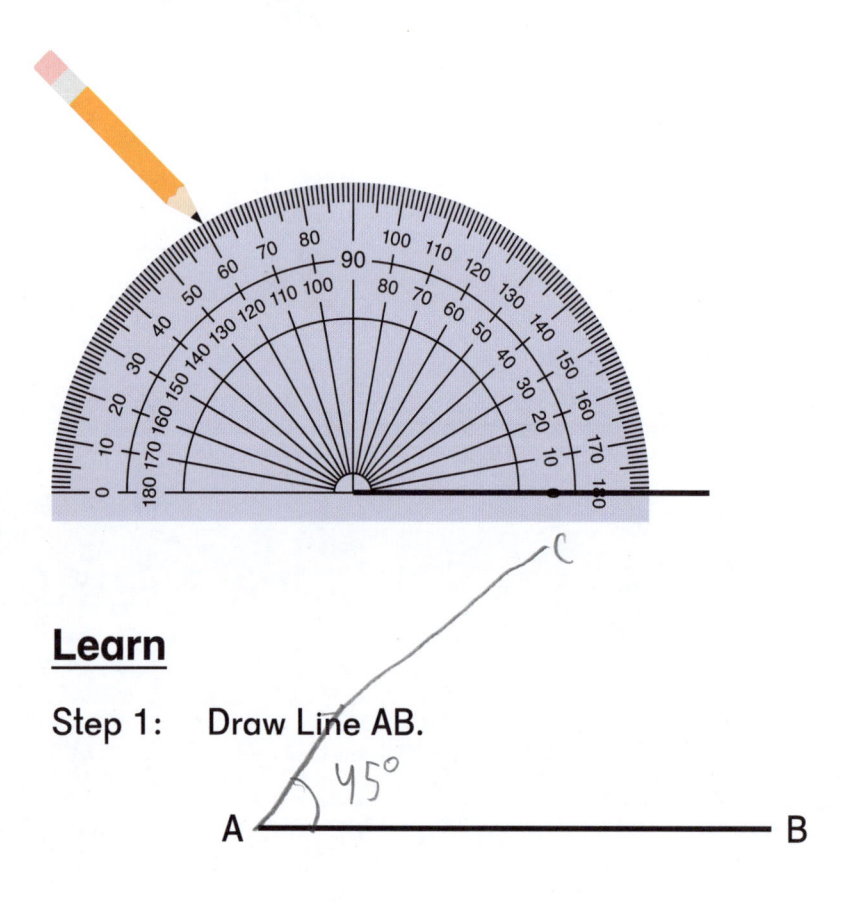

Learn

Step 1: Draw Line AB.

45°

A ——————————— B

Step 2: Line up the center of the protractor with Point A and the base line with Line AB.

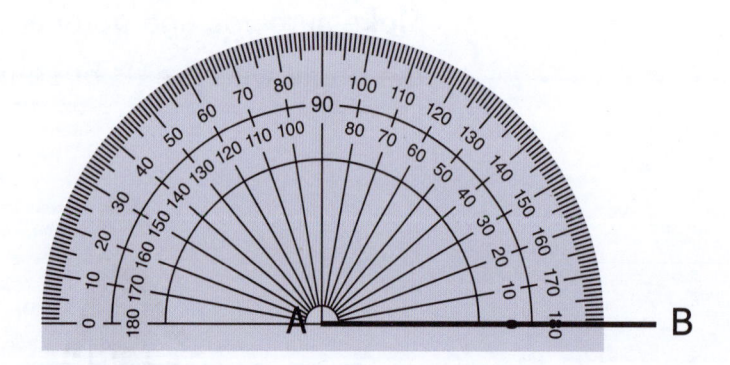

Step 3: For a 45° angle, draw a point at the 45° mark.

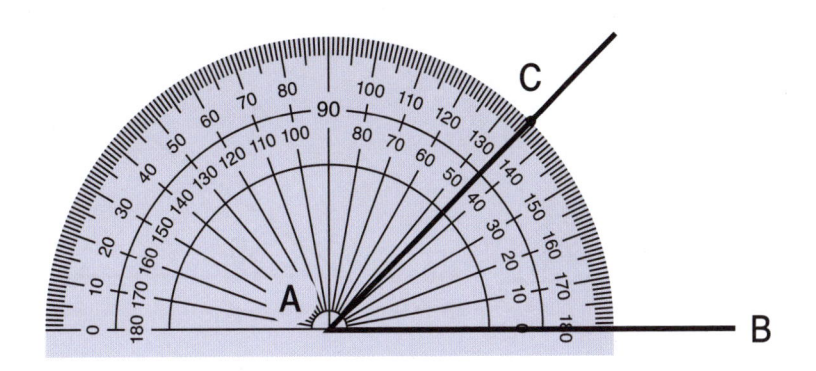

Step 4: Draw a line from Point A through Point C.

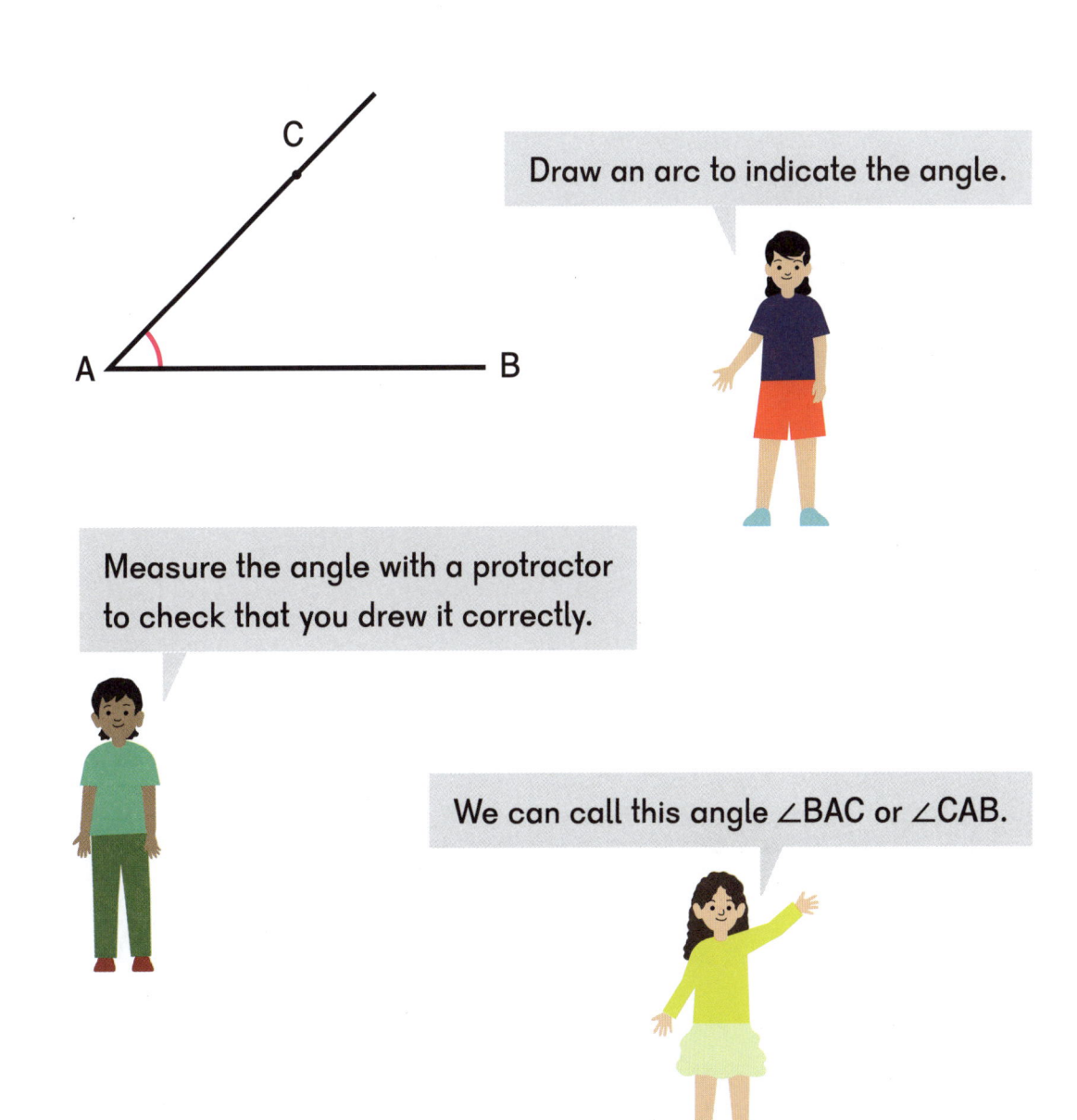

Draw an arc to indicate the angle.

Measure the angle with a protractor to check that you drew it correctly.

We can call this angle ∠BAC or ∠CAB.

15-3 Drawing Angles

Do

① Draw a 35° angle.

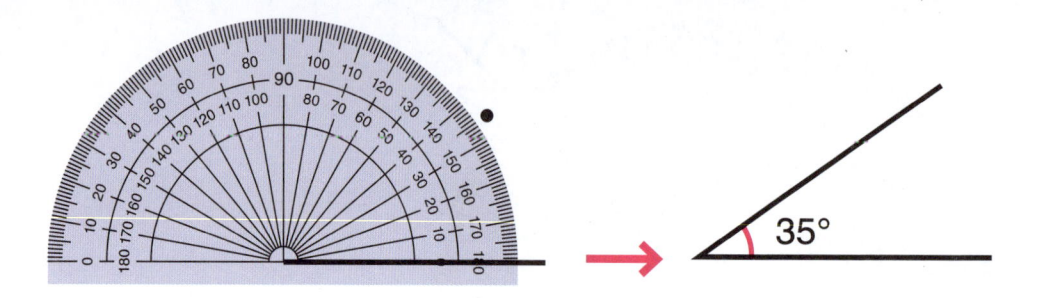

② Draw a 165° angle.

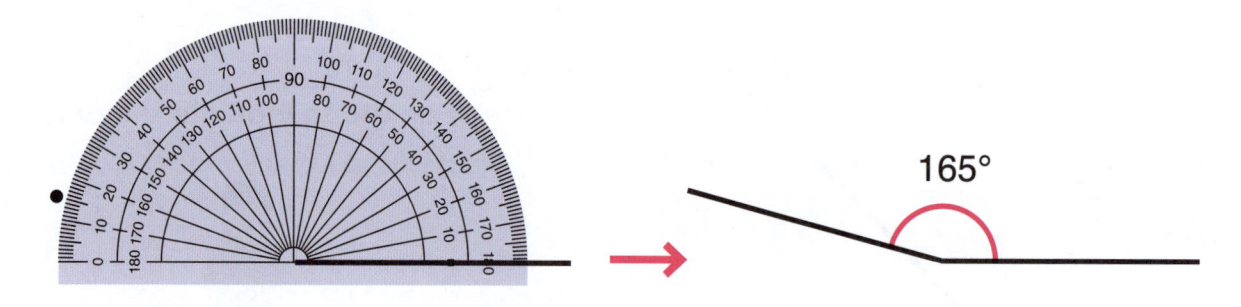

③ Draw a 40° angle with the vertex on the right.

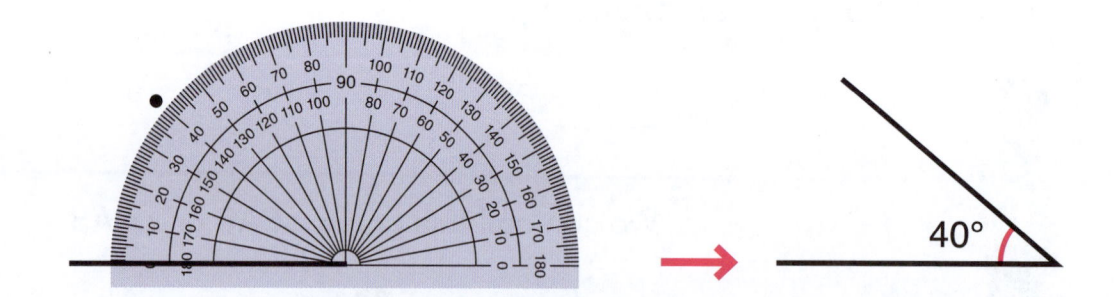

4 Draw two 60° angles in different orientations.

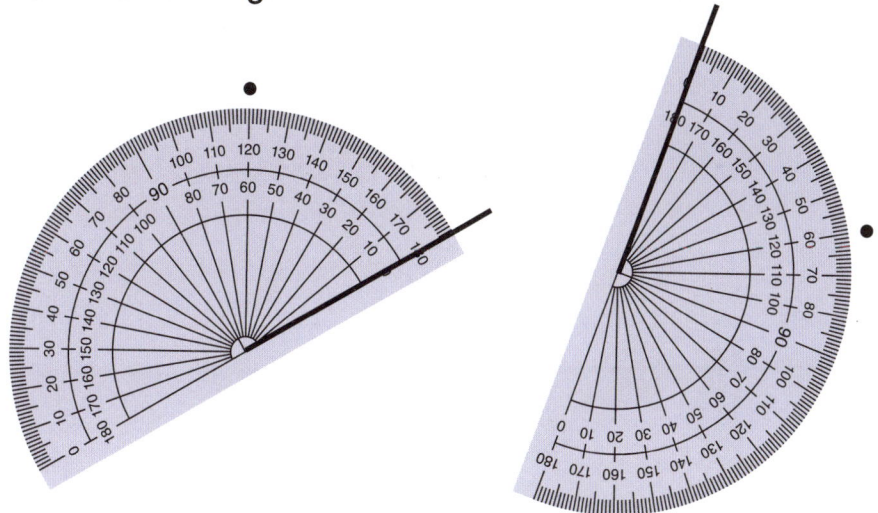

5 Use a protractor to draw three right angles with different orientations.

6 Draw angles with the following measurements.

(a) 10°

(b) 55°

(c) 170°

(d) 125°

Exercise 3 • page 139

Lesson 4
Adding and Subtracting Angles

Think

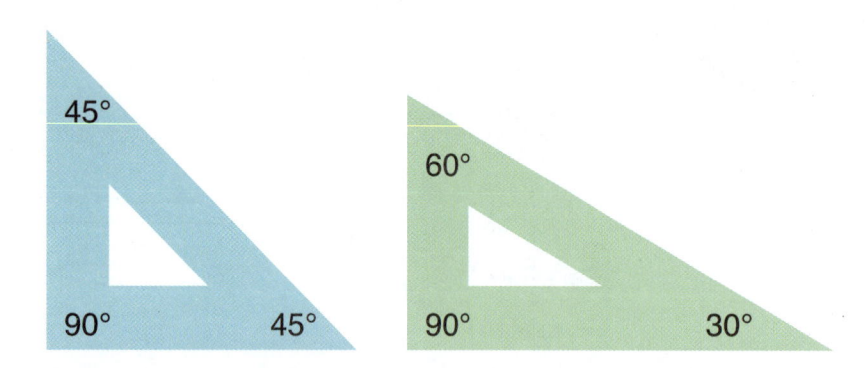

Combine your set squares to draw acute or obtuse angles of different sizes. Write the size of the angle.

This angle is the same size as two of the angles on the set square put together.

186 15-4 Adding and Subtracting Angles

Learn

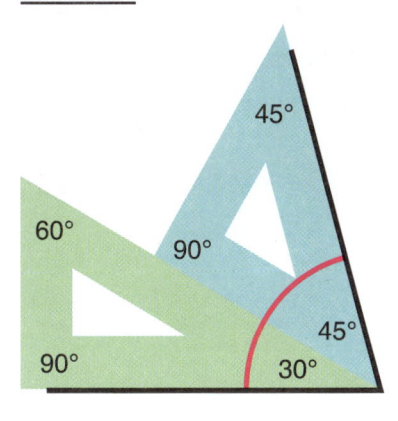

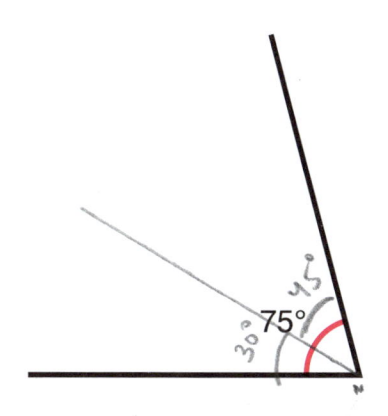

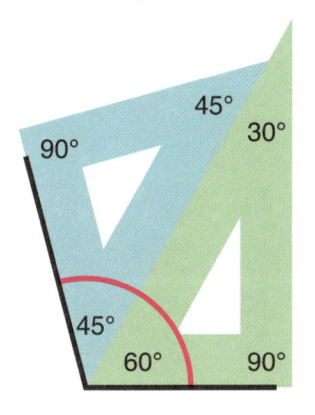

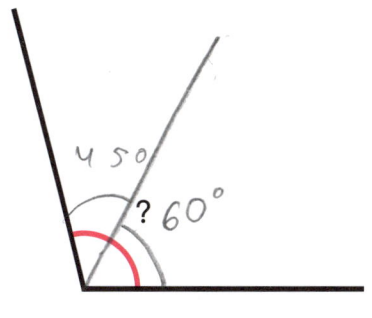

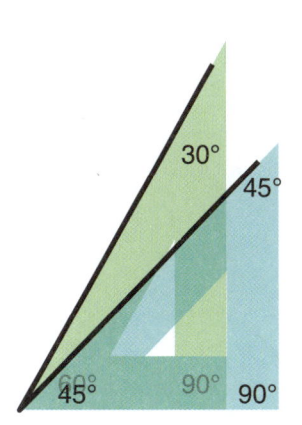

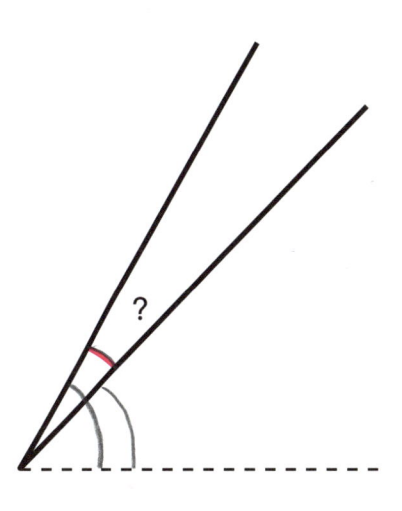

$30° + 45° = 75°$

$45° + 60° = \boxed{105}°$

$60° - 45° = \boxed{15}°$

What other size angles can you make with the set squares?

15-4 Adding and Subtracting Angles

Do

① Put two similar set squares together to form right angles.

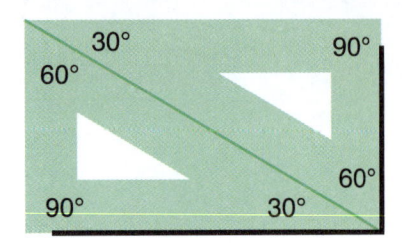

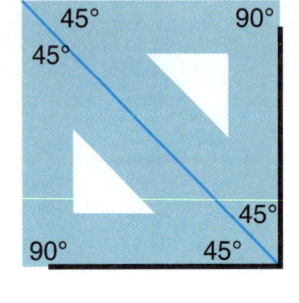

30° + 60° = ☐°   45° + 45° = ☐°

Can you think of another way to make a 90° angle with set squares?

② What is the measure of the angle formed by the set squares?

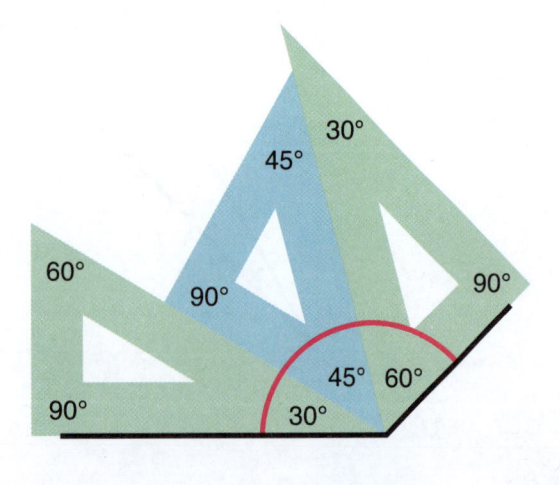

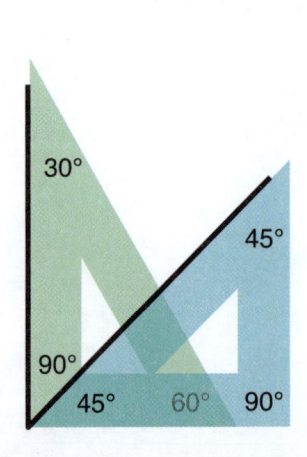

30° + 45° + 60° = 135°   90° − 45° = 45°

3. Find the measure of the unknown angles.

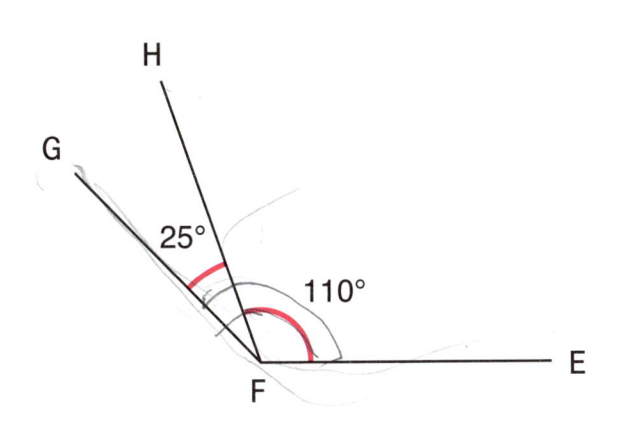

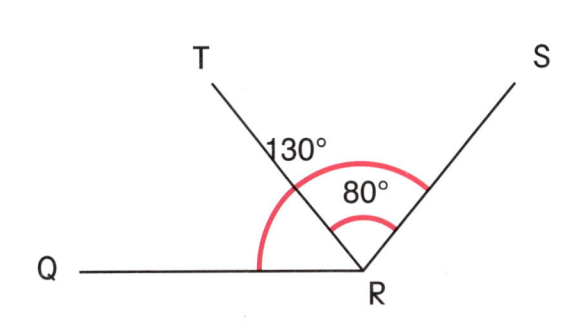

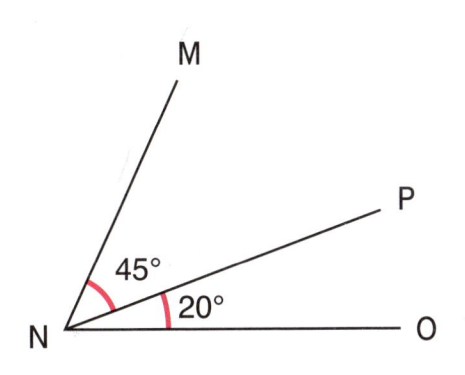

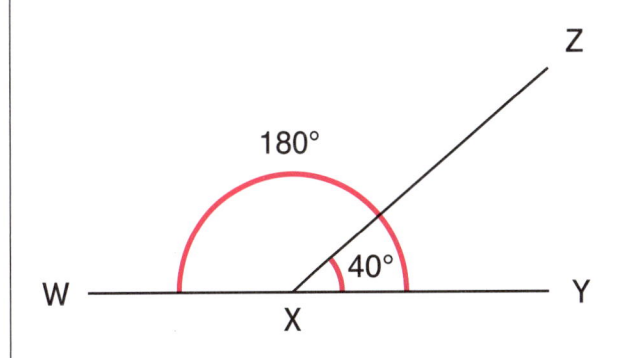

∠GFE = 25° + 110° = 135°

∠QRT = 130° − 80° = 50°

∠MNO = 45° + 20° = 65°

∠WXZ = 180° − 40° = 140°

4. ABCD is a rectangle. What is the measure of ∠ACD?

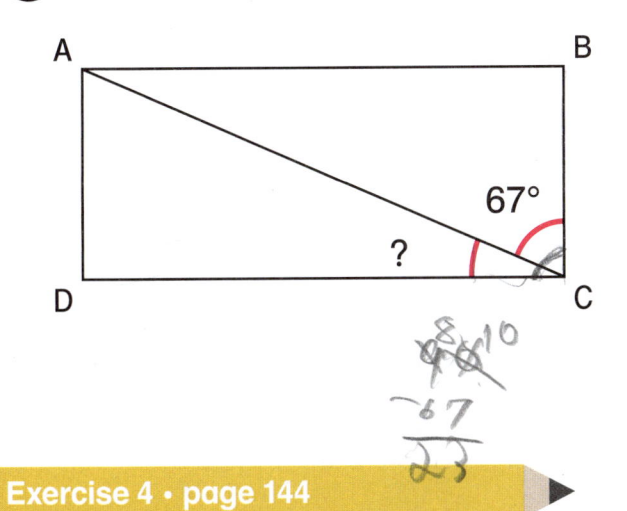

The corners of a rectangle are right angles.

Exercise 4 • page 144

15-4 Adding and Subtracting Angles 189

Lesson 5
Reflex Angles

Think

Sofia drew a reflex angle by putting together set squares like this.

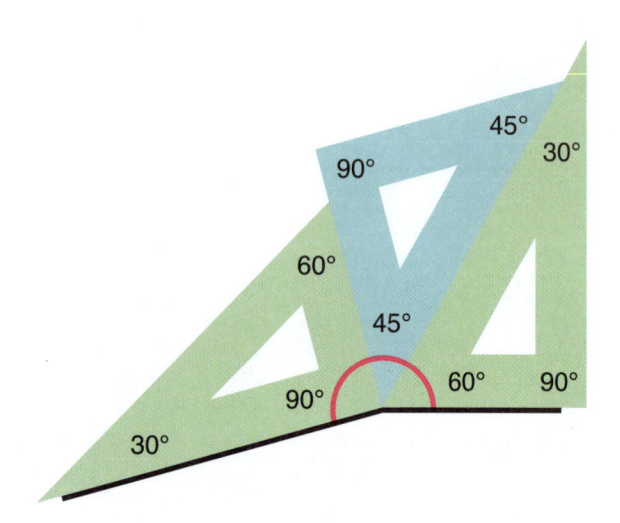

It is greater than 180°.

(a) What is the measure of the angle?

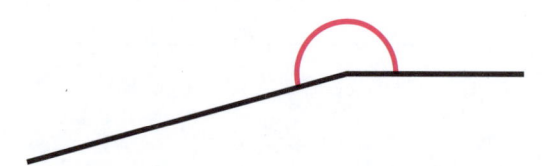

(b) What is the measure of the angle on the opposite side?

It is less than 180°.

190   15-5 Reflex Angles

Learn

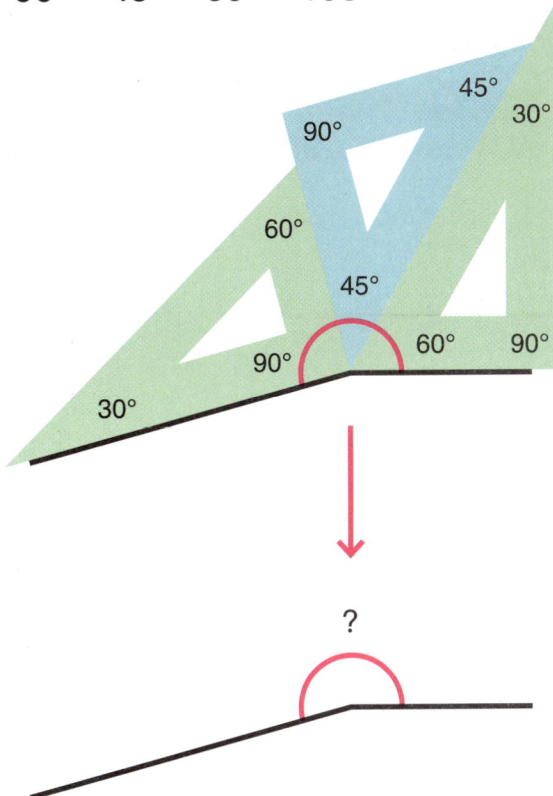

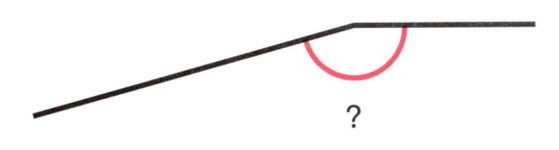

(a) 90° + 45° + 60° = 195°

(b) 360° − 195° = 165°

A complete turn is 360°.

15-5 Reflex Angles

Do

1 Put set squares together to make angles that are greater than 180°. Write the measure of the angle you made.

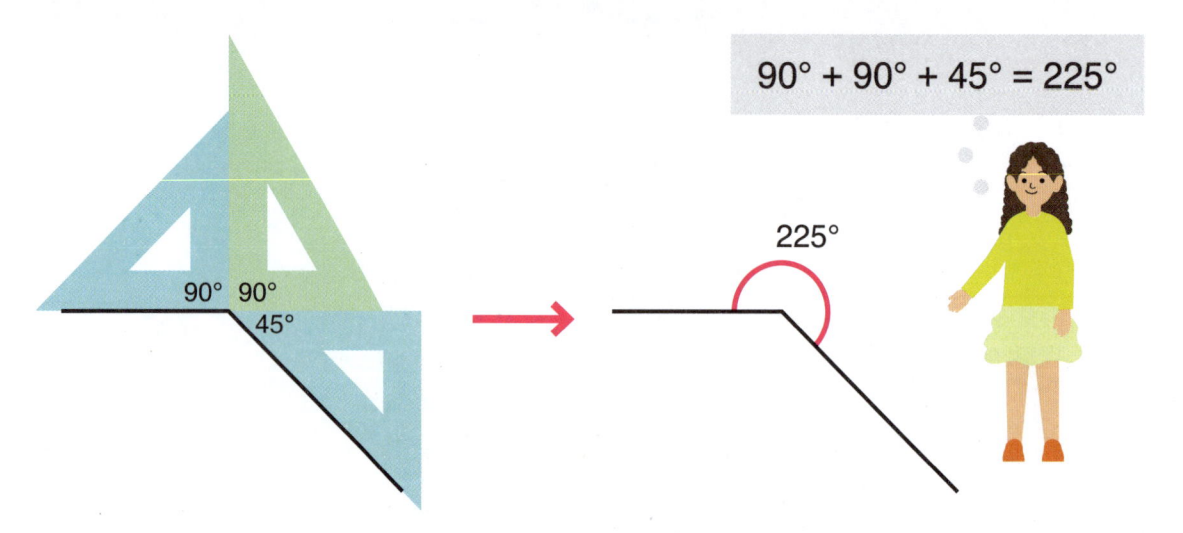

90° + 90° + 45° = 225°

90° 90° 45°

225°

2 How can we measure ∠a using a protractor?

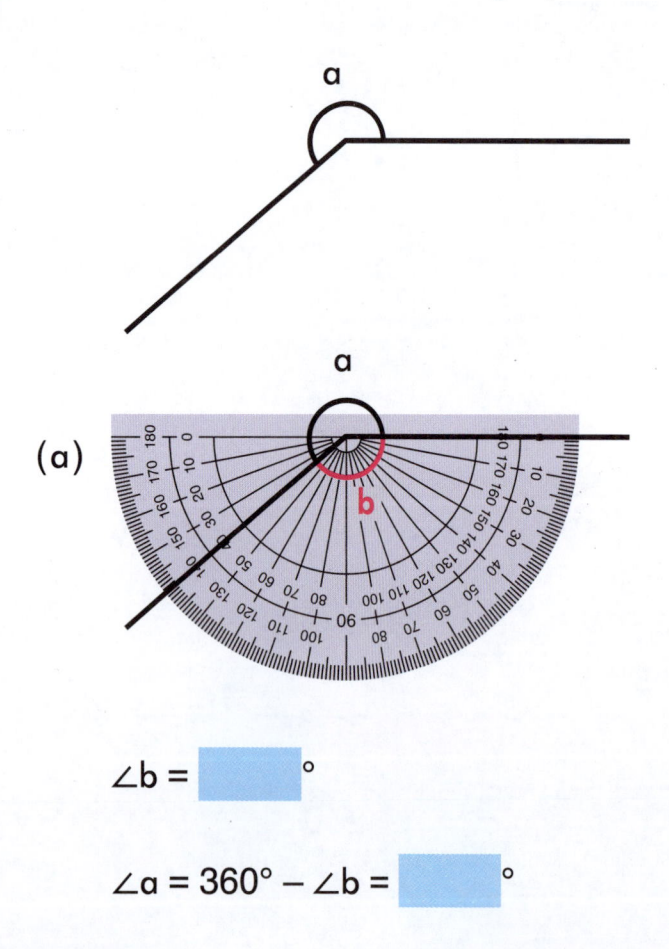

(a)

∠b = ▢ °

∠a = 360° − ∠b = ▢ °

(b)

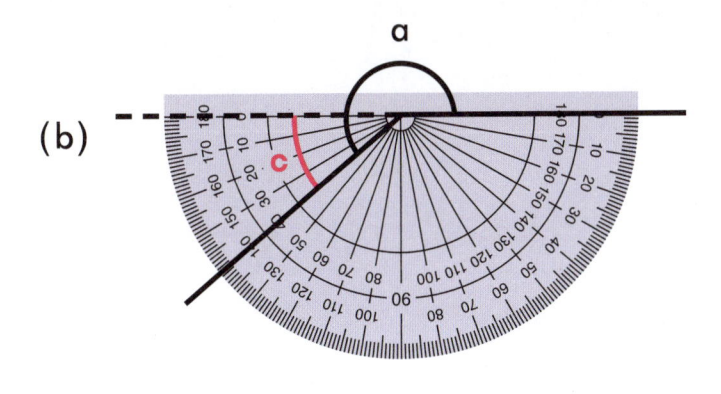

$\angle c =$ ____ °

$\angle a = \angle c + 180° =$ ____ °

3 What is the measure of Angle f?

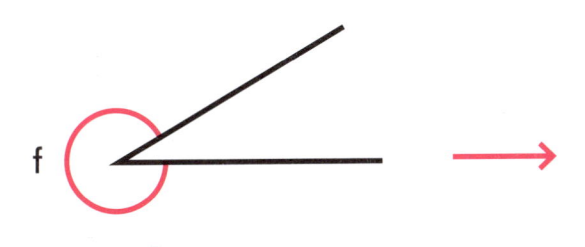

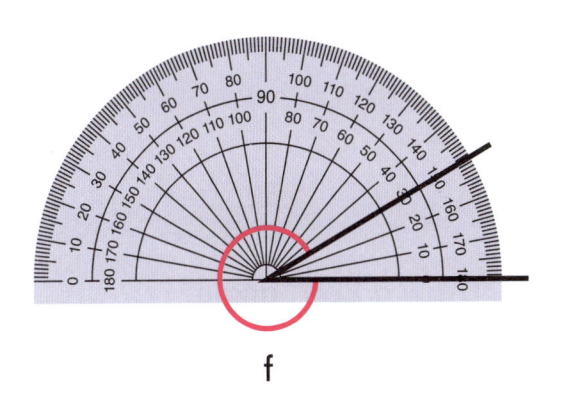

4 What is the measure of each angle?

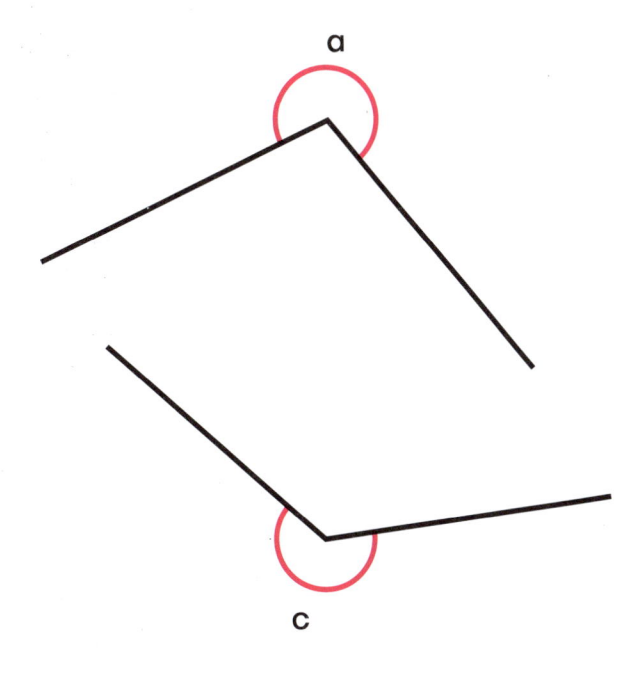

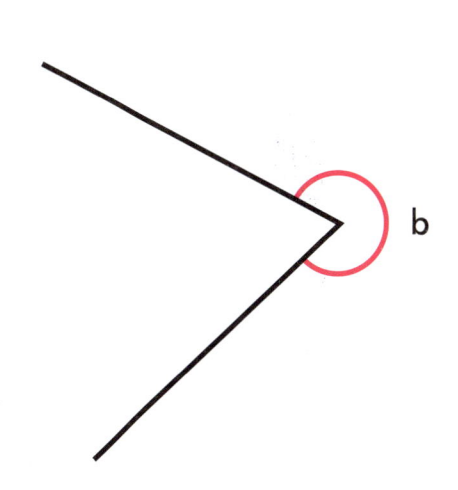

15-5 Reflex Angles   193

5. Draw a 300° angle.

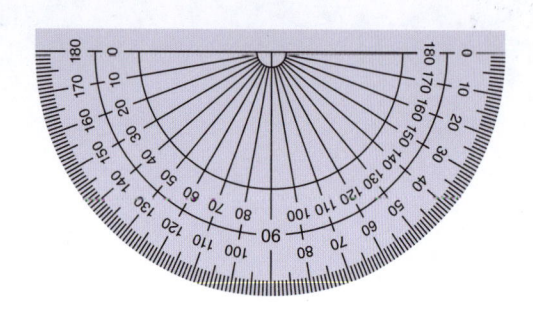

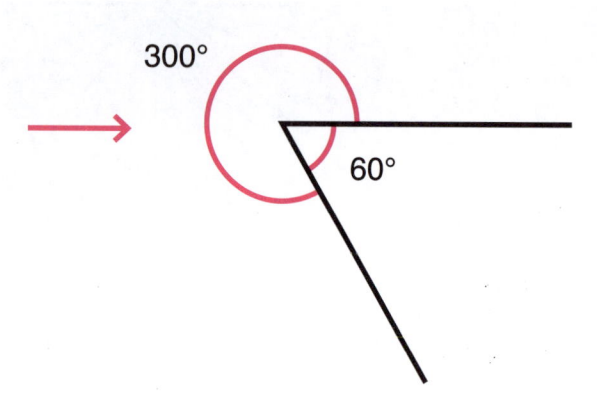

360° − 300° = 60°

6. Draw a 260° angle.

7. Find the measure of ∠a.

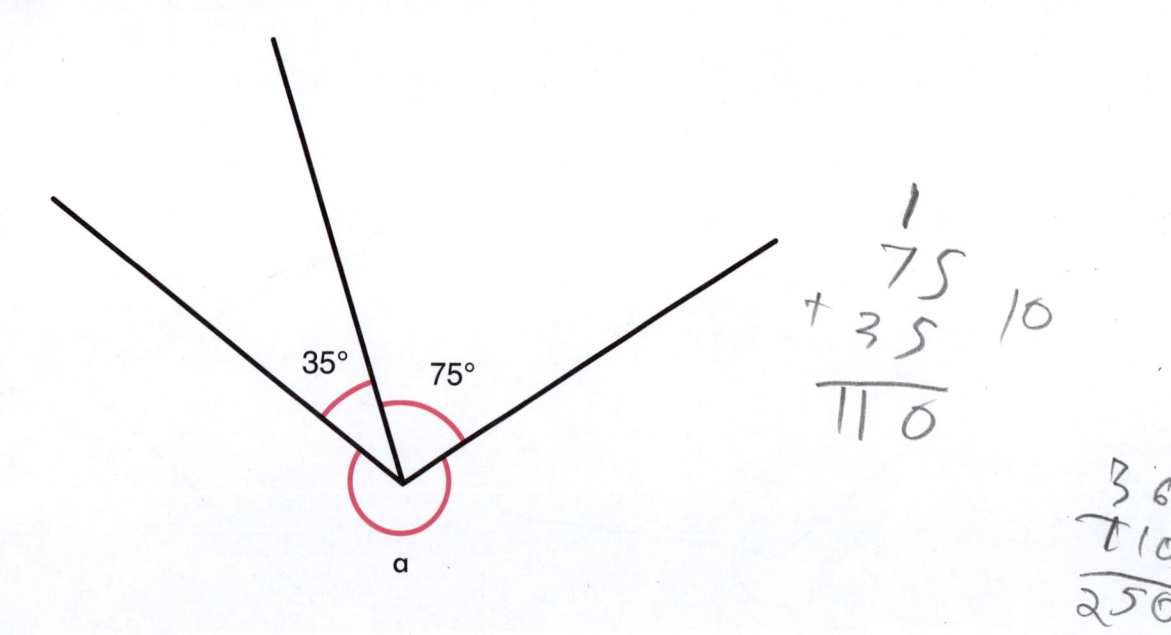

35° 75°

a

Exercise 5 • page 147

15-5 Reflex Angles

Lesson 6
Practice

P 6

1 Two paper strips are put together to make angles. What is the measure of these angles?

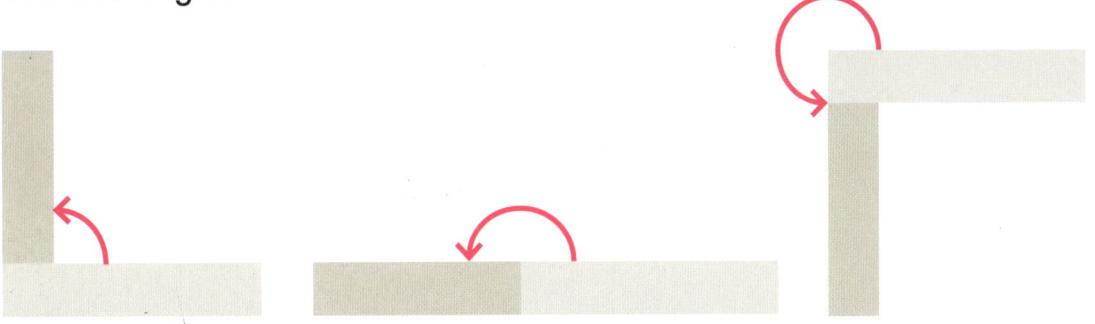

2 Which of the following angles are acute and which are obtuse? Measure each angle.

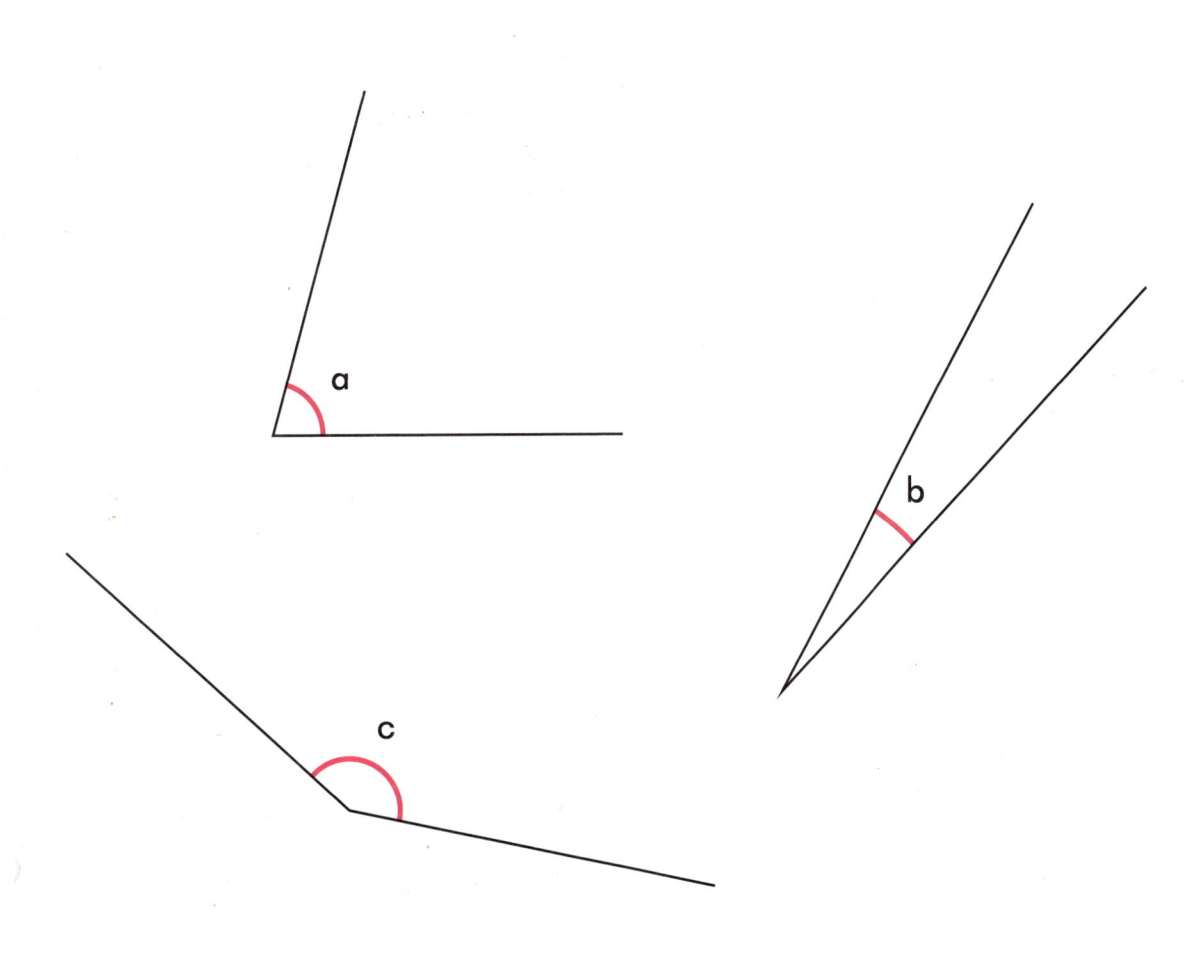

15-6 Practice 195

3 Measure each reflex angle.

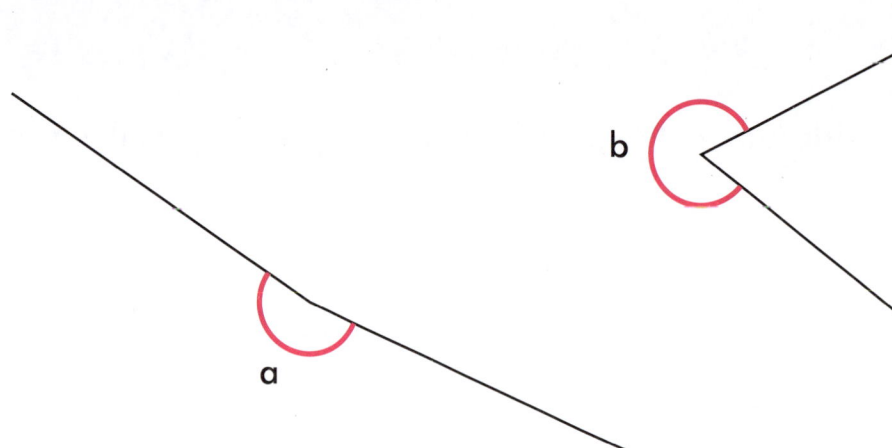

a

b

4 Draw angles with the following measurements.

(a) 65°

(b) 140°

(c) 92°

(d) 128°

(e) 245°

(f) 310°

5 ABCD is a rectangle. Find the measure of ∠ADB and ∠DCE.

A   B

32°

C   133°

D

E

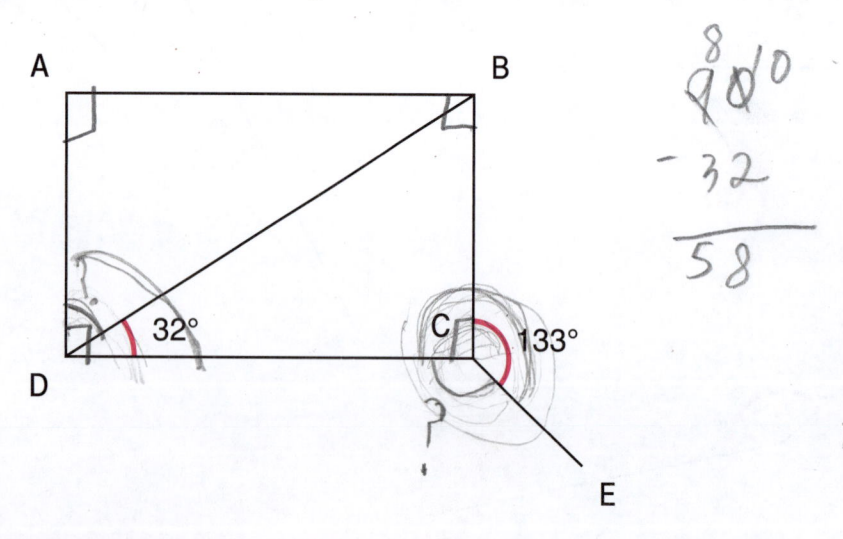

Exercise 6 • page 151

Chapter 16

Lines and Shapes

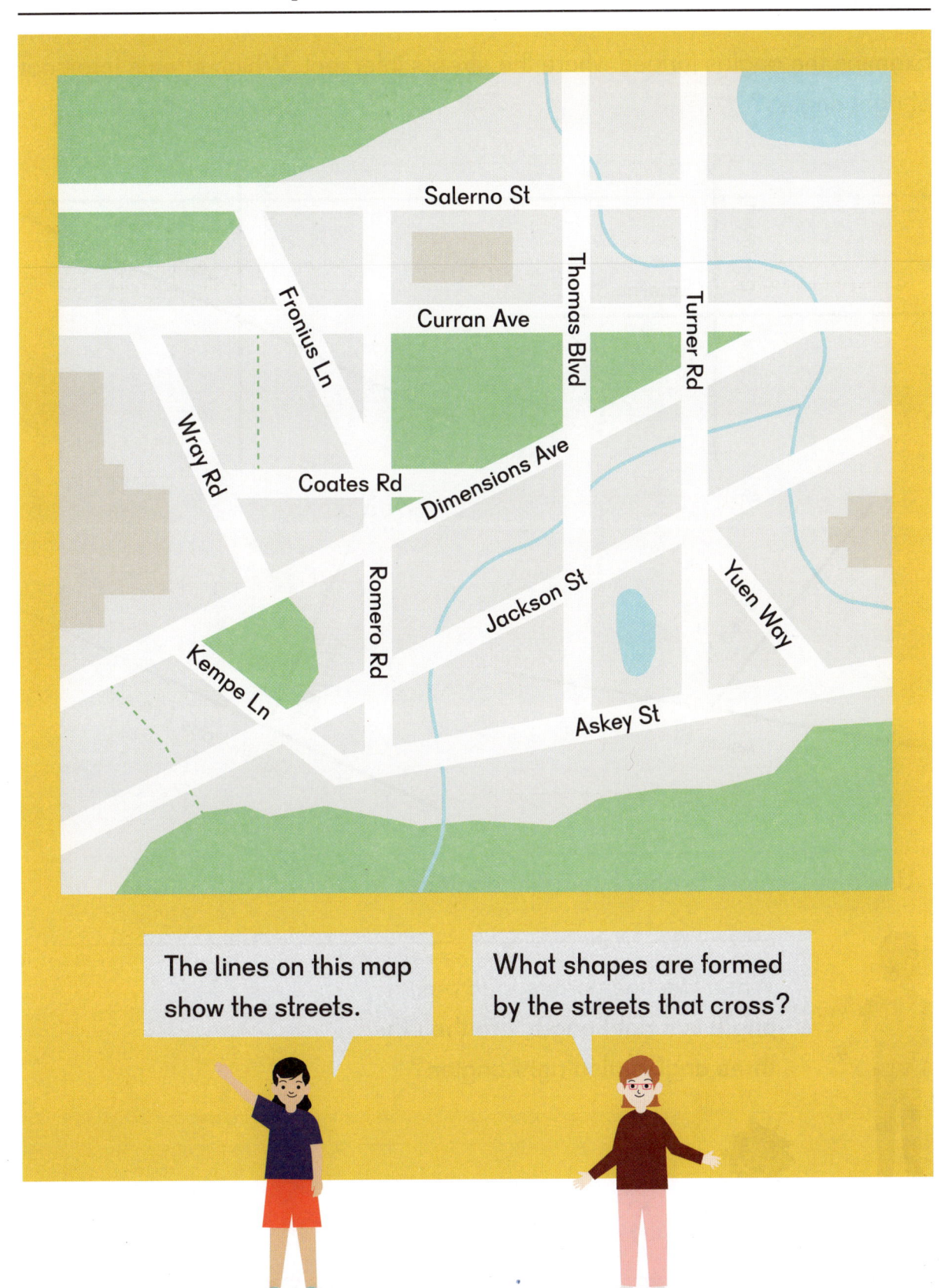

The lines on this map show the streets.

What shapes are formed by the streets that cross?

197

Lesson 1
Perpendicular Lines

Think

Examine the angles formed where the streets intersect. Which streets intersect at right angles?

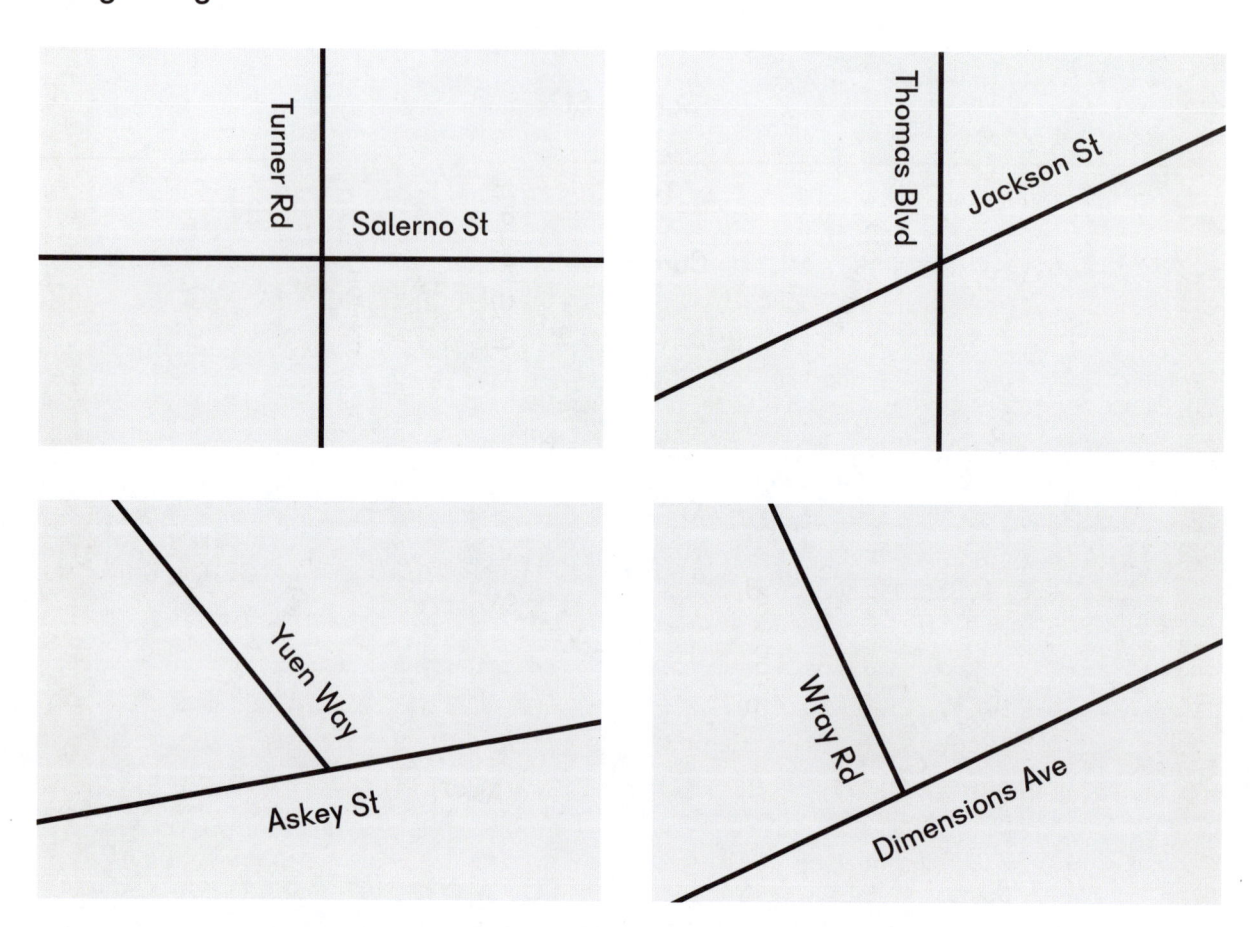

Use a set square to check for right angles.

When two lines cross, and one angle is a right angle, are the other three angles also right angles?

Learn

Lines that meet at right angles are called **perpendicular lines**.

These lines are perpendicular.

These lines are not perpendicular.

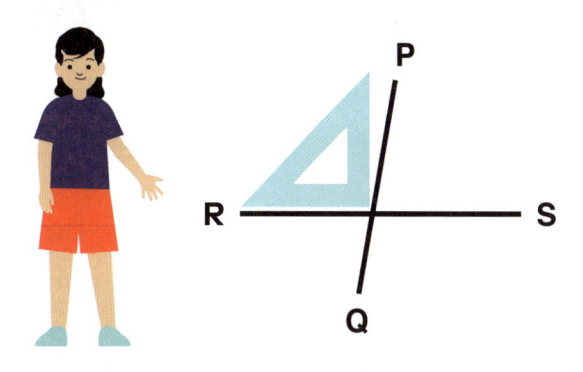

AB is perpendicular to CD.
AB ⊥ CD

PQ is not perpendicular to RS.

⊥ means "is perpendicular to." We mark one right angle with a small square to show that the lines are perpendicular.

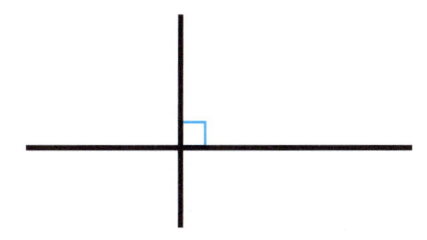

These lines are also perpendicular to each other because if we extend one they will intersect at a right angle.

Do

1 Fold a paper and then fold it again as shown below.

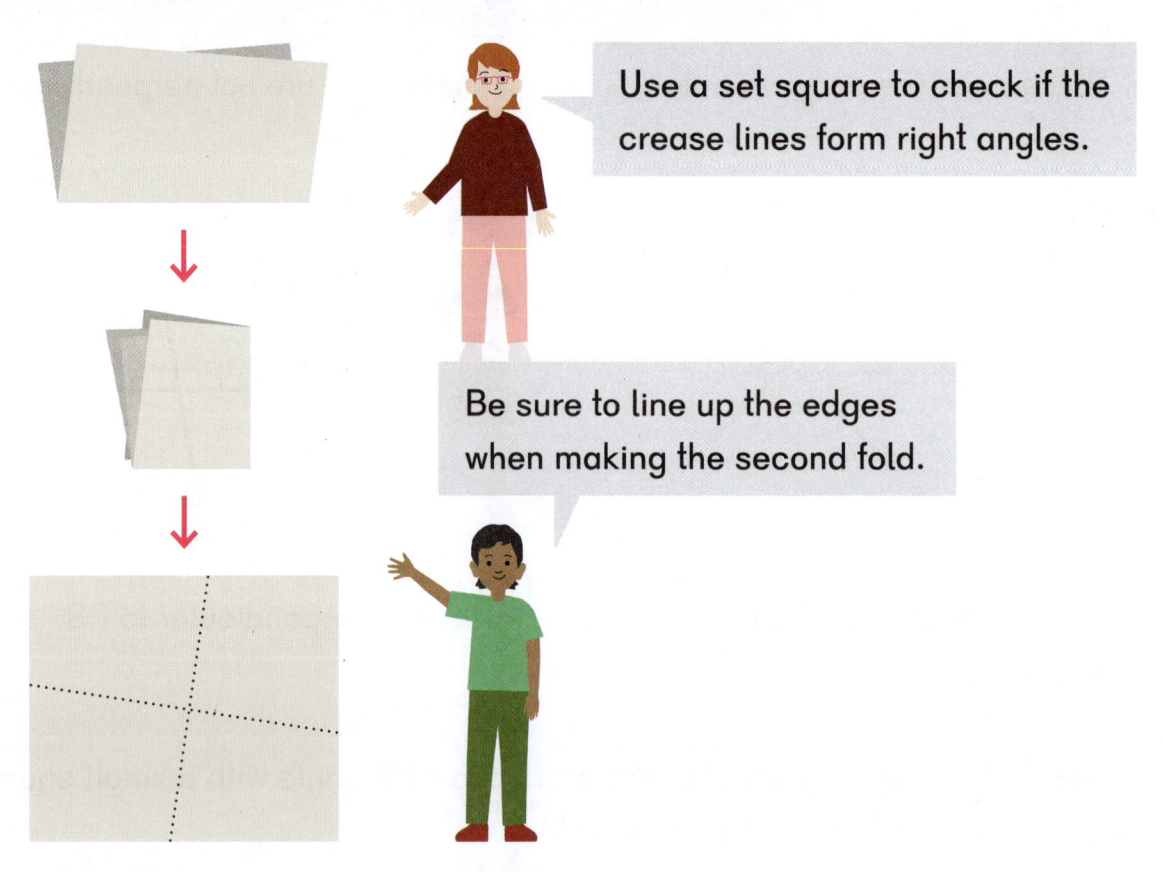

Use a set square to check if the crease lines form right angles.

Be sure to line up the edges when making the second fold.

Are the crease lines perpendicular to each other?

2 Which sides are perpendicular to each other in Rectangle ABCD?

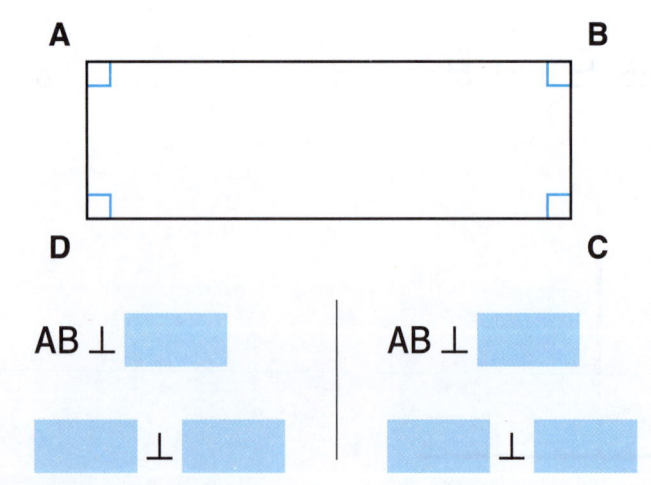

A   B

D   C

AB ⊥ ▭ | AB ⊥ ▭

▭ ⊥ ▭ | ▭ ⊥ ▭

16-1 Perpendicular Lines

3 Which sides are perpendicular to each other in each right triangle?

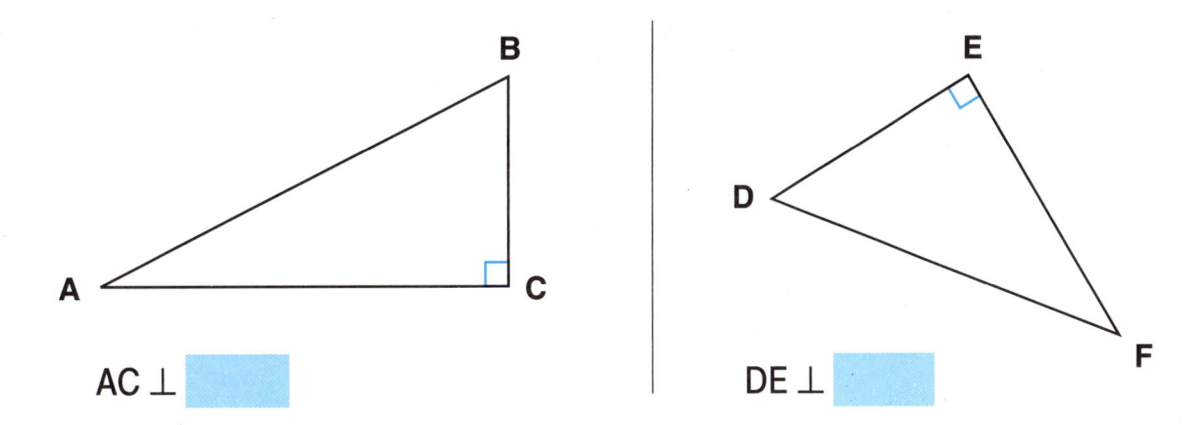

AC ⊥ ☐

DE ⊥ ☐

4 Name each pair of perpendicular sides in the following polygons.

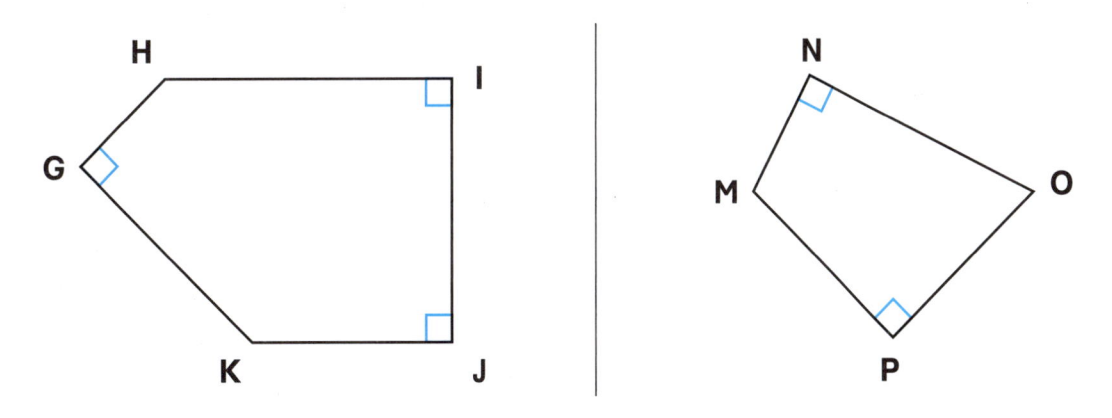

5 Which pairs of lines are perpendicular to each other? Use a set square to check.

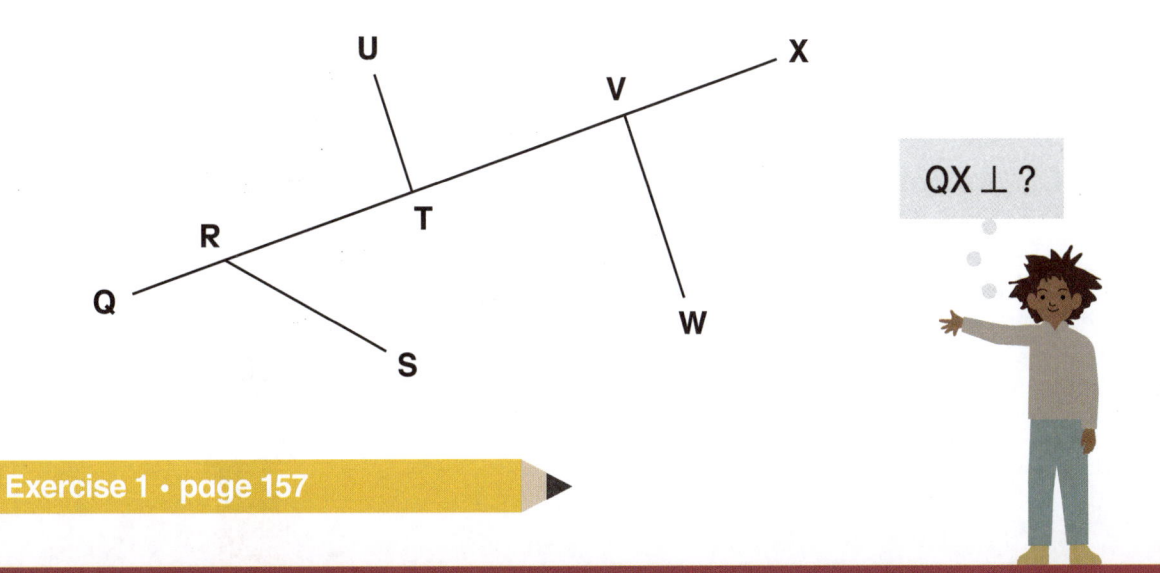

QX ⊥ ?

Exercise 1 • page 157

16-1 Perpendicular Lines

Lesson 2
Parallel Lines

Think

Use a set square to examine the angles formed where these streets intersect. Which streets are perpendicular to each other?

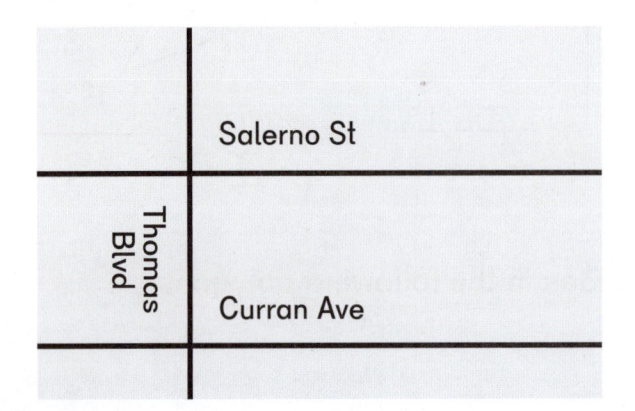

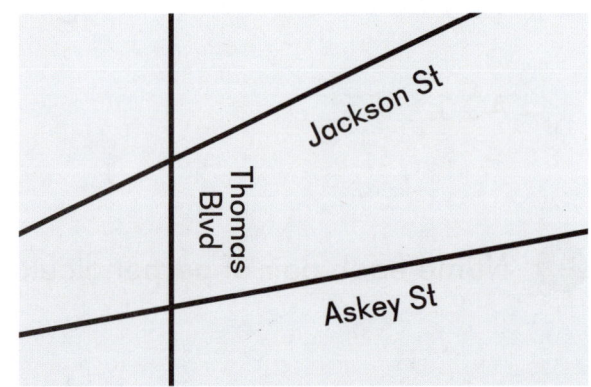

Learn

Two lines that are perpendicular to the same line are called **parallel lines**.

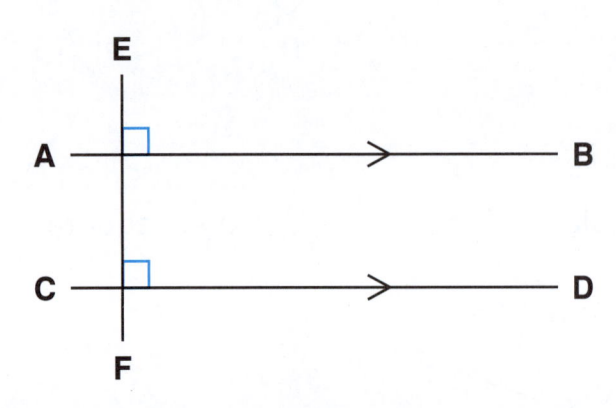

We use arrowheads to indicate which lines are parallel.

AB and CD are both perpendicular to EF.

AB is parallel to CD.

AB || CD

|| means "is parallel to."

Do

① Fold a paper and then fold it again as shown below.

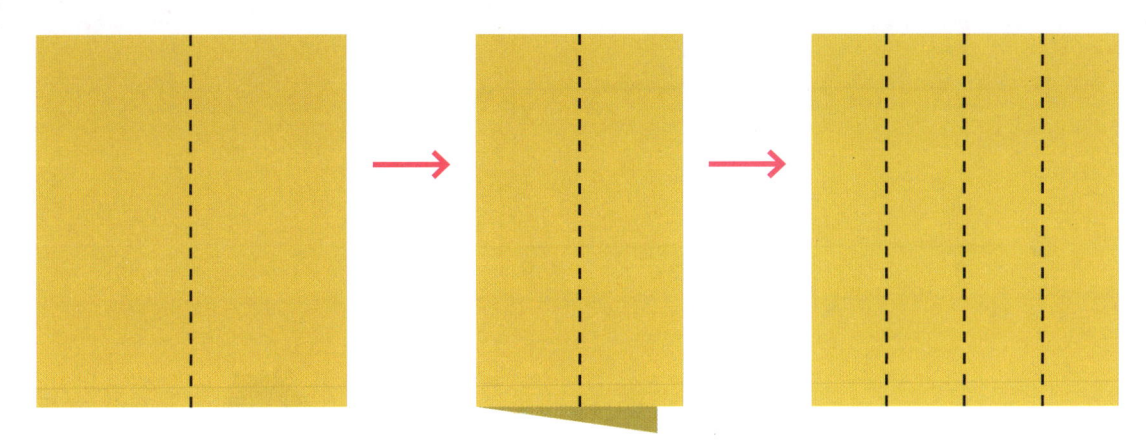

Are the crease lines parallel?

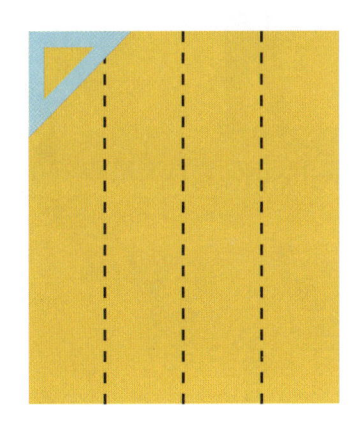

Use a set square to see if the lines are perpendicular to the edges of the paper.

② Which sides are parallel to each other in Rectangle ABCD?

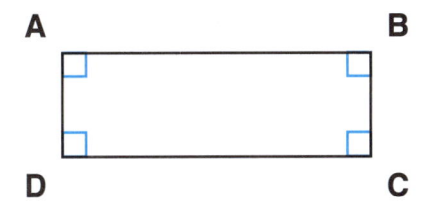

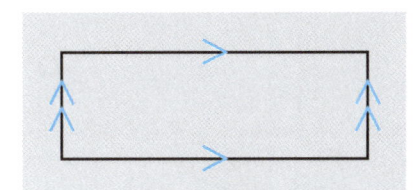

AB ∥ ☐

☐ ∥ ☐

16-2 Parallel Lines

3. PR is parallel to QS. Use a compass or ruler to see if TU, VW, and XY are the same length.

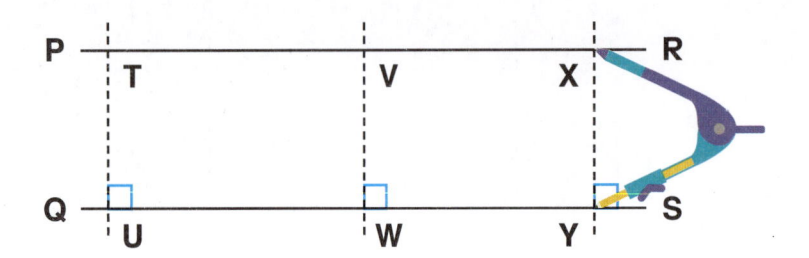

The perpendicular distance between two parallel lines is the same everywhere.

AB is not parallel to CD.

4. PQ and RS are parallel to each other. Which point on RS is the shortest distance from Point E?

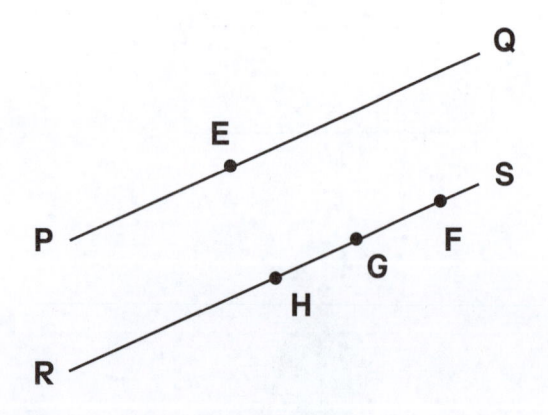

If we draw lines from Point E to each point on RS, which line would be perpendicular to PQ?

5 Name each pair of parallel lines in the following polygons.

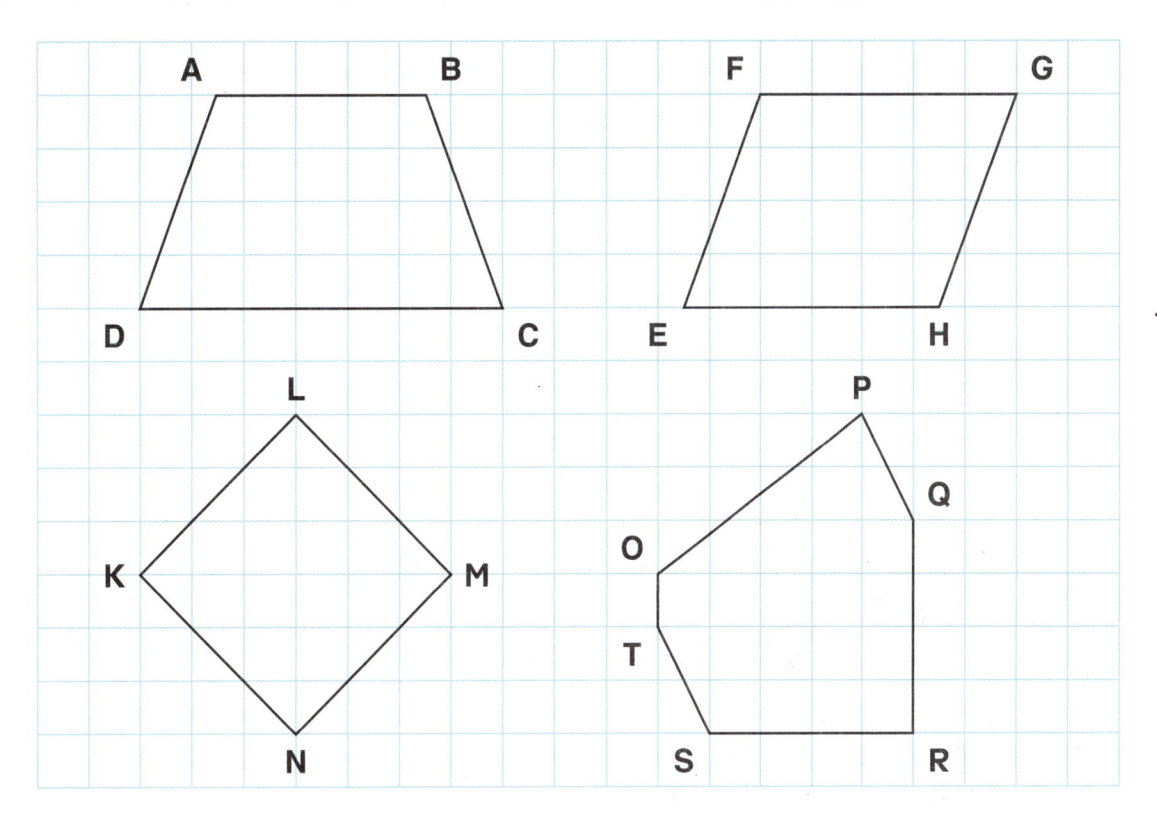

6 Which pairs of lines below are parallel lines? Use a set square to check.

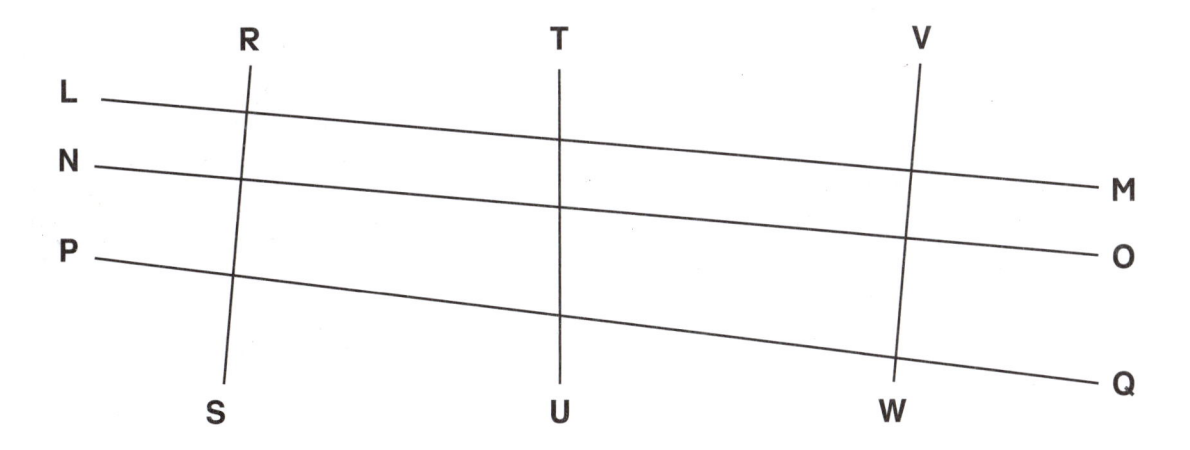

LM and NO are both perpendicular to VW.

Exercise 2 • page 160

16-2 Parallel Lines

Lesson 3
Drawing Perpendicular and Parallel Lines

Think

Use a ruler and a set square.

(a) Draw a line perpendicular to AB that passes through Point C.

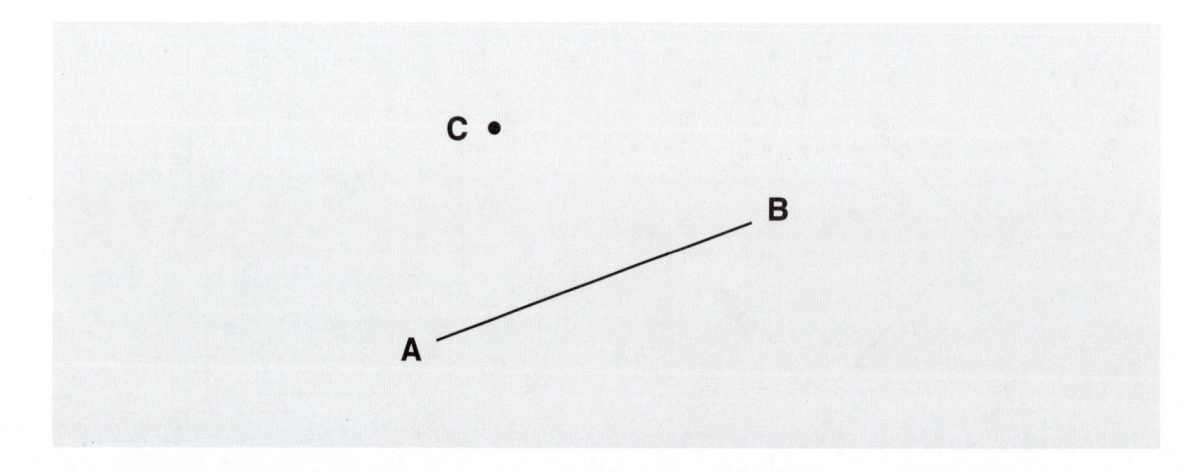

(b) Draw a line parallel to PQ that passes through Point R.

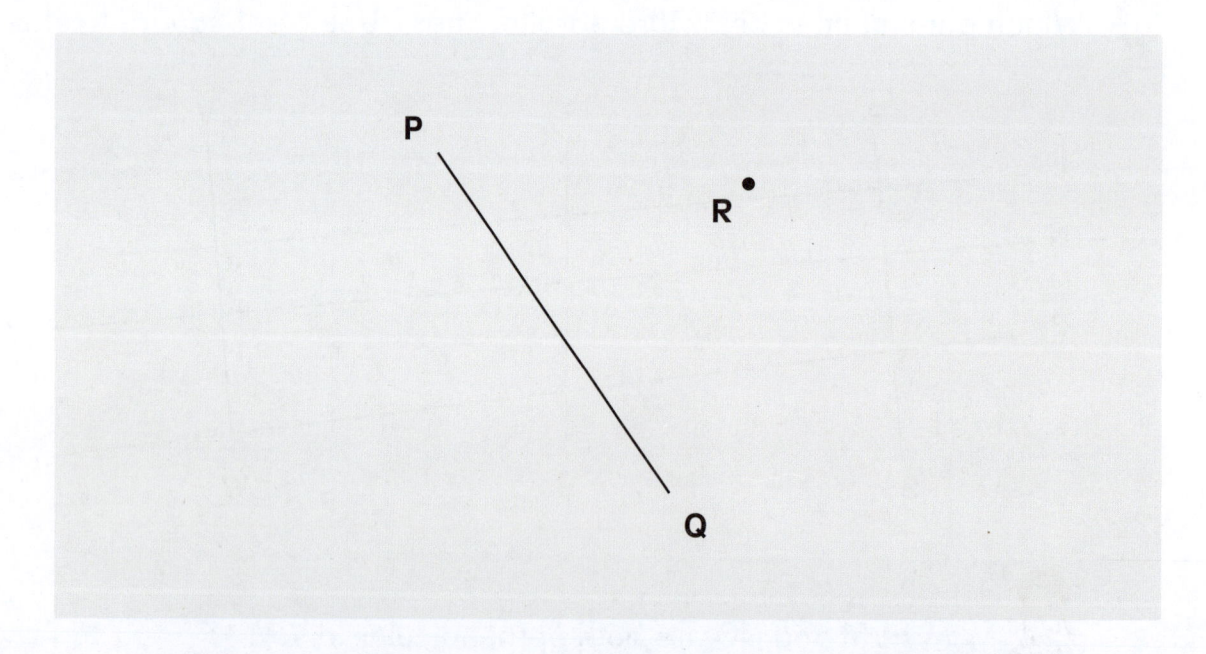

(c) Draw parallel lines that are 8 cm apart.

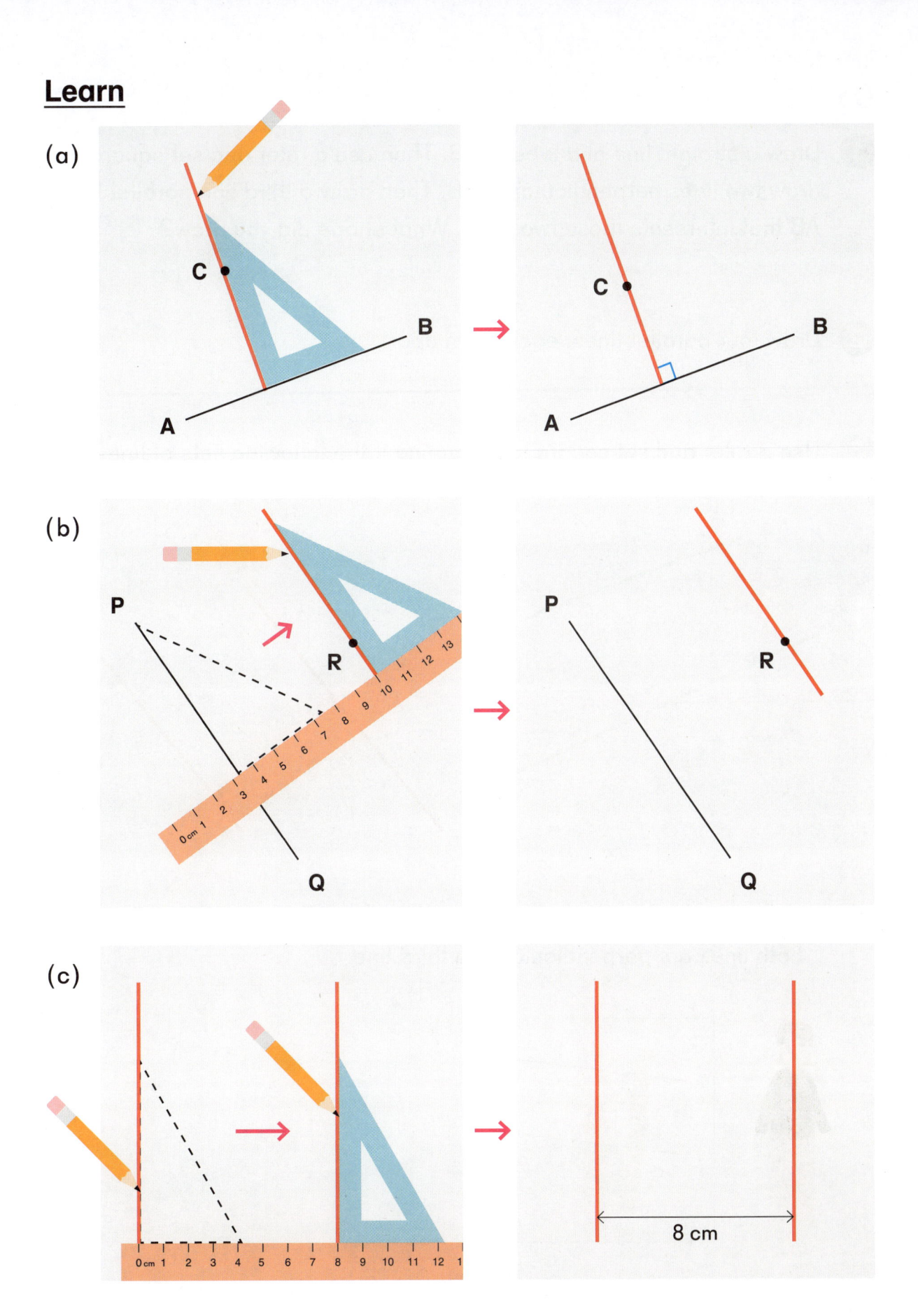

Learn

(a)

(b)

(c)

16-3 Drawing Perpendicular and Parallel Lines

Do

1. Draw a straight line and label it AB. Then use a ruler and set square to draw two lines perpendicular to AB. Then draw a third line parallel to AB that intersects those two lines. What shape did you draw?

2. Draw four parallel lines, each 3 cm apart.

3. Use a ruler and set square to determine if the following sets of lines are parallel.

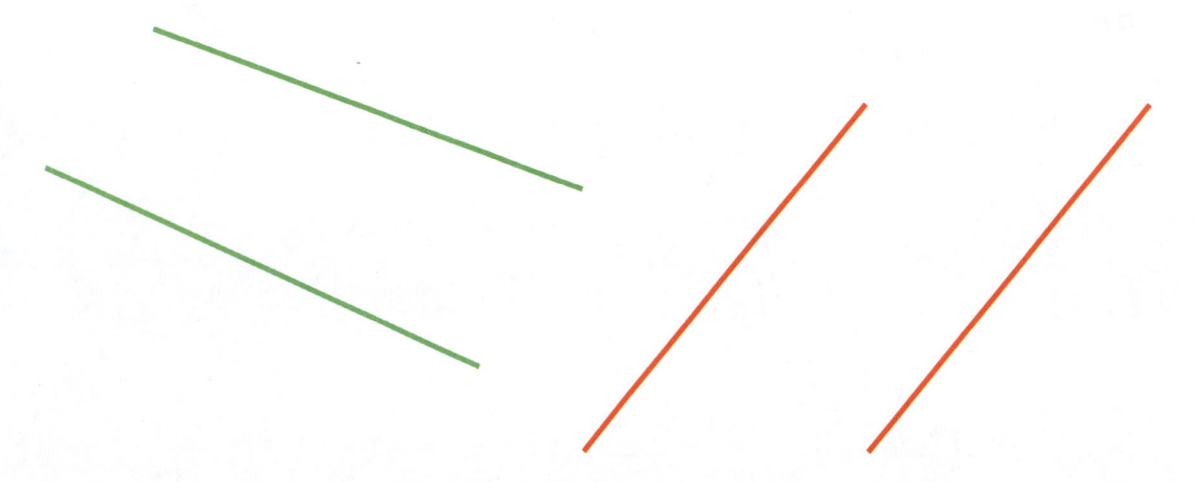

We can use a set square and a ruler to see if both lines are perpendicular to a third line.

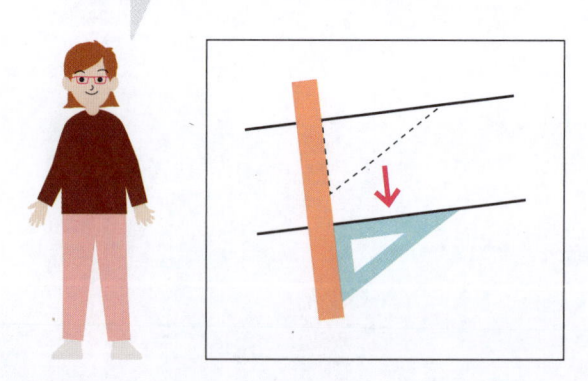

4 Use a ruler and set square to draw perpendicular and parallel lines on grid paper. Have the lines end at an intersection of the graph lines. Some examples are shown below.

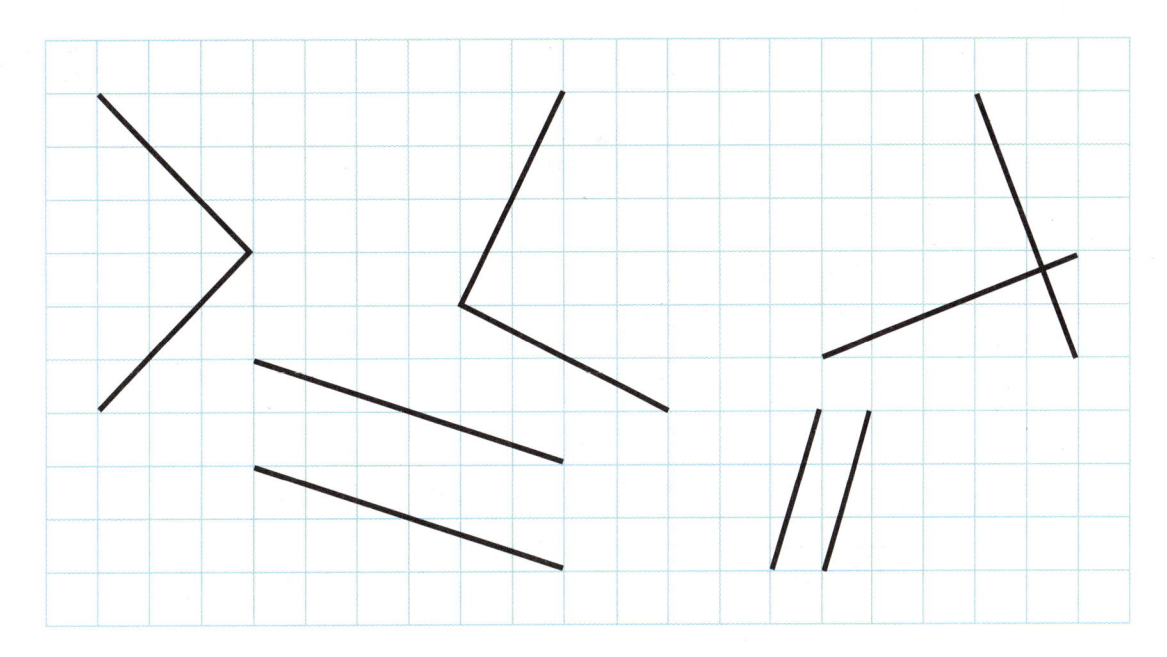

5 Which pairs of lines below are parallel lines? How can you tell?

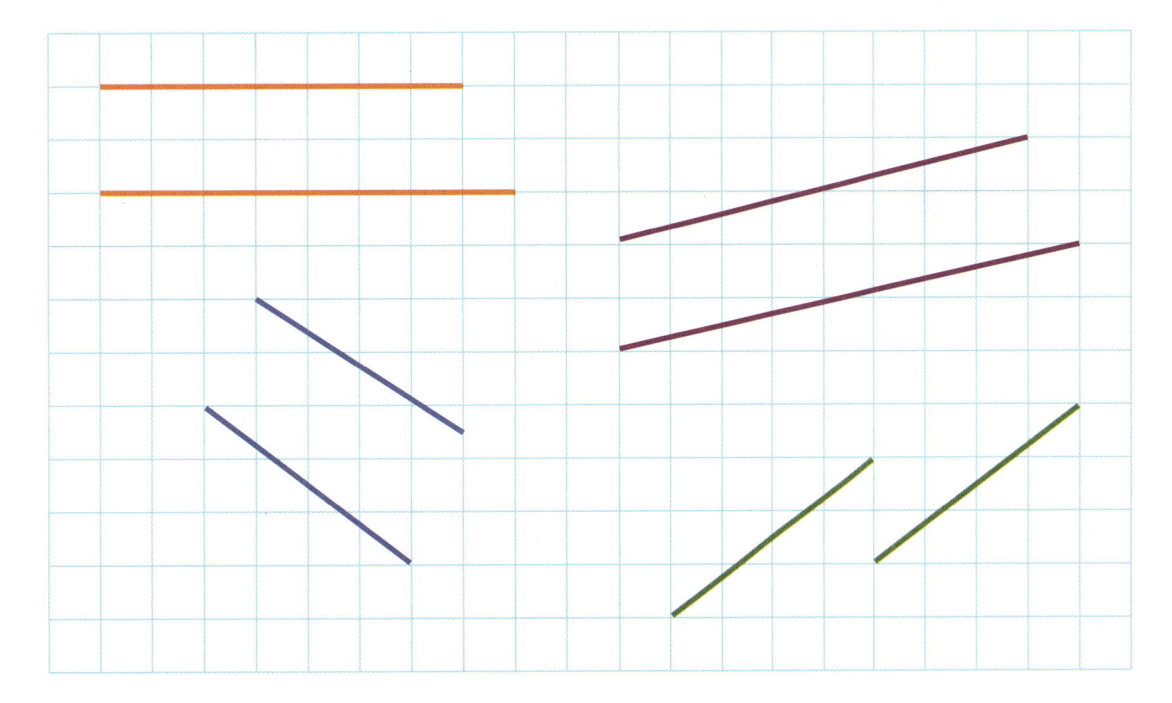

Exercise 3 • page 162

16-3 Drawing Perpendicular and Parallel Lines

Lesson 4
Quadrilaterals

Think

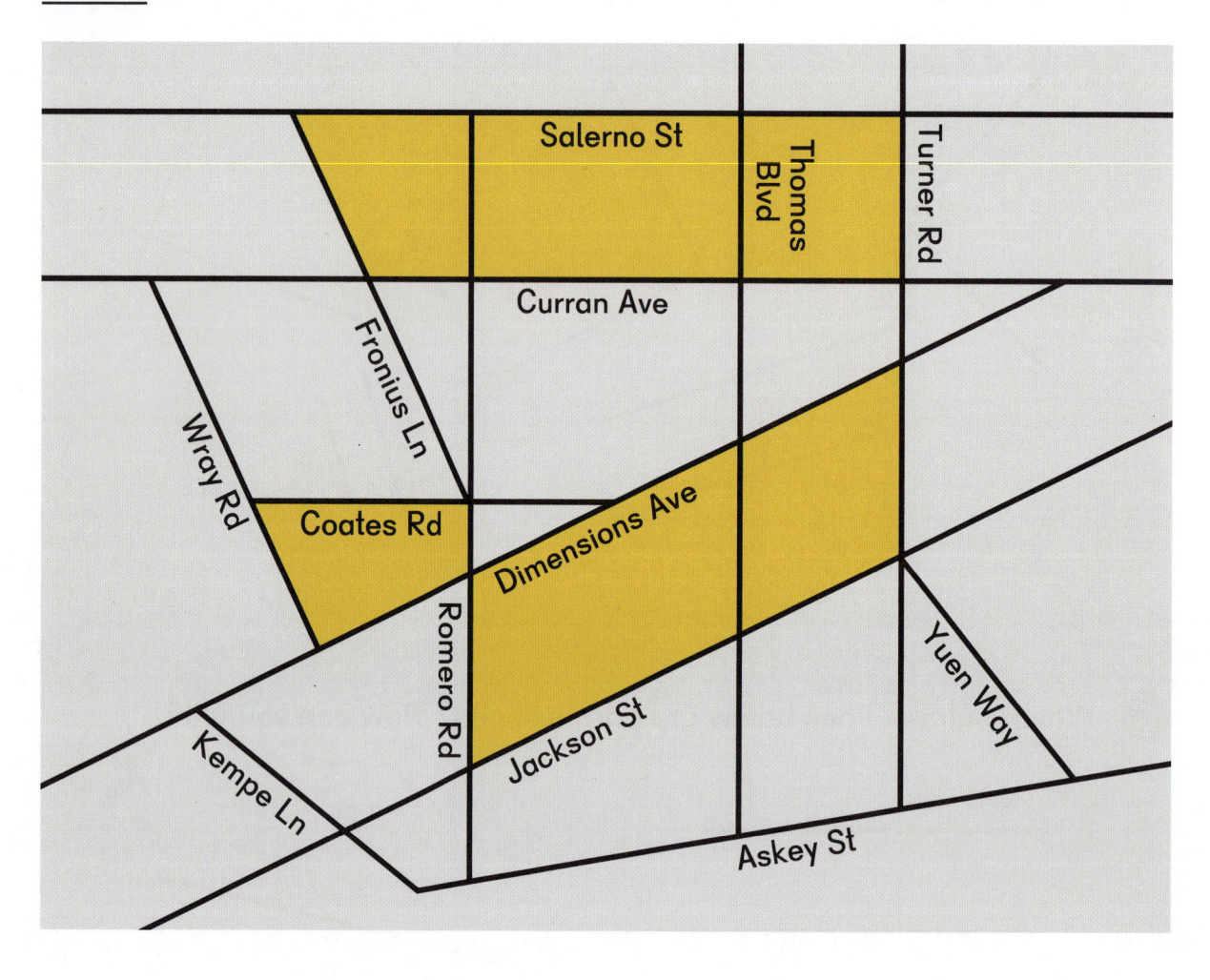

Look at the four-sided figures formed by the intersections of the streets.

(a) Which figure has no parallel sides?

(b) Which figures have at least one pair of parallel sides?

(c) Which figures have two pairs of parallel sides?

(d) Which figures have right angles?

Learn

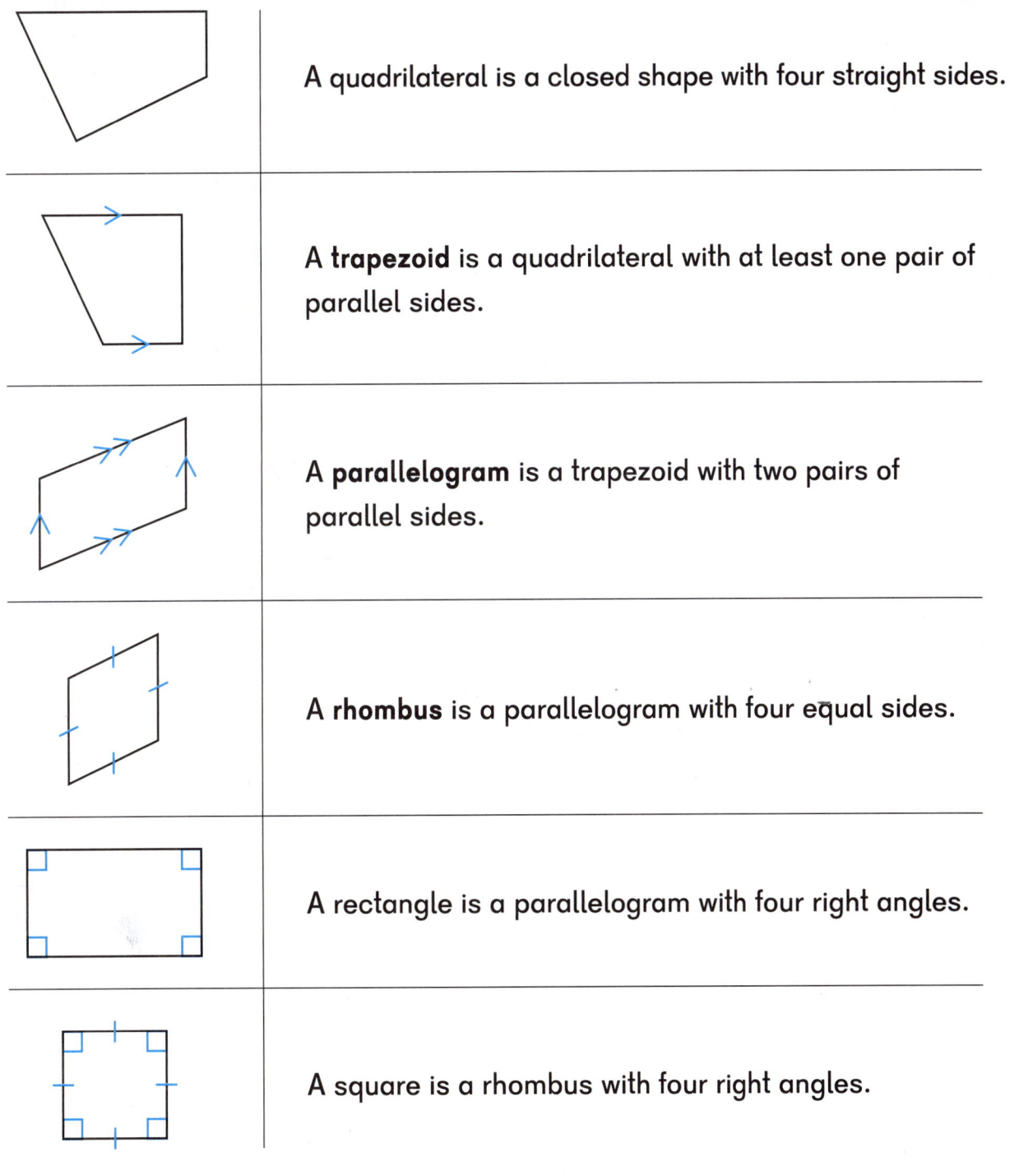

	A quadrilateral is a closed shape with four straight sides.
	A **trapezoid** is a quadrilateral with at least one pair of parallel sides.
	A **parallelogram** is a trapezoid with two pairs of parallel sides.
	A **rhombus** is a parallelogram with four equal sides.
	A rectangle is a parallelogram with four right angles.
	A square is a rhombus with four right angles.

Find other trapezoids and parallelograms on the map.

Do

① Draw a diagonal on a rectangular sheet of paper. Cut the paper along the diagonal.

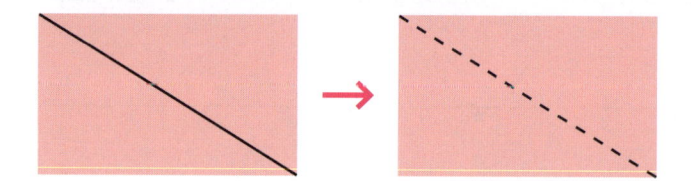

Put the two right triangles together to make a different parallelogram.

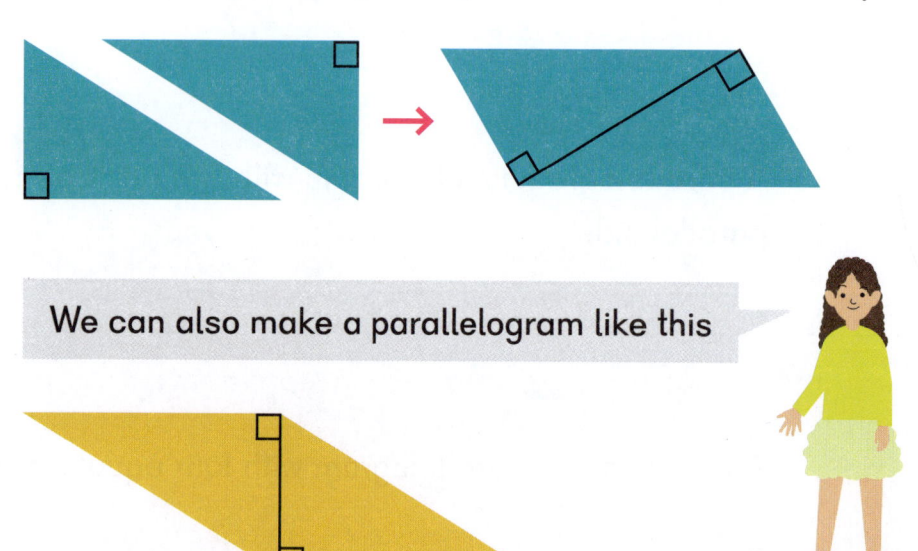

We can also make a parallelogram like this

② Which parallelograms below are rhombuses?

You can use a compass to see if the sides are the same length.

212　16-4 Quadrilaterals

3️⃣ Compare the lengths of the sides of this parallelogram.

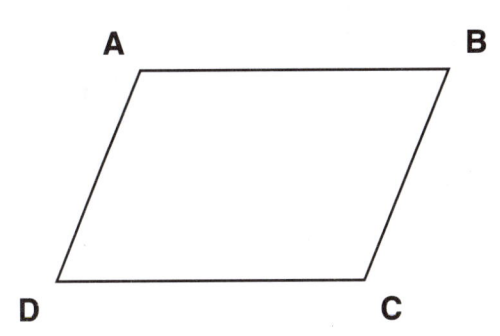

(a) Which sides have the same length?

(b) What can you say about the lengths of the opposite sides of a parallelogram?

> Are opposite sides the same length for all trapezoids?

4️⃣ Identify and name the parallel sides of the parallelograms below.

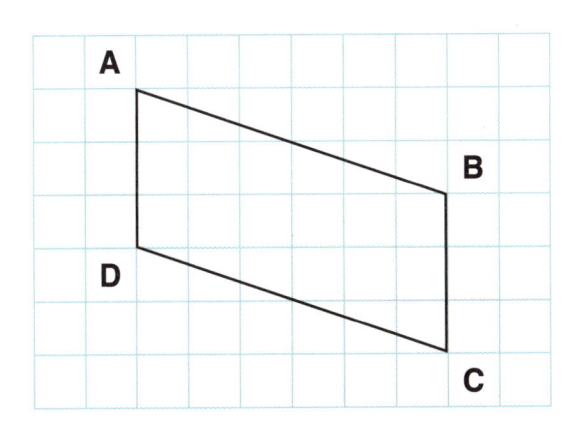

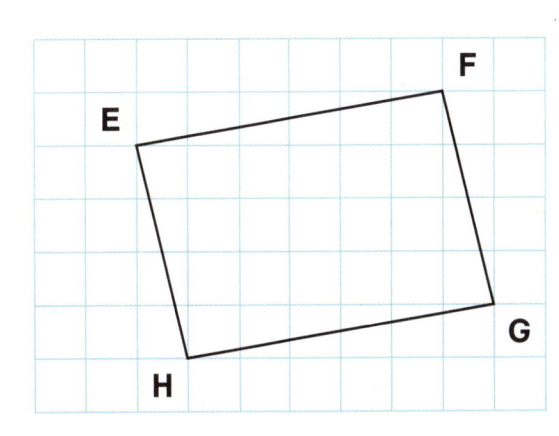

16-4 Quadrilaterals   213

5. Identify the parallel sides of the trapezoids below.

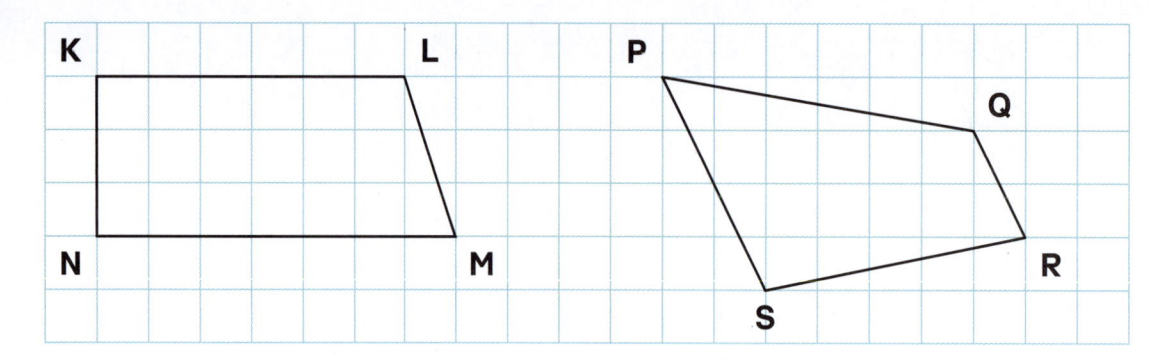

6. Identify and name two trapezoids in the diagram below. Which one is a parallelogram?

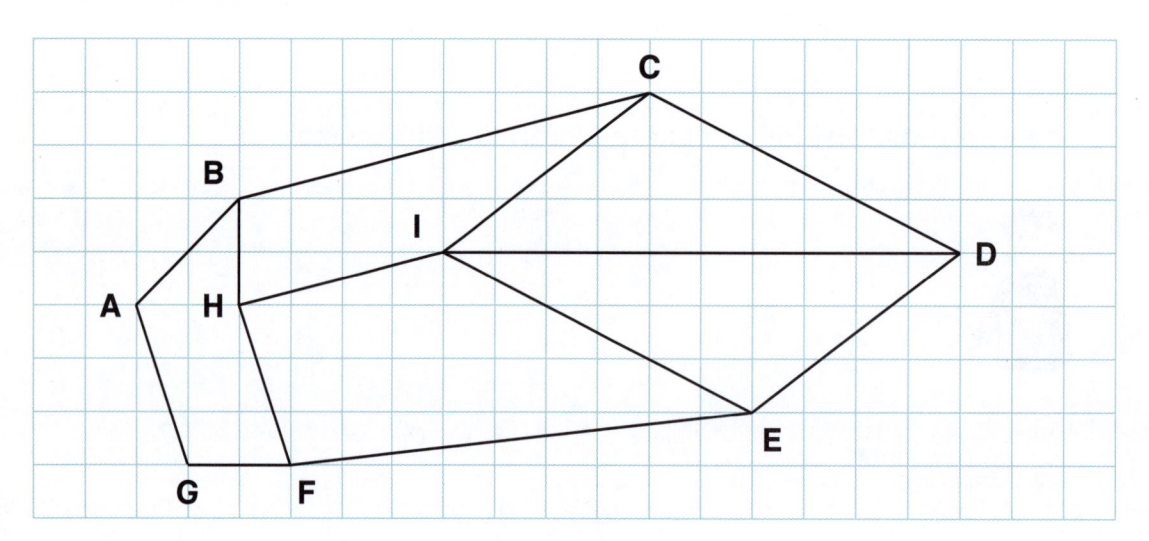

7. Draw different parallelograms and trapezoids on grid paper.

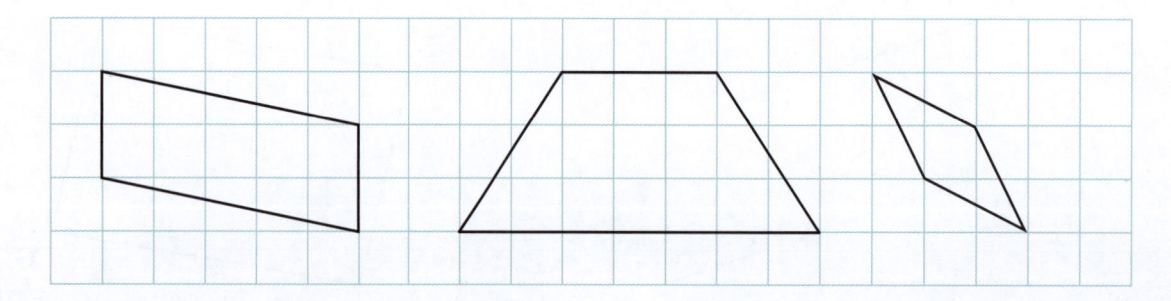

Exercise 4 • page 166

Lesson 5
Lines of Symmetry

Think

Fold a paper and draw a picture where one edge of the picture is along the fold. Cut out the picture and open it up. What do you notice about the two sides?

Learn

A figure where both sides match when it is folded in half is a **symmetrical** figure.

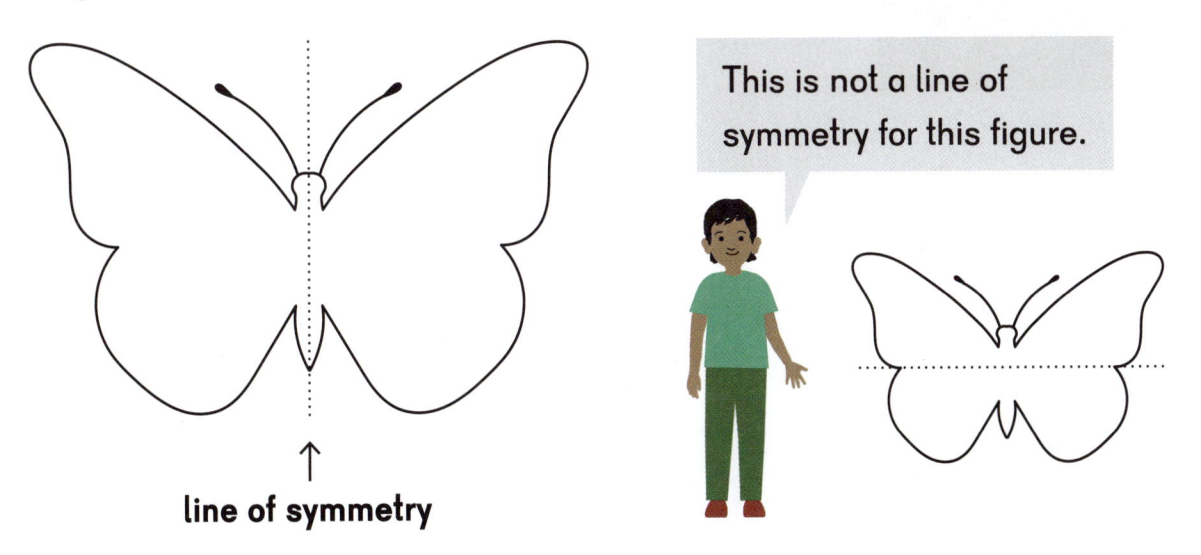

line of symmetry

This is not a line of symmetry for this figure.

Do

1 Fold a rectangular sheet of paper in half different ways and then unfold it. Which creases are lines of symmetry?

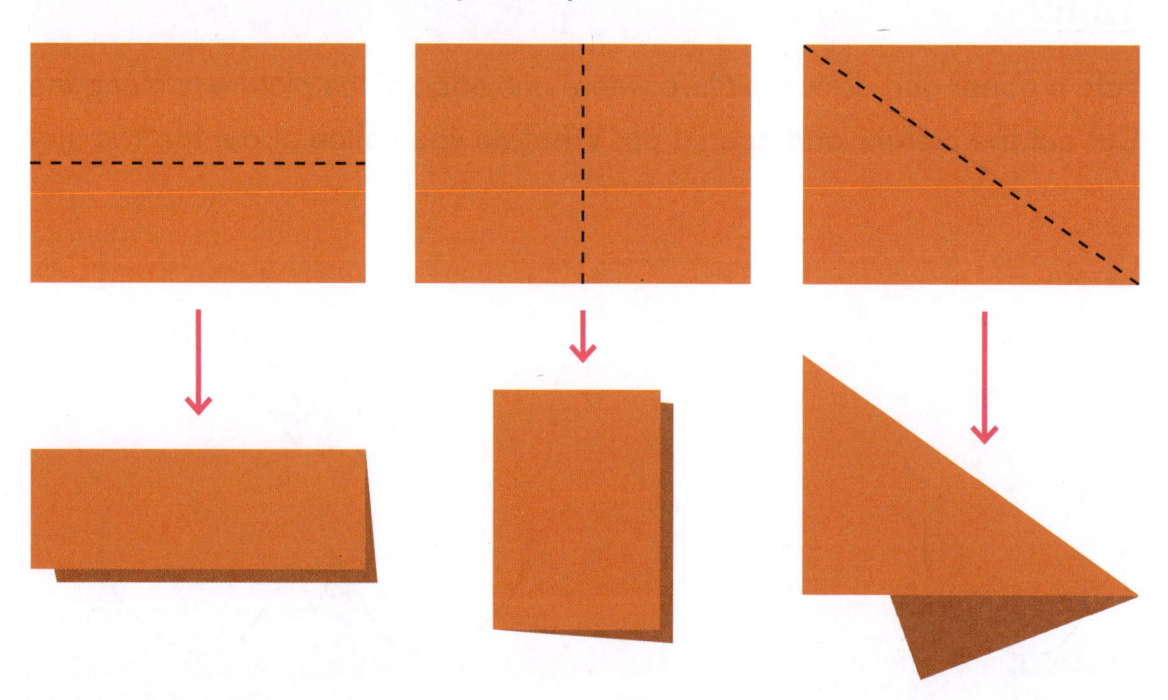

2 How many lines of symmetry does a square have?

3 How many lines of symmetry does this parallelogram have?

216   16-5 Lines of Symmetry

4. How many lines of symmetry does this rhombus have?

5. How many lines of symmetry does a triangle with 3 equal sides have?

A triangle in which all three sides are of equal length is called an **equilateral triangle**.

6. How many lines of symmetry does a triangle with only two equal sides have?

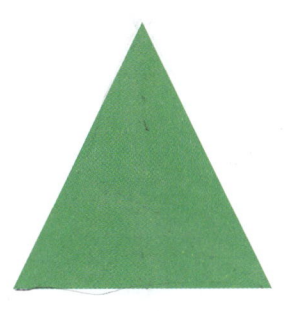

A triangle in which only two sides are of equal length is called an **isosceles triangle**.

7. Which of these right triangles has a line of symmetry?

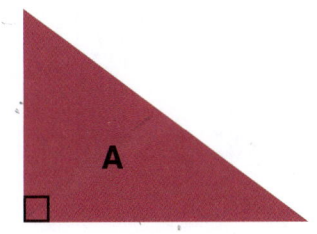

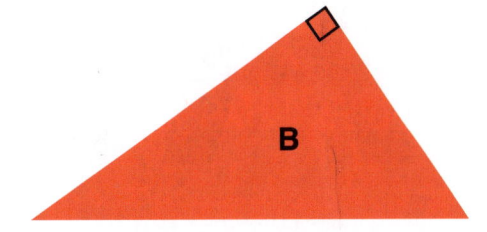

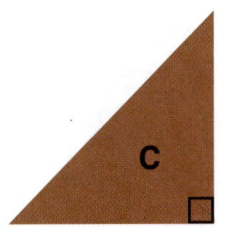

A   B   C

16-5 Lines of Symmetry

8 How many lines of symmetry does a circle have?

A circle has an infinite number of lines of symmetry.

9 Which of these shapes are symmetrical figures?

A   B   C

10 Identify lines of symmetry in these letters.

MATH

Exercise 5 • page 170

218   16-5 Lines of Symmetry

Lesson 6
Symmetrical Figures and Patterns

Think

Two symmetrical figures are partially drawn on grid paper. The dotted lines are lines of symmetry. Copy and complete the drawing.

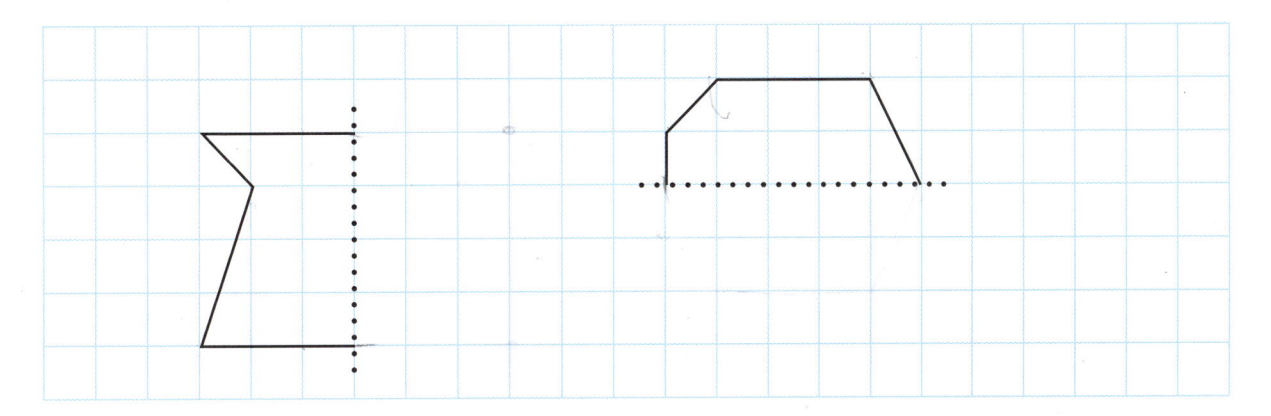

Learn

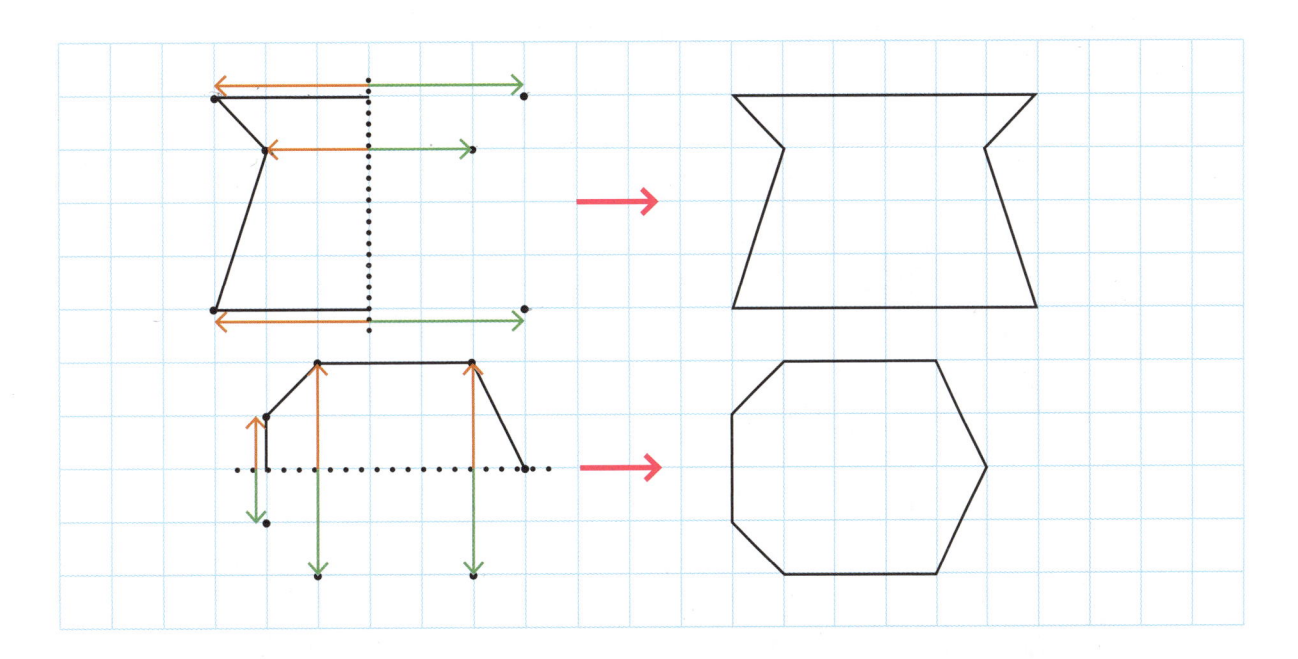

To create a symmetrical figure we can first draw points on the other side of the line of symmetry that are the same perpendicular distance from the line of symmetry.

16-6 Symmetrical Figures and Patterns 219

Do

① Copy and complete each figure so that the dotted line is a line of symmetry.

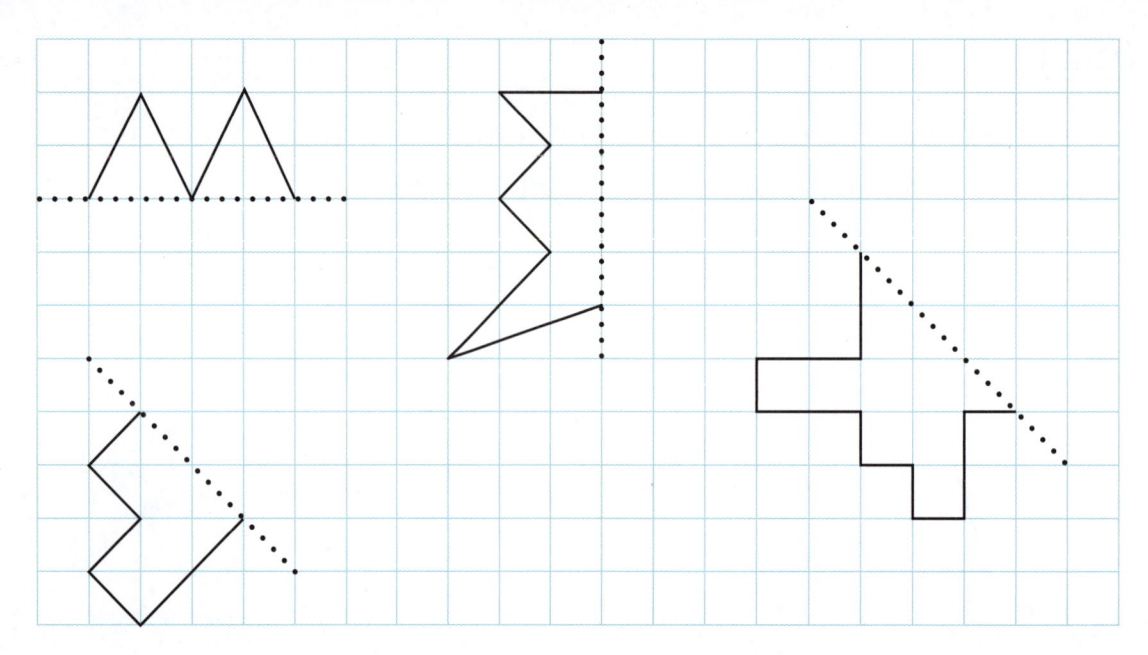

② A symmetrical pattern is made with squares. What do you notice about the squares on each side of the line of symmetry?

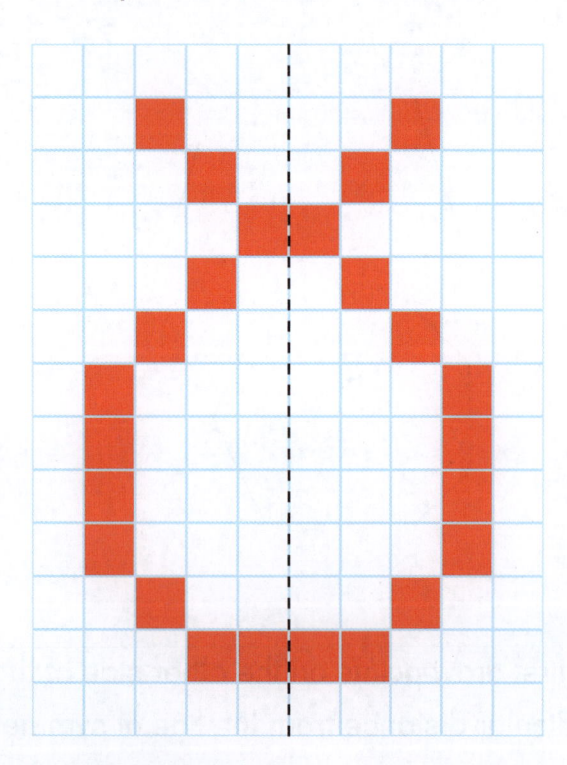

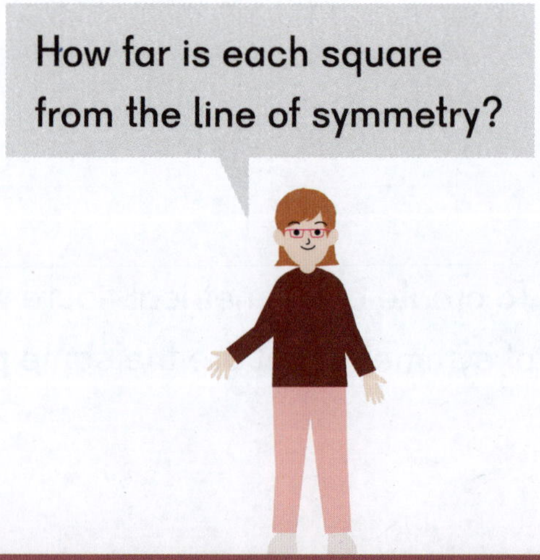

How far is each square from the line of symmetry?

220   16-6 Symmetrical Figures and Patterns

3 Copy and complete each figure so that the dotted line is a line of symmetry.

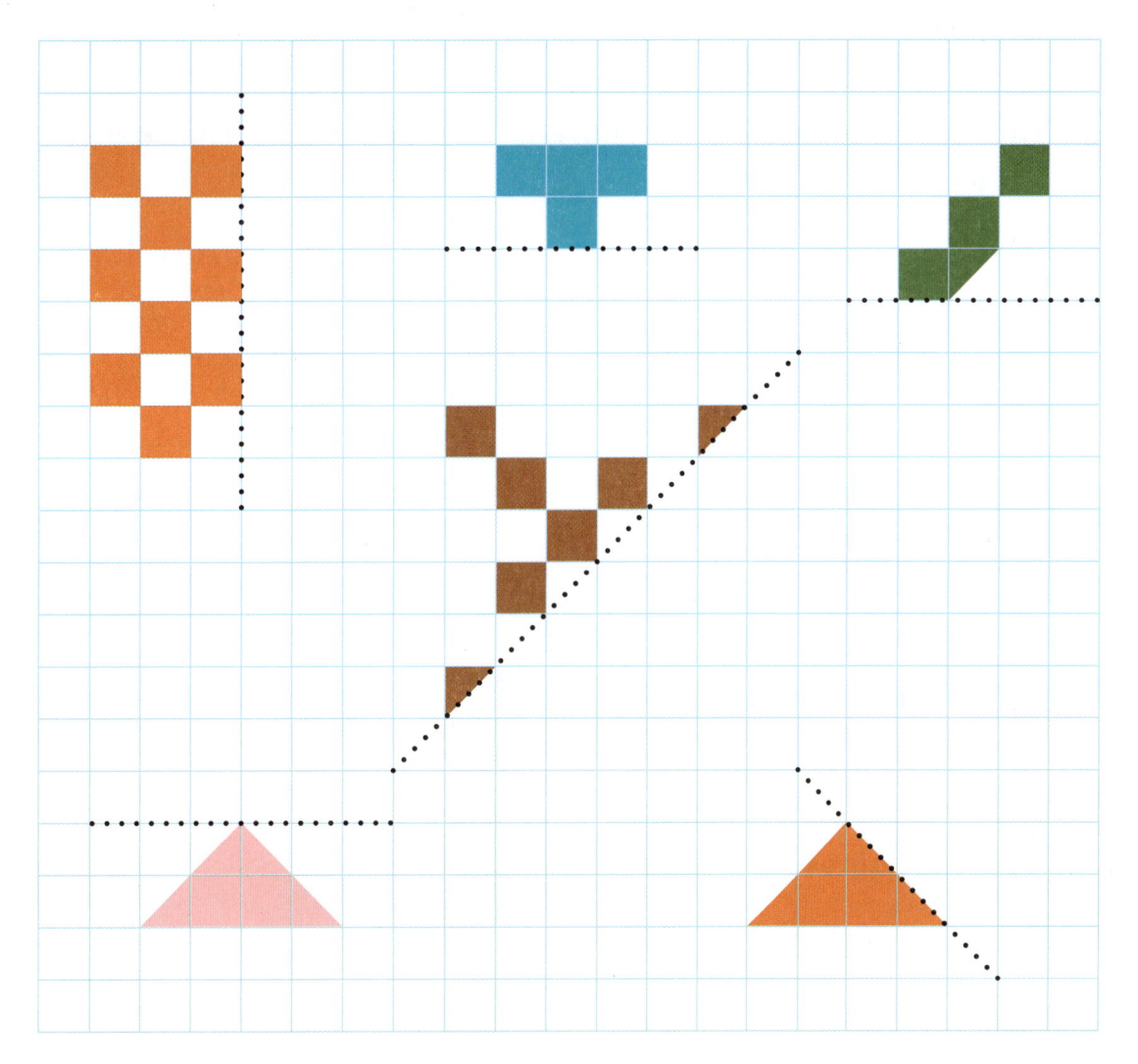

4 Draw three symmetrical figures on grid paper with different lines of symmetry. Each one should have a different orientation for the line of symmetry.

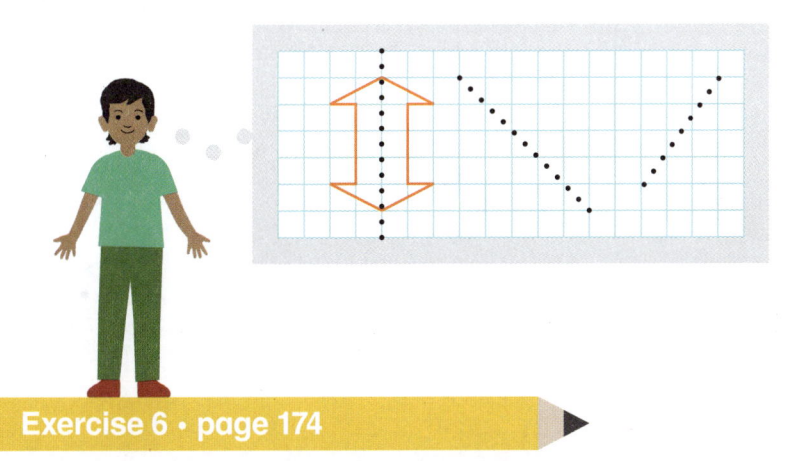

Exercise 6 • page 174

Lesson 7
Practice

P 7

1 Which pairs of lines are perpendicular? Which pairs of lines are parallel?

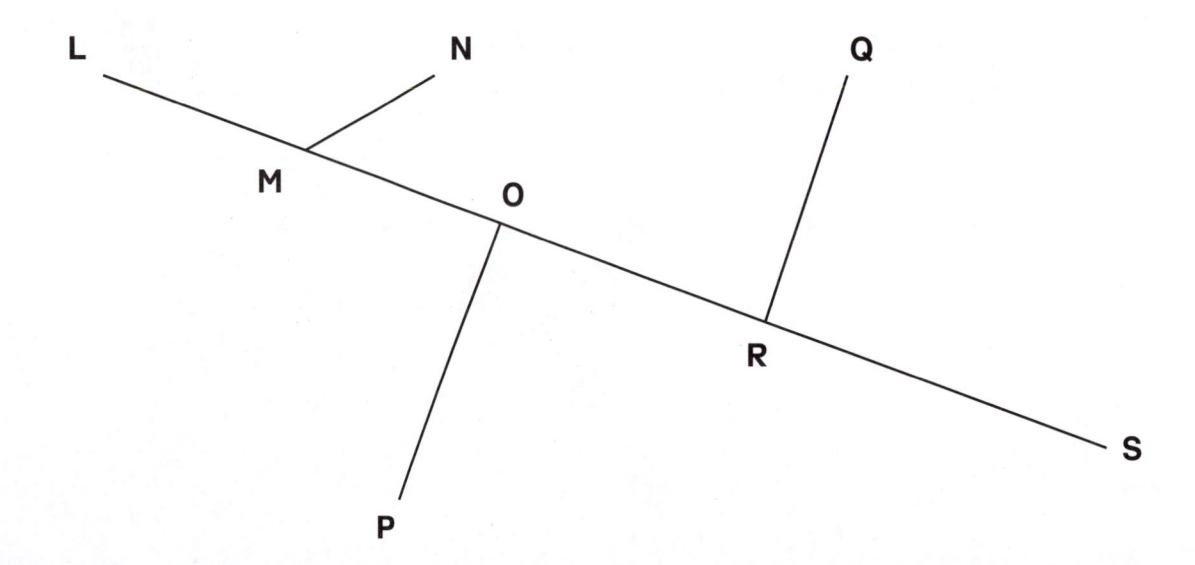

2 List the pairs of perpendicular lines and the pairs of parallel lines in the following figures.

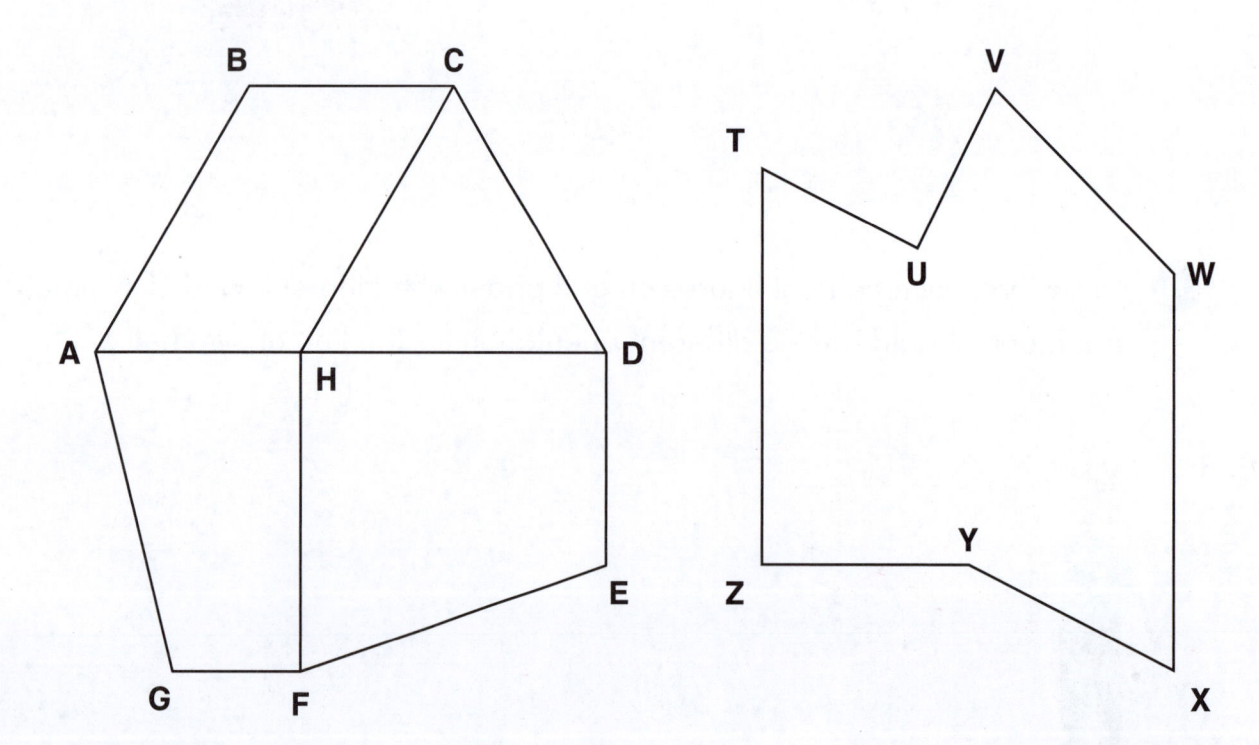

222 16-7 Practice

3

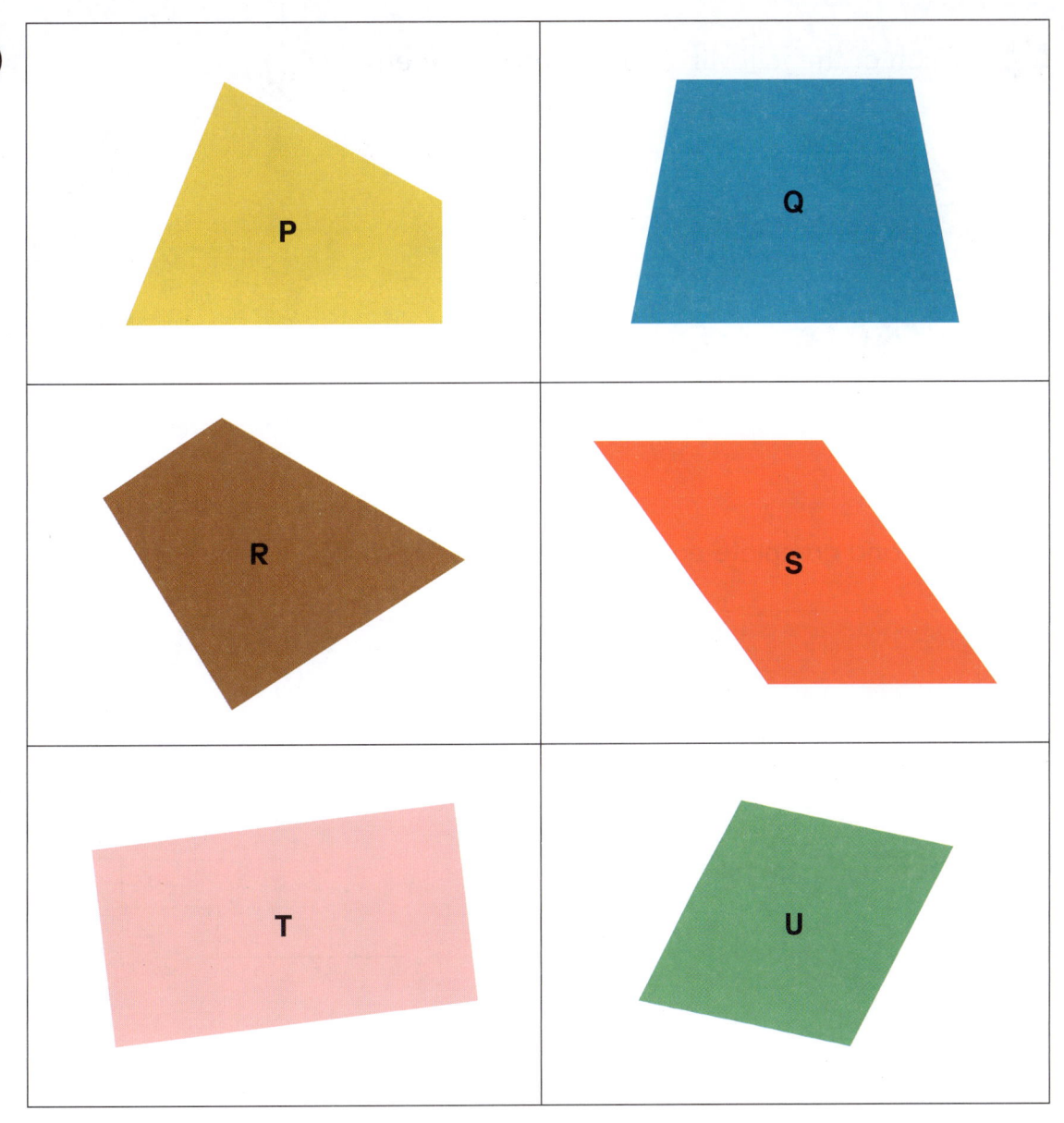

(a) How many pairs of perpendicular lines are in each shape?

(b) How many pairs of parallel lines are in each shape?

(c) Which of the shapes are trapezoids?

(d) Which of the shapes are parallelograms?

(e) Which of the shapes have a line of symmetry?

16-7 Practice

④ Which of the following figures are symmetrical?

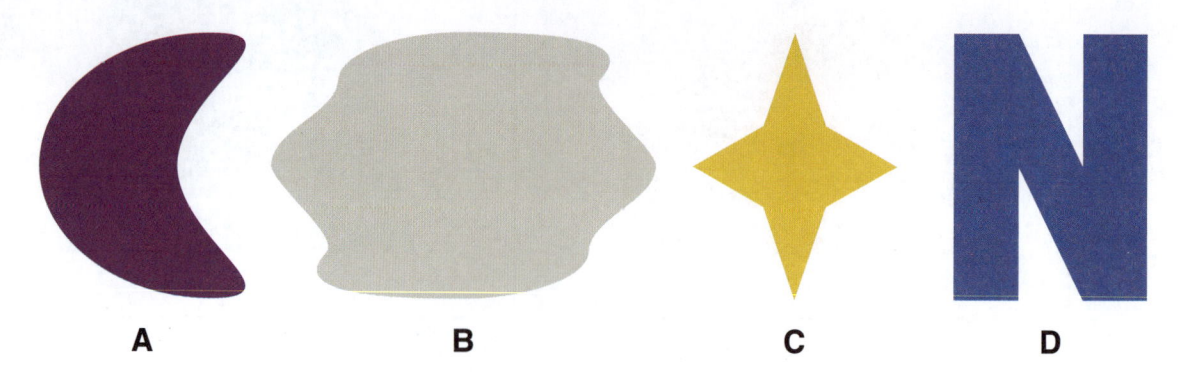

A   B   C   D

⑤ Copy and complete each figure so that the dotted line is a line of symmetry.

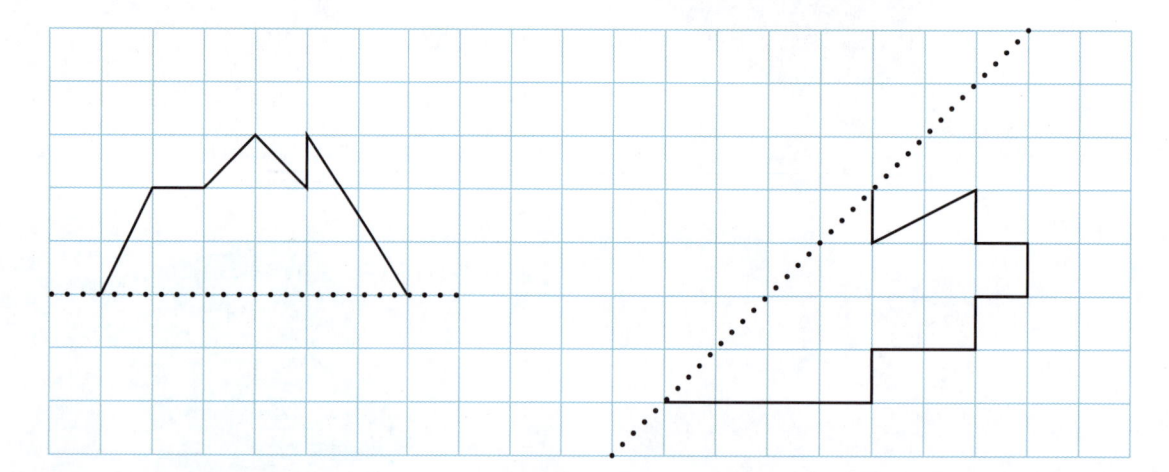

⑥ Copy and complete the figure so that the dotted line is a line of symmetry.

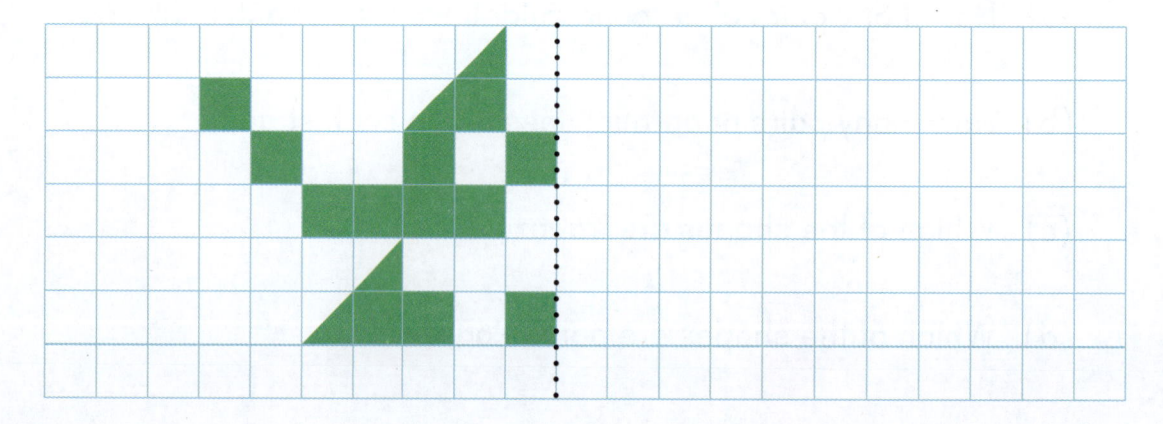

Exercise 7 • page 177

Chapter 17

Properties of Cuboids

Dion and Sofia are packing and stacking boxes.

Why are boxes so easy to stack?

I wonder if it has something to do with the angles of the sides and the edges.

Lesson 1
Cuboids

Think

Examine the faces, edges, and vertices of a cuboid.

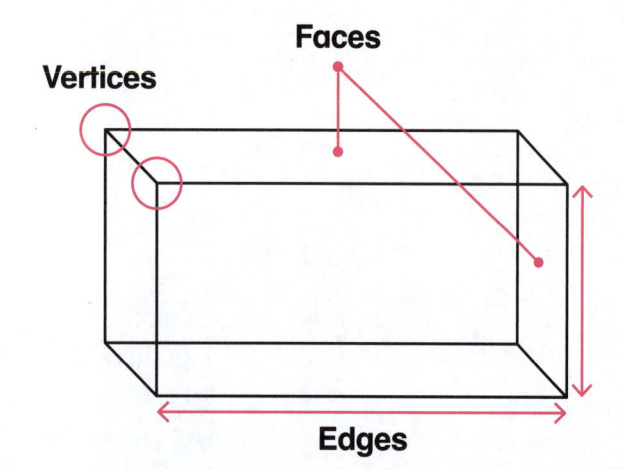

The top and bottom faces are the same size and shape.

(a) How many vertices, faces, and edges are there?

(b) Which faces are the same size and shape?

(c) Which edges are the same length?

Learn

A cuboid is a solid figure. A cuboid is also called a **right rectangular prism**.

(a) A cuboid has 6 faces, 8 vertices, and 12 edges.

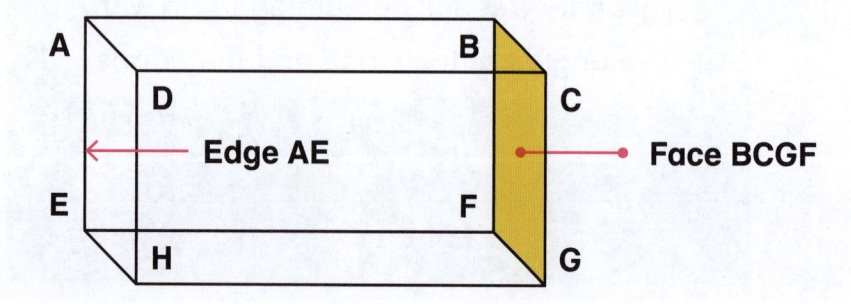

(b) Opposite faces are the same size and shape.

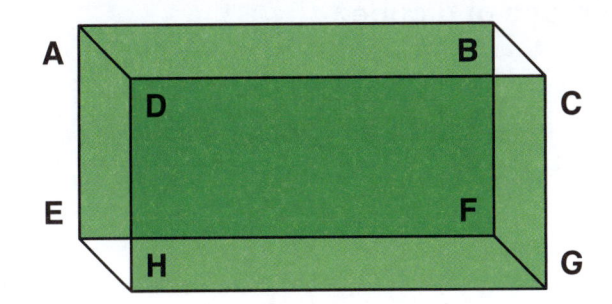

Face ABFE is the same size and shape as Face DCGH.

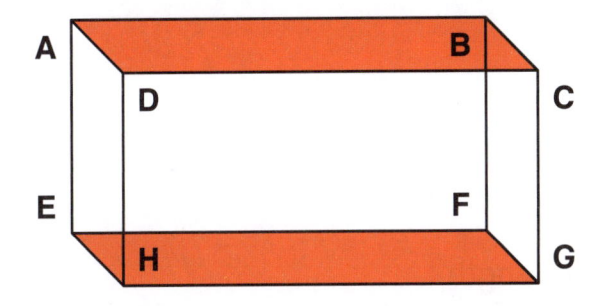

Face ABCD is the same size and shape as Face EFGH.

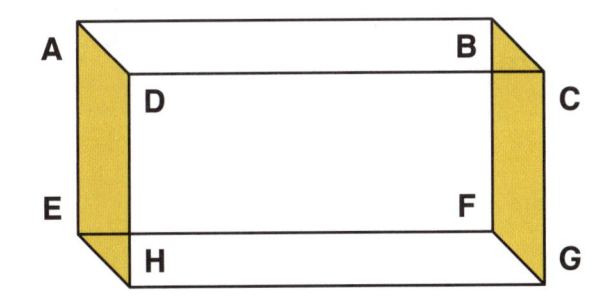

Face ADHE is the same size and shape as Face BCGF.

(c) Opposite pairs of edges are the same length.

AB and DC are the same length as EF and HG.

AD and EH are the same length as BC and FG.

AE and DH are the same length as BF and CG.

Do

1 Examine the faces, edges, and vertices of a cube.

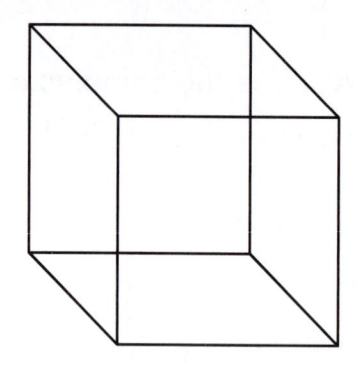

(a) How many faces, edges, and vertices does a cube have?

(b) How many edges are the same length?

(c) How many faces are the same size and shape?

2 Examine the edges of the cuboid.

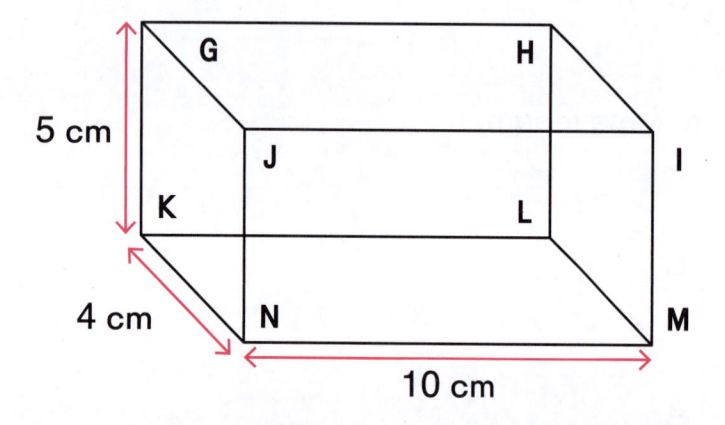

(a) List all the edges that measure 5 cm.

(b) List all the edges that measure 10 cm.

(c) List all the edges that measure 4 cm.

228   17-1 Cuboids

3. Name the faces of the cuboid shown below, then find the area of each face.

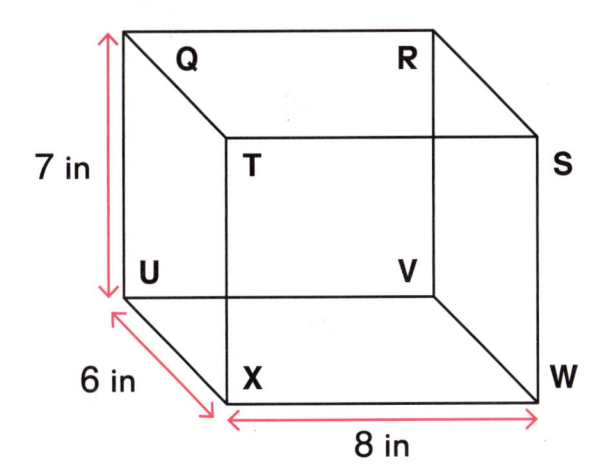

7 in
6 in
8 in

Opposite faces have the same size and shape, so we don't need to find the area of every face.

4. This figure is a cuboid.

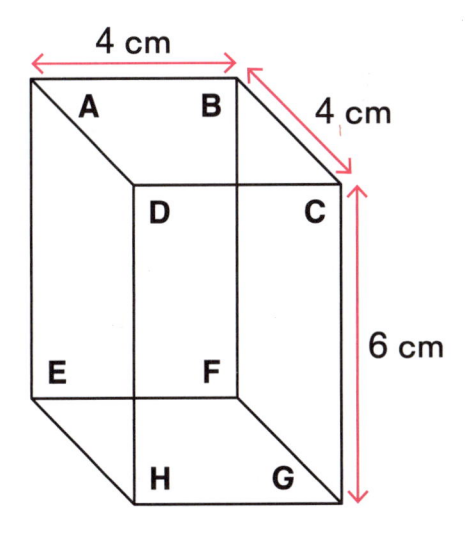

4 cm
4 cm
6 cm

(a) List all the edges that measure 6 cm.

(b) List all the edges that measure 4 cm.

(c) Which face has the same area as Face ABCD?

(d) Which faces have an area of 24 cm²?

Exercise 1 • page 183

17-1 Cuboids   229

Lesson 2
Nets of Cuboids

Think

Cut around the outside edges of each shape. Which shapes can be folded into cubes with no open sides?

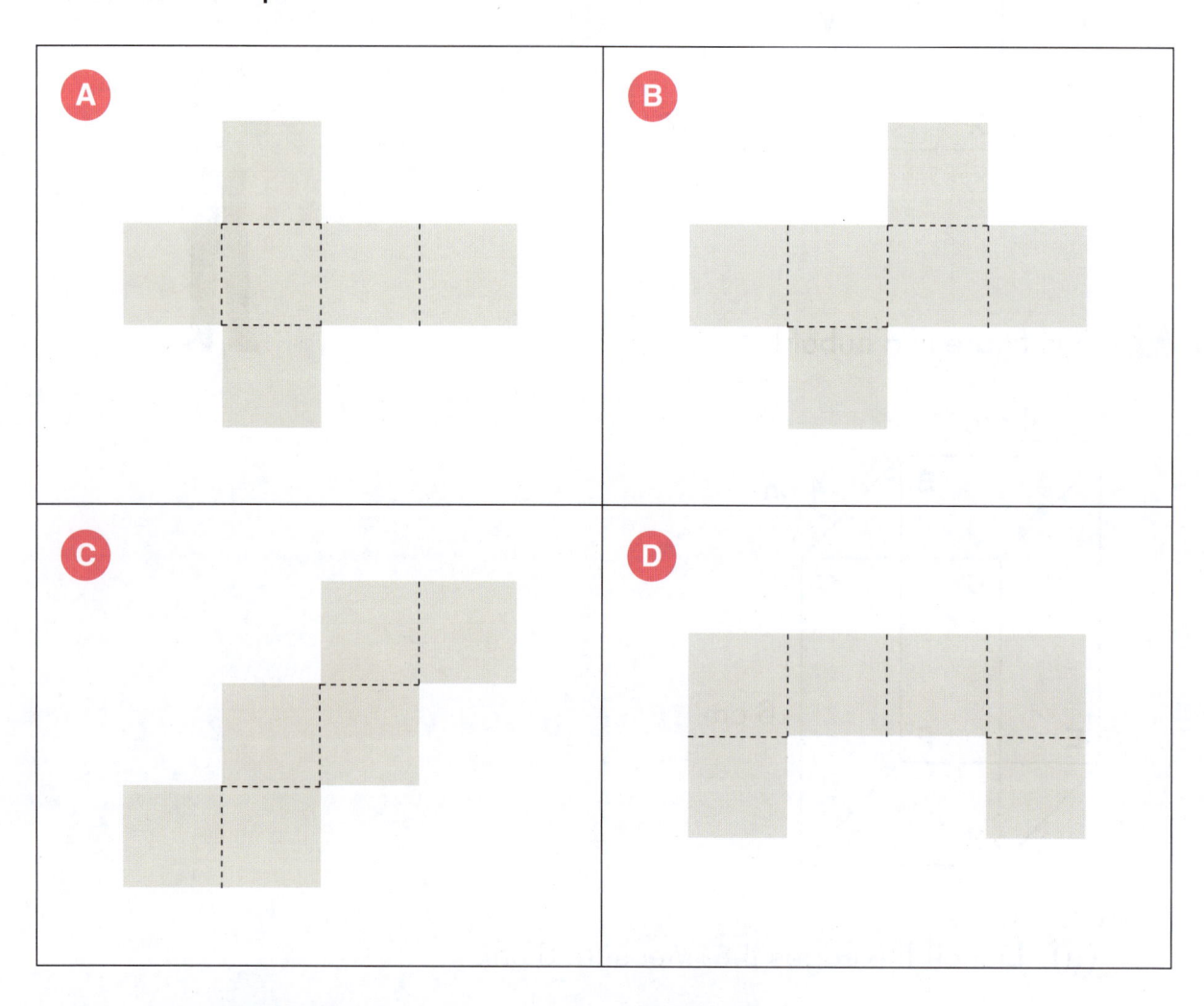

A

B

C

D

How many edges come together when folding the shapes that can make a cuboid?

Learn

A flat shape that can be folded into a solid figure is called a **net**.

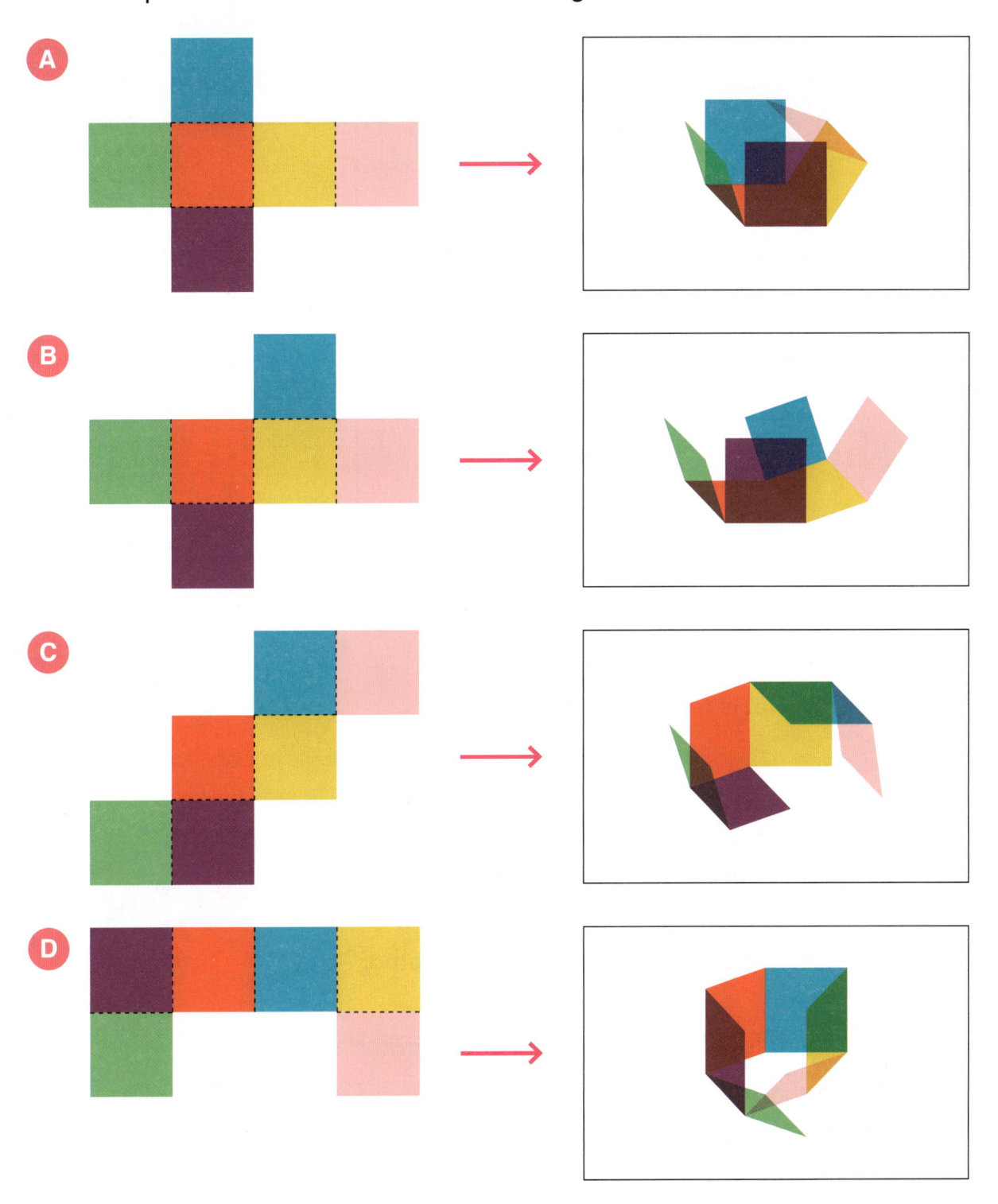

A

B

C

D

Nets A, B, and C will form a cube. Net D will not, since two sides will overlap.

17-2 Nets of Cuboids

231

Do

1 The net of a cuboid is shown below.

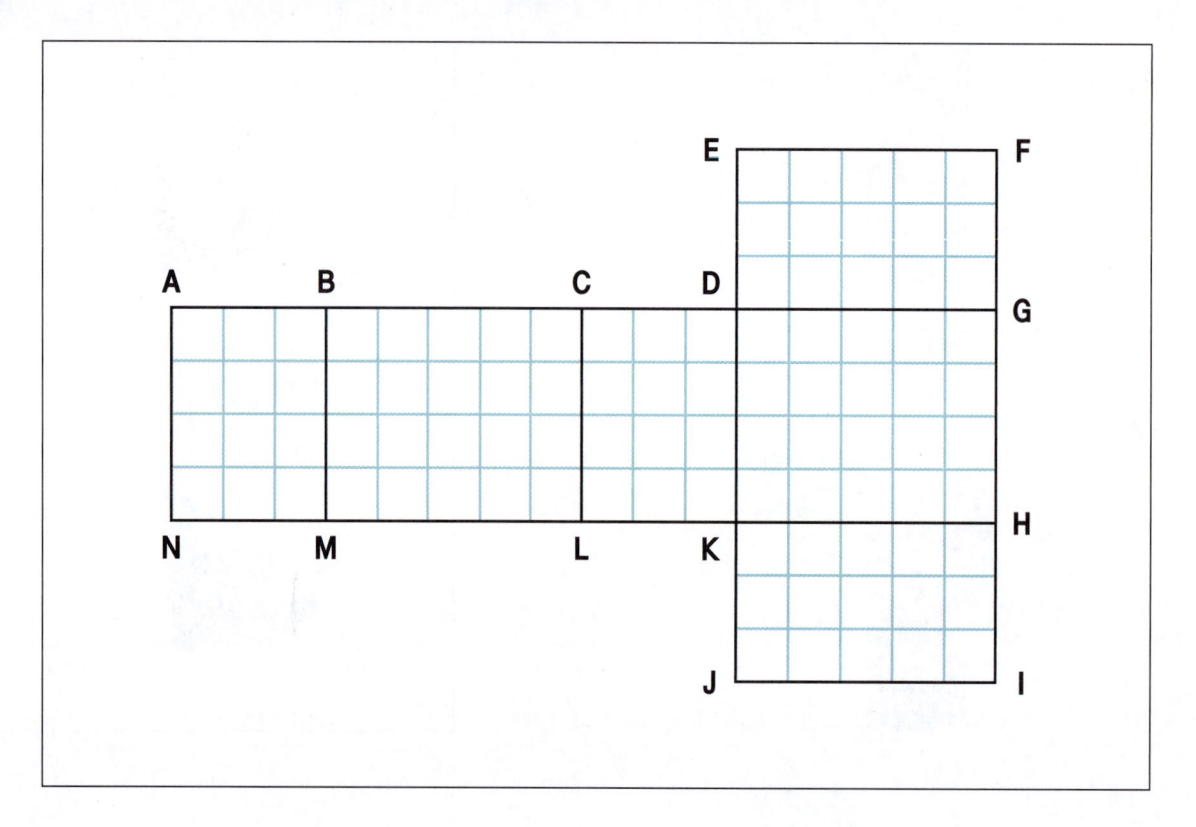

When the net is folded:

(a) Which vertices will touch?

(b) Which edges will touch?

(c) Which faces will be opposite each other?

(d) Which faces have the same shape and size?

(e) How many pairs of edges will match up as it is folded?

(f) Cut out and fold a copy of the net and make the cuboid to verify your answers.

2. Use 6 square cards. Tape some of the edges together to form a net. Fold to see if it will form a cube.

Try to find a net that will form a cube that is different than Nets A, B, and C on page 230.

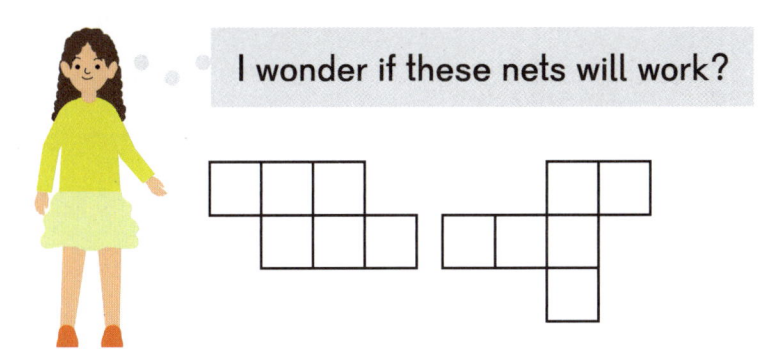

I wonder if these nets will work?

Compare your net with your classmates' nets. How many different nets of a cube were found?

3. Look at the net of this die.

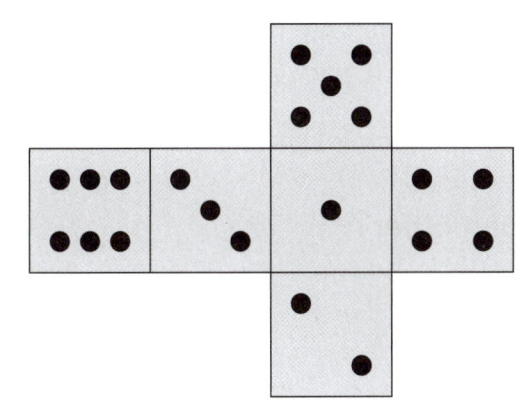

(a) When the net is folded, what numbers of dots will be on the faces that are opposite each other?

(b) What is the sum of the numbers that are on opposite sides of the die?

Exercise 2 • page 186

17-2 Nets of Cuboids

Lesson 3
Faces and Edges of Cuboids

Think

Fold a net to make a cuboid. Use a set square to investigate the angles of the cuboid.

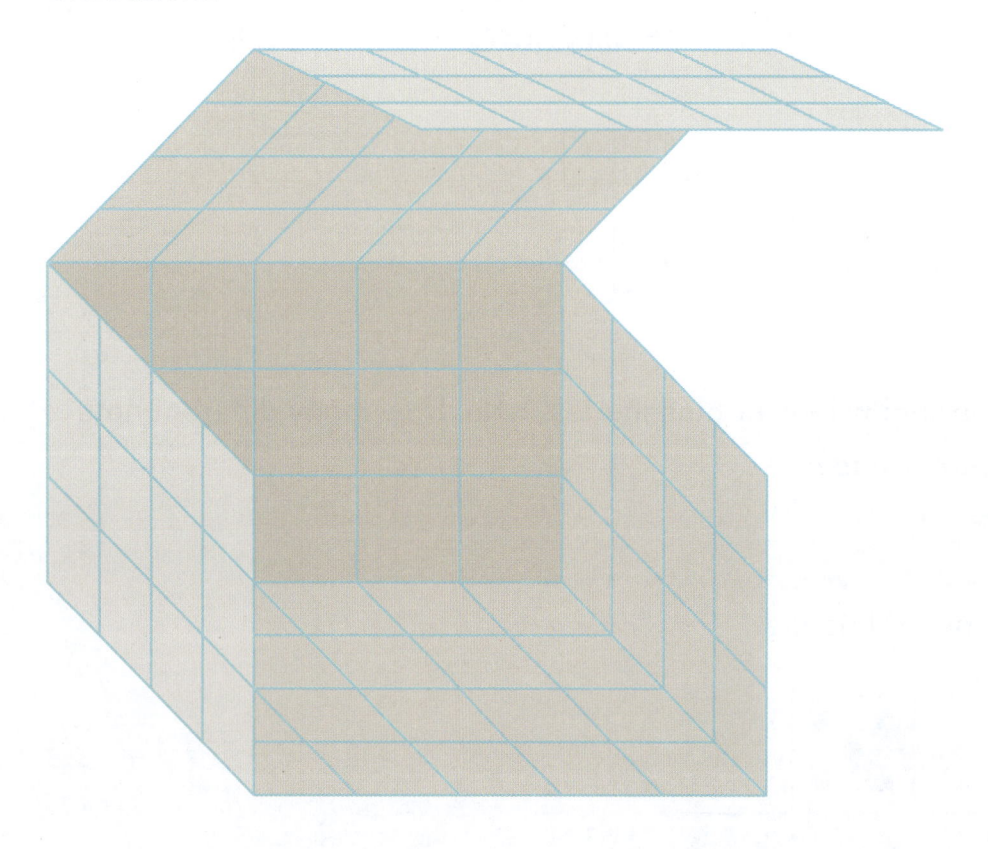

(a) Which faces are perpendicular to each other?

(b) Which faces are parallel to each other?

What kind of angles are formed where the faces of the cuboid meet at an edge?

Some of the edges are parallel to each other.

Learn

(a) For a cuboid, two faces that meet at a common edge are perpendicular to each other.

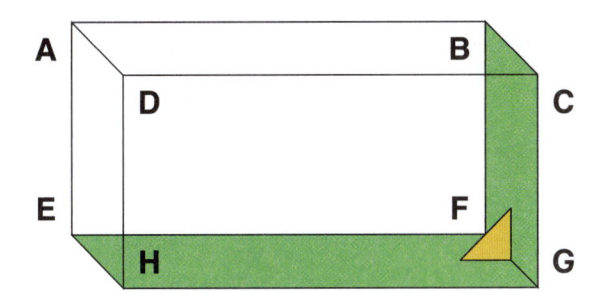

Faces EFGH and BCGF meet at edge FG.

Face BCGF is perpendicular to Face EFGH.

> What other faces are perpendicular to Face EFGH?

(b) For a cuboid, opposite faces are parallel to each other.

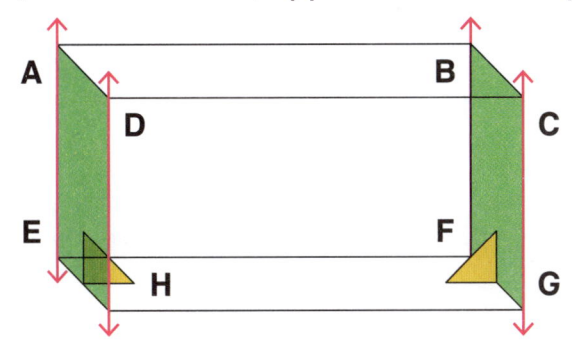

Faces ADHE and BCGF are both perpendicular to Face EFGH.

Face ADHE is parallel to Face BCGF.

> Which other pairs of faces are parallel to each other?

17-3 Faces and Edges of Cuboids

Do

1 Use a set square to investigate the angles formed by the faces of a cube.

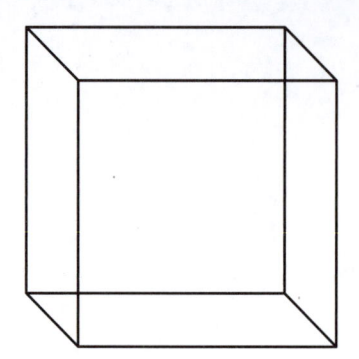

(a) Which faces are perpendicular to each other?

(b) Which faces are parallel to each other?

2 The figure below is a cuboid.

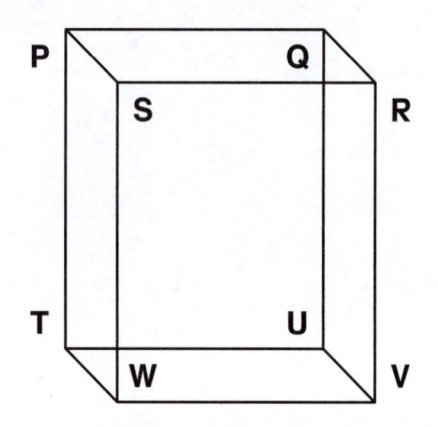

(a) Name two edges that are perpendicular to Edge WV.

(b) Which faces are perpendicular to Face TUVW?

(c) Name two edges that are parallel to Edge QR.

(d) Which face is parallel to Face SRVW?

3 This is a net of a cube.

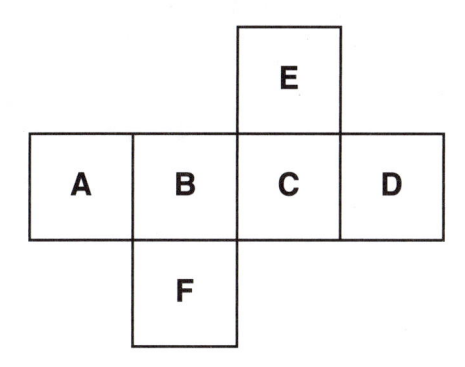

```
        E
    A | B | C | D
        F
```

(a) When folded, which faces will be perpendicular to face E?

(b) Which face will be parallel to face E?

4 Use grid paper and a ruler to draw a cuboid.

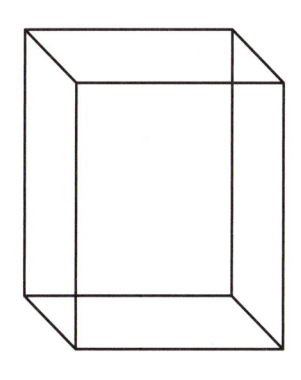

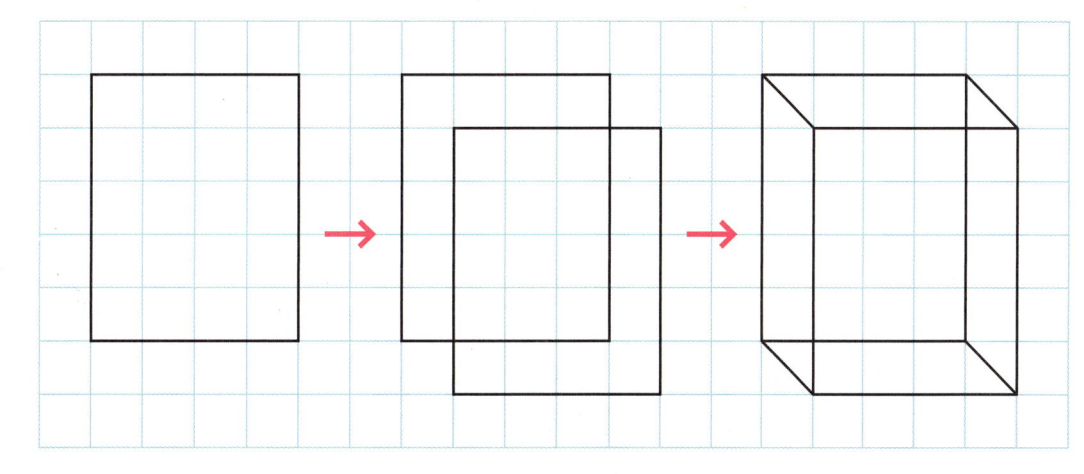

Exercise 3 • page 190

17-3 Faces and Edges of Cuboids

Lesson 4
Practice

1 This figure is a cuboid.

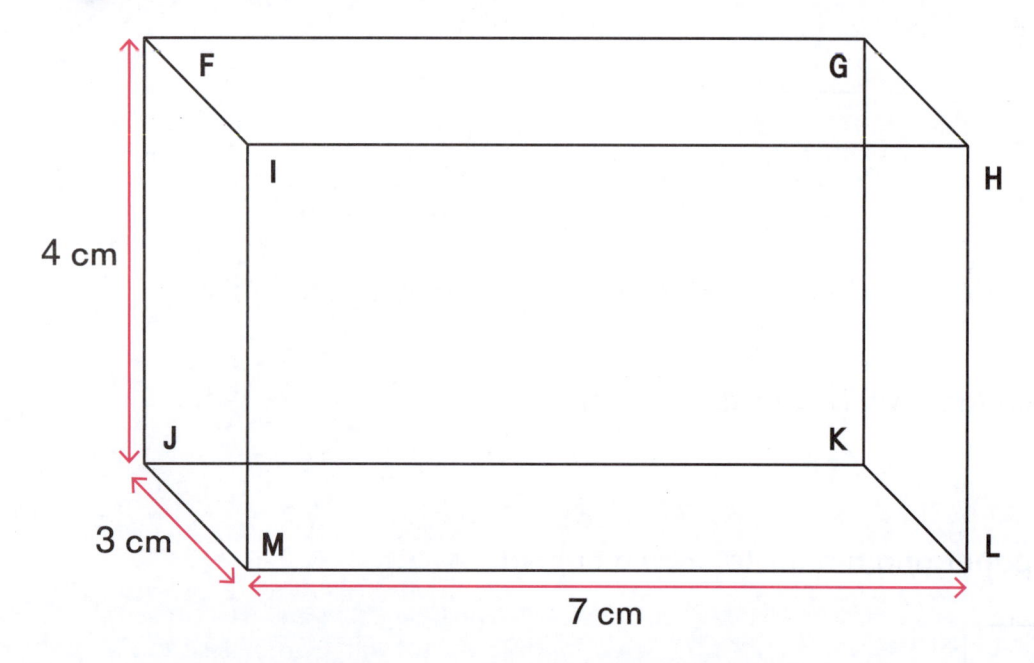

[Cuboid FGHL-JIKM... with edges: height 4 cm (J to F), depth 3 cm (J to M), length 7 cm (M to L). Vertices labeled F, G, H, I, J, K, L, M.]

(a) Which edges are the same length?

(b) Which sides have the same size and shape?

(c) What is the area of each face?

(d) Name a pair of perpendicular edges.

(e) Which faces are perpendicular to each other?

(f) Name a pair of parallel edges.

(g) Which faces are parallel to each other?

(h) Draw a net of this cuboid on centimeter grid paper.

2 This is a net of a cube.

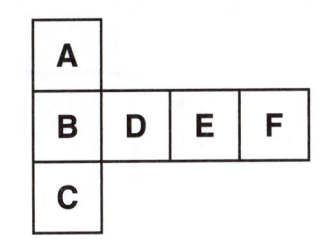

A			
B	D	E	F
C			

(a) When folded, which faces will be perpendicular to Face E?

(b) Which face will be parallel to Face E?

3 This is the net of a cuboid.

(a) Which faces have the same size and shape?

(b) Which faces will be parallel to each other?

(c) When the net is folded which edges will touch?

17-4 Practice   239

4 Which nets below can form a cuboid? For those that cannot form a cuboid, explain why not.

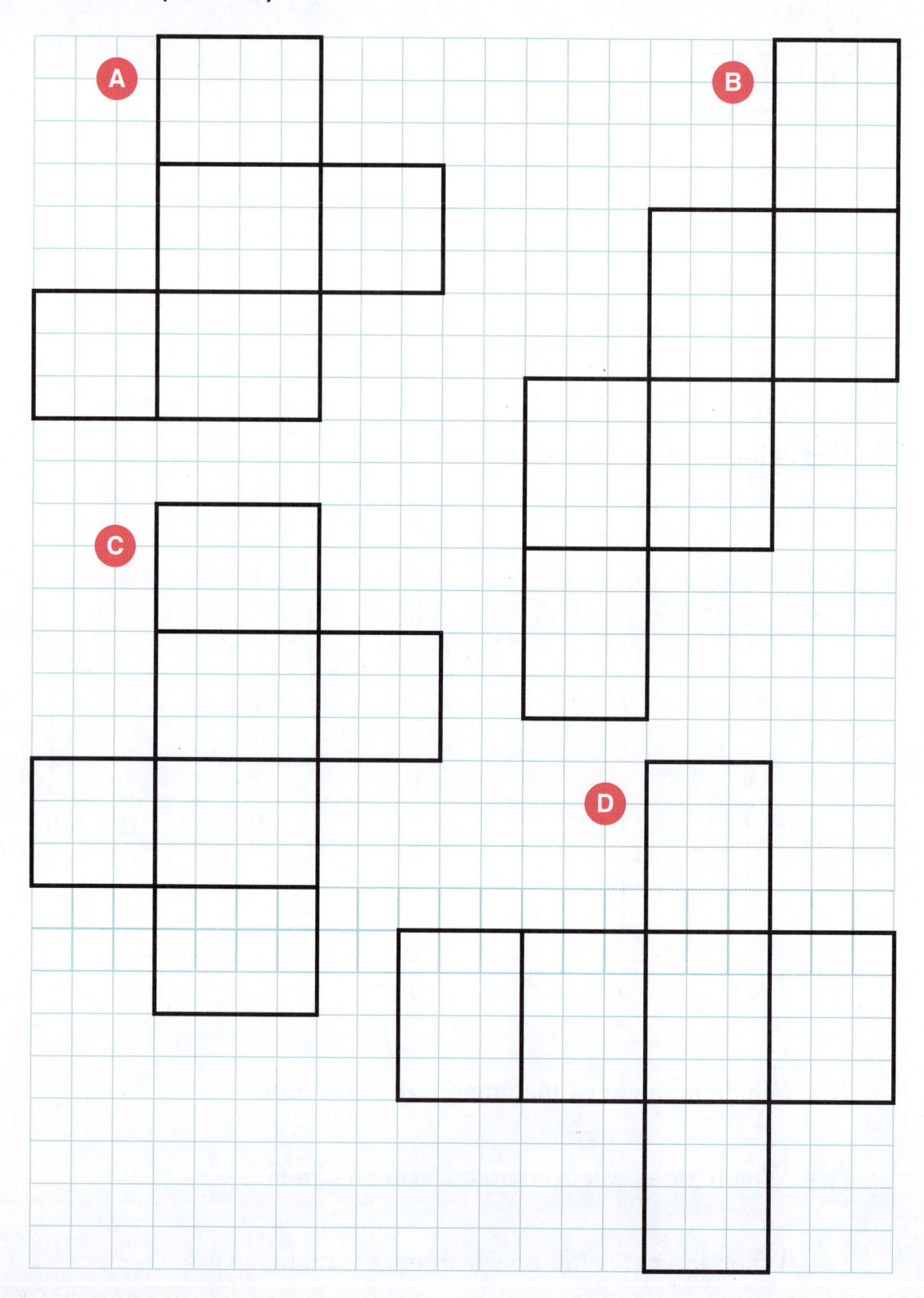

Review 4

1 Find the values. Express the answer as a quotient and remainder.

(a) 8,987 ÷ 4

(b) 4,098 ÷ 6

(c) 9,999 ÷ 7

2 Estimate and then find the values.

(a) 85,987 + 856   (b) 6,172 − 1,752   (c) 40,345 − 728

(d) 6,459 × 7   (e) 58 × 49   (f) 482 × 64

(g) 33.3 + 0.9   (h) 5.98 + 17.5   (i) 21 − 7.4

(j) 16.21 − 7.5   (k) 9.6 × 5   (l) 0.08 × 4

(m) 3.56 × 9   (n) 0.9 × 7   (o) 11.6 ÷ 4

(p) 7.68 ÷ 3   (q) 7.56 ÷ 7   (r) 4.08 ÷ 6

3 Express the values as a fraction or as a mixed number in simplest form.

(a) 3 ÷ 5   (b) 6 ÷ 9   (c) 8 ÷ 3

(d) 14 ÷ 5   (e) 56 ÷ 6   (f) 42 ÷ 8

4. Express the values as a fraction or mixed number in simplest form.

(a) $\frac{3}{4} + \frac{3}{8}$

(b) $1\frac{2}{3} - 1\frac{1}{12}$

(c) $7\frac{1}{10} - \frac{3}{5}$

(d) $7\frac{1}{2} - 2\frac{5}{8}$

(e) $18 \times \frac{2}{3}$

(f) $\frac{3}{4} \times 24$

(g) $\frac{4}{7} \times 14$

(h) $3 \times \frac{2}{5}$

(i) $\frac{7}{12} \times 8$

5. The graph shows the number of tornadoes each month of 2018 in the U.S.

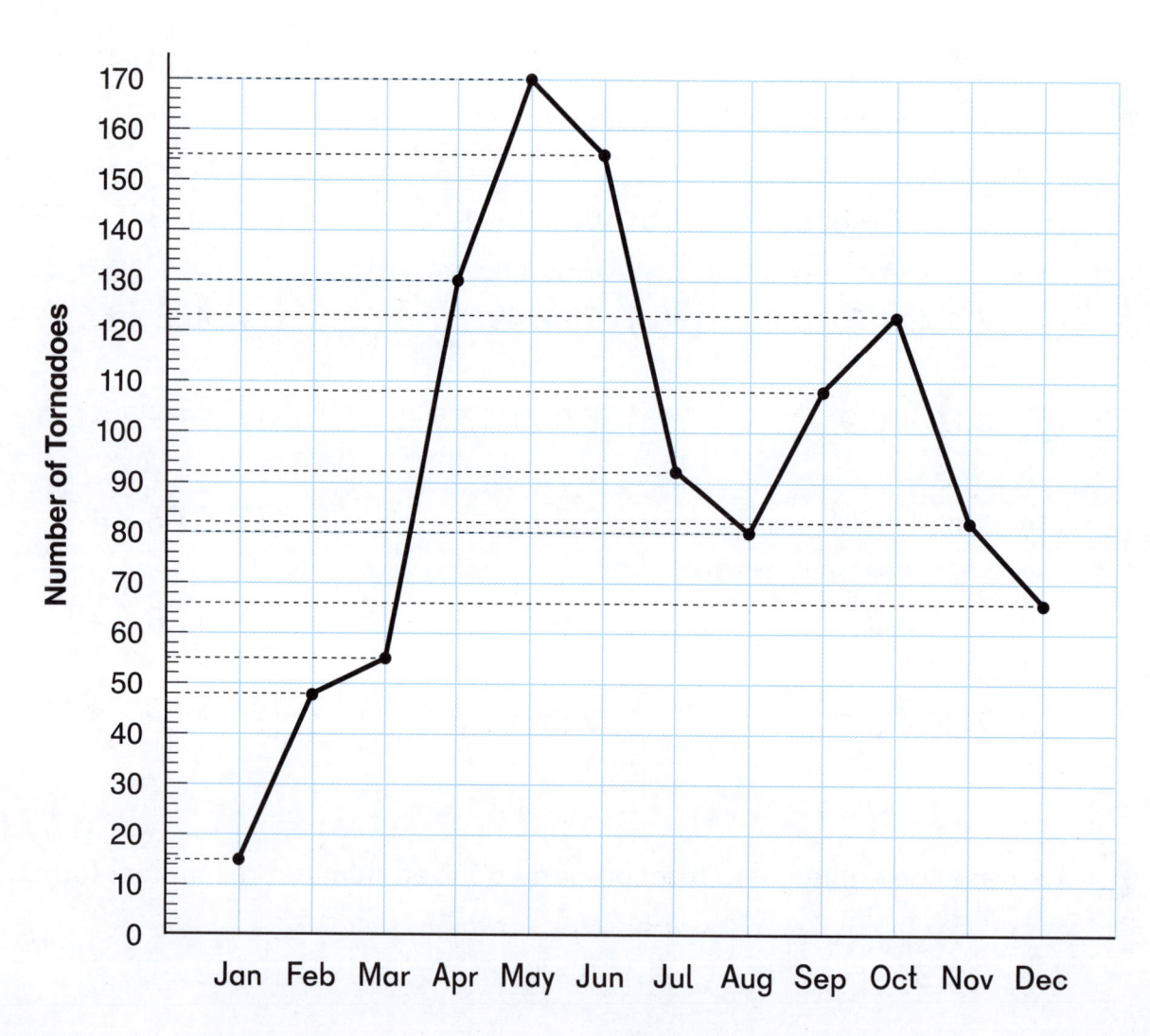

(a) Which month had the greatest number of tornadoes? How many?

(b) Which month had the least number of tornadoes? How many?

(c) Between which two months was there the sharpest rise in the number of tornadoes?

(d) Which two months had almost the same number of tornadoes?

(e) How many fewer tornadoes were there in October than in May?

(f) Which three-month period, Jan–Mar, Apr–Jun, Jul–Sep, or Oct–Dec, had the most tornadoes? How many tornadoes were there during that period?

(g) How many tornadoes were recorded for 2018?

6 A number between 20 and 50 is a multiple of 8. When it is divided by 6, there is a remainder of 4. What is the number?

7 Which of the following numbers are composite numbers?

| 18 | 49 | 67 | 101 | 134 |

8 Which of the following numbers are common factors of 12 and 30?

| 2 | 4 | 6 | 12 | 30 |

Review 4   243

9 Andrew has the same amount of money in pennies, in nickels, in dimes, and in quarters.

   (a) What is the least number of each type of coin he could have?

   (b) What is the total amount of money for all the coins in the answer for (a)? Express the answer in dollars.

10 Measure each marked angle.

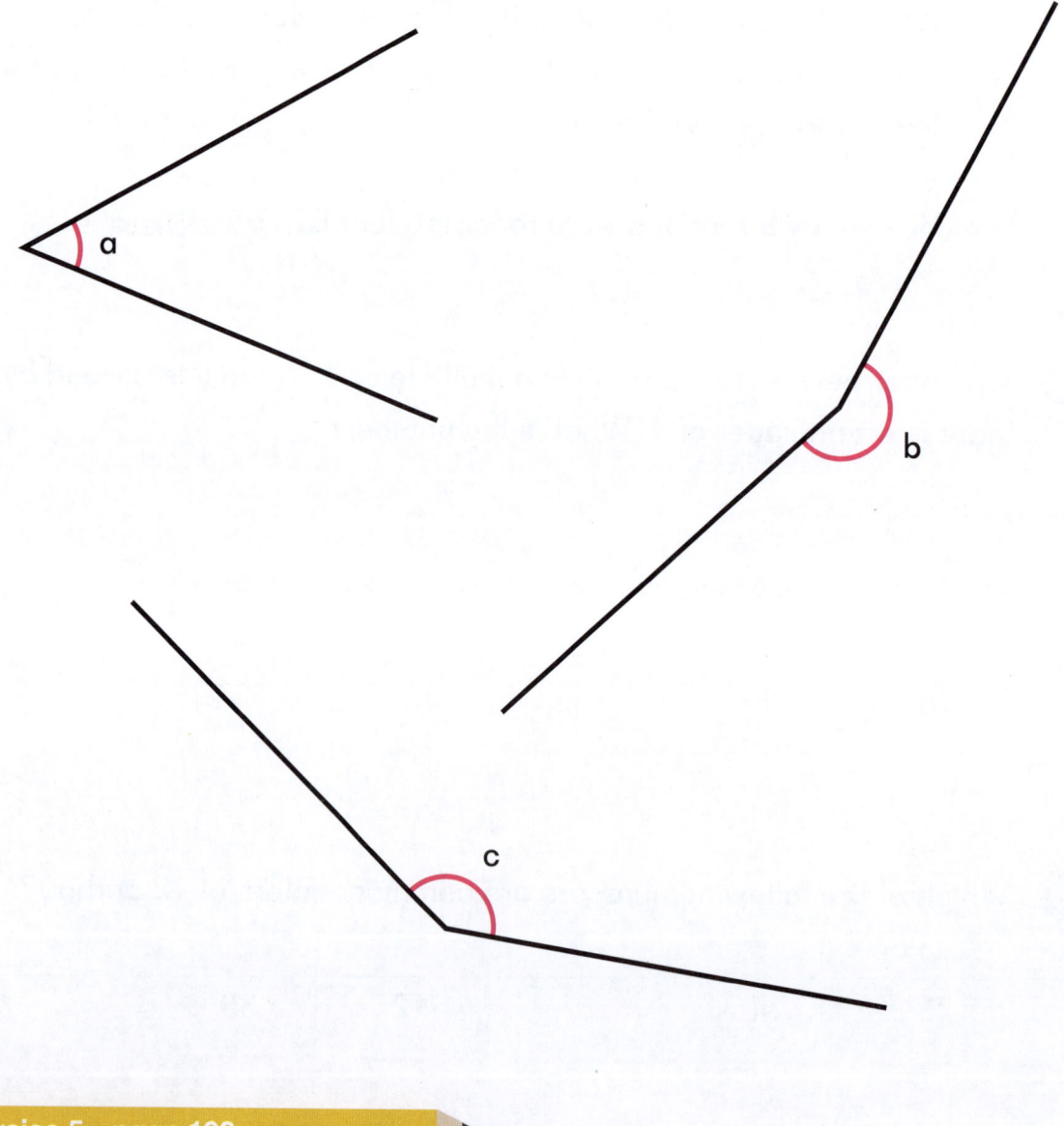

Exercise 5 • page 198

Review 5

1. The line plot shows the length of some rattlesnakes in a reptile exhibit, measured to the closest fourth of a foot.

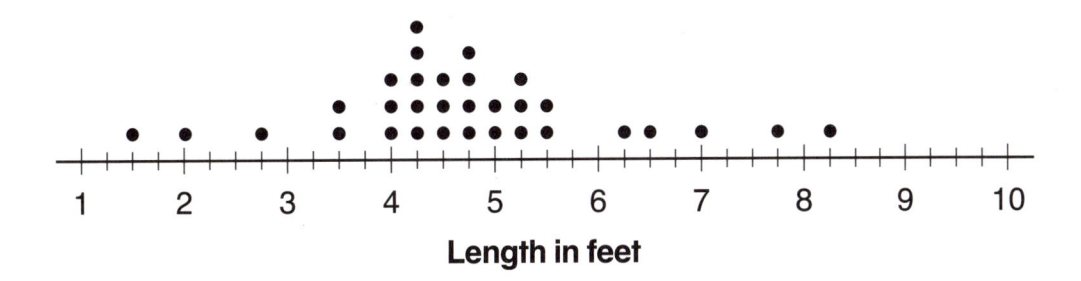

Length in feet

(a) How many rattlesnakes were measured?

(b) How many rattlesnakes were longer than 6 feet 4 inches?

(c) What is the difference in length between the shortest and the longest rattlesnake? Express the answer in feet as a mixed number, in feet and inches, and in inches.

(d) What fraction of the total number of rattlesnakes were between 3 feet and 6 feet long? Express the answer in simplest form.

(e) One of the rattlesnakes weighs 5 lb 4 oz. Express this weight in ounces only, and in pounds as a mixed number.

(f) Two other rattlesnakes weigh 4 lb 10 oz and 6 lb 2 oz. What is the sum of the weights of these two rattlesnakes? Express the answer in compound units.

2 Add or subtract. Express the answers using compound units where possible.

(a) 3 m 25 cm + 2 m 80 cm

(b) 5 km 280 m − 2 km 700 m

(c) 6 L − 2 L 15 mL

(d) 6 cm 9 mm + 3 cm 8 mm

(e) 4 lb 8 oz + 2 lb 9 oz

(f) 4 ft 7 in − 1 ft 10 in

3 A baker uses 1.25 lb of flour to make a loaf of sourdough bread. How many pounds of flour does she need to make 8 loaves of this bread?

4 Maya ran the same distance each day Monday through Friday. She ran a total of 17.5 km. How far did she run each day? Express the answer in kilometers as a mixed number.

5 A red ribbon is 4 times as long as a blue ribbon. The total length of both ribbons is $10\frac{4}{5}$ m. How long is each ribbon in meters? Express the answers as decimals.

6 Jesse had $45. He spent $\frac{2}{3}$ of his money on a book, then $1.65 on a snack. How much money did he have left?

7 What is the measure of Angle a?

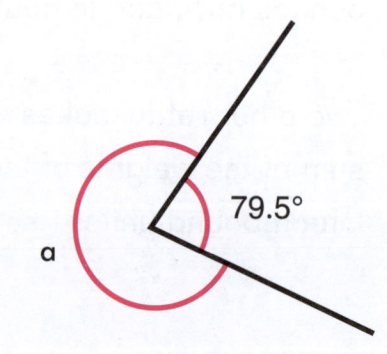

79.5°

a

Review 5

8 The garden shown below has a rectangular pond in the center and a lawn around the pond. What is the area of the lawn?

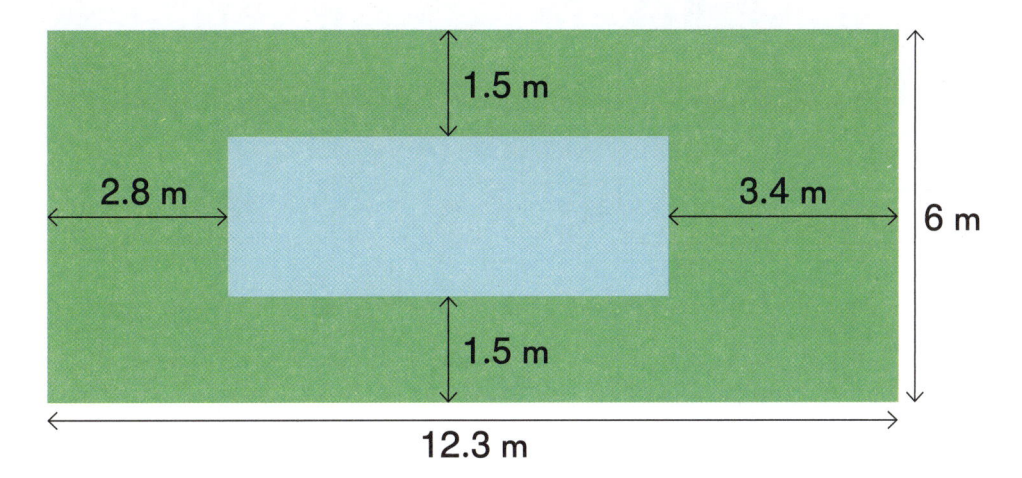

9 The figure below is symmetrical. All sides meet at right angles.

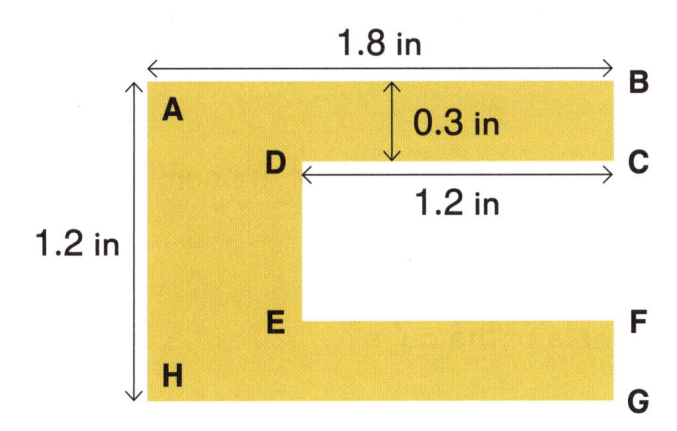

(a) Which sides are perpendicular to AH?

(b) Which sides are parallel to AH?

(c) Express the perimeter in inches both as a decimal and as a mixed number in simplest form.

(d) The shape is cut in half along a line of symmetry. Express the perimeter of each half both as a decimal and as a mixed number in simplest form.

Review 5

10 This figure is a cuboid.

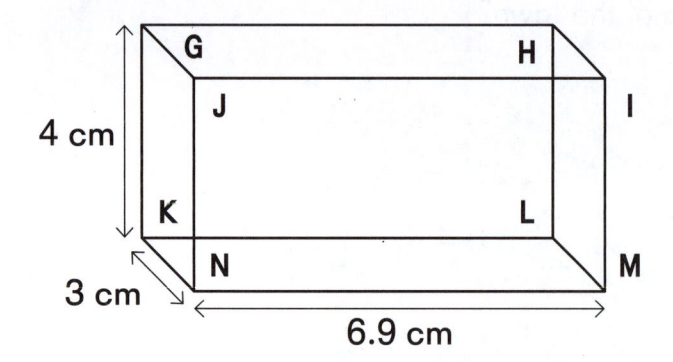

(a) Which faces are parallel to each other?

(b) What is the area of each face?

(c) Which faces are perpendicular to each other?

11 On a cube where the faces are numbered 1–6, the sum of the numbers on parallel faces is 7.

(a) Which of the following could be nets of the cube?

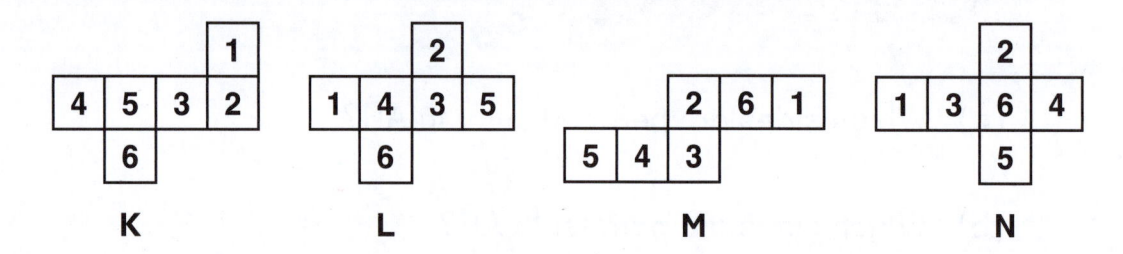

			1	
4	5	3	2	
		6		

K

			2	
1	4	3	5	
		6		

L

		2	6	1
5	4	3		

M

			2	
1	3	6	4	
			5	

N

(b) Copy the nets below and write 1–6 on the faces so that they could be a net of the cube.

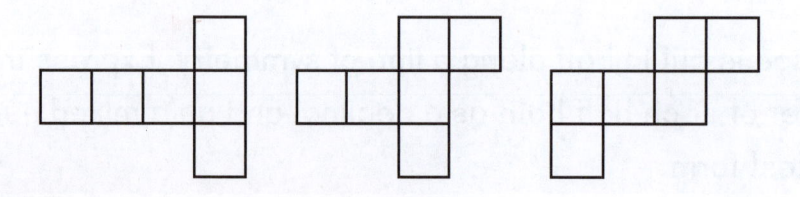

Exercise 6 • page 204

248   Review 5